D0101106

The LIFE 101 Quote Book

Selected by Peter McWilliams

Arranged by Jean Sedillos

Desktop Publishing by Jean Bolt

Prelude Press

8159 Santa Monica Blvd. #201
Los Angeles, California 90046

800–LIFE–101
800 – 5 4 3 – 3 1 0 1

For Andy.
Thank you.

Most of the published books by
Peter McWilliams are available for free
browsing, reading, downloading, or
burning on the Internet.

http://mcwilliams.com

CONTENTS

WARNING: THIS INTRODUCTION IS TOO LONG

"I read your book," people say to me with enthusiasm. I sense a compliment coming on. I see praise on the horizon. It is dawn. I begin to feel increasingly humble—as egomaniacs tend to feel when it's feeding time.

My mind reels at Pentium speed through the list of appreciative responses:

- The all-purpose "Thank you" is always appropriate, especially if accompanied by a slight bowing of the head, as though the weight of the praise is momentarily too much to bear.

- "You're so kind," compliments the complimentee in return; very tasteful.

- If the applause of the reader makes that transcendental leap into ovation, the true megalomaniac is permitted a plaintive "Please!" accompanied by a raising of one's hand in a carefully rehearsed but seemingly unconscious gesture of "Stop!"

While reviewing these and 16,345 other options, my mind is nevertheless—like a bear awaiting the next drop of honey to trickle from the hive—completely focused on the next panegyric* to pour from the mouth of the obviously intelligent and deeply sensitive person before me.

My grateful response is chosen. I am ready to receive.

My benefactor speaks: "The quotes are great!" A pause. I sense with my praise-radar—developed over years of exhaustive research, use, and refinement—that the complete compliment has been given. There will be no more. The shade is drawn. Dusk.

My ego, already salivating over what promised to be an all-you-can-eat gourmet buffet, will have to make do with a handful of Cheetos.

---

* I paid $3.95 for my thesaurus and I intend to use it.

Being complimented for *selection* is hardly the same as being complimented for *achievement*. Yes, one who chooses Hayden over hip-hop deserves commendation, but nowhere near the same acclamation as is due Hayden himself.

Shattered, I am simultaneously faced with the thorny problem of how to respond. What can I say? If I say "Thank you," it seems as though I'm taking credit for some of the tastiest examples of 5000 years of the written word. Although I'm certainly willing, waiting, and wanting to do so, even *I* can't bring myself to that level of pretension.

If I say of the quotes, "Yes, they are," then it may imply that I'm tooting my own horn about my ability to choose. To retain the outer trappings of humility, one must be like the conductor of a symphony orchestra and get other people to toot your horns for you. (It is, however, perfectly acceptable to point at them with a stick and let them know when, how loudly, and for how long they are to toot.)

So, while my ego licks its wounds and I remind myself, "It's better to have half a loaf than to be kicked down the stairs at 3:00 in the morning the week after your medical insurance has lapsed," I smile and say the neutral but pontifically correct: "I love quotes, too!"

And I do. As Christopher McMullen said (what would an introduction to a quote book be without a quote or two?), "I have the attention span of a hummingbird." Me too. I look at a page of solid text and, like Mozart's tone-deaf patron, think, "Too many words." Sound bites seem excessively long. A penetrating in-depth interview is any discussion with more than one question.

It's not that I'm a child of the TV generation; it's just that the world has finally caught up with my God-given mental limitations. As the world gets dumber and dumber, I feel more and more at home.

For attention-span challenged people such as myself, quote books are essential. They provide a link to our cultural past, a commune with the noblest minds in history, a way to get one-up on someone who is trying to impress the same stunningly attractive person we just met at a dignified cocktail party we have no business being at. When asked by our rival, "Have you read Hemmingway (Locke, Voltaire, Spinoza, Madonna, etc.)?" how else could we with any degree of integrity answer, "Yes, of course—some."

The triumphant follow-up to my internationally successful *The Bible by Peter McWilliams and God* was, of course, *The Complete Works of William Shakespeare Quotes*. In that Introduction I wrote:

> Now during otherwise-wasted 30-second intervals in the day, you can read the complete works of Shakespeare with all the boring bits removed. You can read all the parts worth reading from *Henry V* and all those other king plays during commercials on *Larry King Live!* While stopped at a traffic light you can read the good parts of six or seven sonnets. Now you can, with complete honesty, shame those co-workers who think Jackie Collins is more culturally significant than Joan Collins by blithely tossing into the conversation, "As I was reading in Shakespeare last night . . ."

So here are the quotes from all the books in The LIFE 101 Series:
- You Can't Afford the Luxury of a Negative Thought
- WEALTH 101: Wealth Is Much More Than Money
- LOVE 101
- WE GIVE TO LOVE: Giving Is Such a Selfish Thing
- LIFE 101
- DO IT! Let's Get Off Our Buts

All the parts that I wrote—the boring bits—have been whacked away by a team of machete-wielding Library Science majors. What's left I acknowledge as the best (he said, proud of his humility).

Faithfully yours,

Peter McWilliams
Four in the morning,
the end of December, 1995

ABUNDANCE
See also MONEY, WEALTH

There is enough in the world for everyone to have plenty to live on happily and to be at peace with his neighbors.

—HARRY S. TRUMAN

Abundance consists not alone in material possession but in an uncovetous spirit.

—CHARLES SHELDON

Wealth is not of necessity a curse, nor poverty a blessing. Wholesome and easy abundance is better than either extreme; better that we have enough for daily comfort; enough for culture, for hospitality, for Christian charity. More than this may or may not be a blessing. Certainly it can be a blessing only by being accepted as a trust.

—ROSWELL D. HITCHCOCK

To have life more abundant, we must think in the limitless terms of abundance.

—THOMAS DREIER

If we do more with less, our resources will be adequate to take care of everybody.

—R. BUCKMINSTER FULLER

ACCEPTANCE

All nature is but art unknown to thee; All chance, direction which thou canst not see; All discord, harmony not understood; All partial evil, universal good; And, spite of pride, in erring reason's spite, One truth is clear, Whatever is, is right.

—ALEXANDER POPE

MAE WEST: For a long time I was ashamed of the way I lived. *INTERVIEWER:* Did you reform? *MAE WEST:* No; I'm not ashamed anymore.

There is no good in arguing with the inevitable. The only argument available with an east wind is to put on your overcoat.

—JAMES RUSSELL LOWELL

Paradise is where I am.

—VOLTAIRE

In the valleys you look for the mountains In the mountains you've searched for the rivers There is no where to go You are where you belong You can live the life you dreamed.

—JUDY COLLINS

The person who says, believes, and acts on the phrase "I ain't taking any shit from anybody" is a very busy person indeed. This person must be ever vigilant against news vendors who shortchange him, cab drivers who take him the wrong way around, waiters who serve the other guy first, florists who are charging ten cents more per tulip than the one down the block, pharmacists who make you wait too long and cars that cut you off at the light: they are a veritable miasma of righteous indignation and never have a minute to relax and have a good time.

—CYNTHIA HEIMEL

Mr. Salter's side of the conversation was limited to expressions of assent. When Lord Copper was right he said, "Definitely, Lord Copper"; when he was wrong, "Up to a point." "Let me see, what's the name of the place I mean? Capital of Japan? Yokohama, isn't it?" "Up to a point, Lord Copper." "And Hong Kong belongs to us, doesn't it?" "Definitely, Lord Copper."

—EVELYN WAUGH

Everyone is in the best seat.

—JOHN CAGE

I can detach myself from the world. If there is a better world to detach oneself from than the one functioning at the moment I have yet to hear of it.

—P. G. WODEHOUSE

If you accept your limitations you go beyond them.

—BRENDAN FRANCIS

And that's the way it is.

—WALTER CRONKITE

Take what you can use and let the rest go by.

—KEN KESEY

If we live, we live; if we die, we die; if we suffer, we suffer; if we are terrified, we are terrified. There is no problem about it.

—ALAN WATTS

Vex not thy spirit at the course of things; they heed not thy vexation. How ludicrous and outlandish is astonishment at anything that may happen in life.

—MARCUS ANTONINUS

ACCOMPLISHMENT
See also ACTION, SUCCESS

Do or do not. There is no try.

—YODA

It's all right to have butterflies in your stomach. Just get them to fly in formation.

—DR. ROB GILBERT

The really idle man gets nowhere. The perpetually busy man does not get much further.

—HENEAGE OGILVIE

Everything I did in my life that was worthwhile I caught hell for.

—EARL WARREN

The world is moving so fast these days that the man who says it can't be done is generally interrupted by someone doing it.

—HARRY EMERSON FOSDICK

We may affirm absolutely that nothing great in the world has been accomplished without passion.

—GEORG HEGEL

Who begins too much accomplishes little.

—GERMAN PROVERB

To accomplish our destiny it is not enough merely to guard prudently against road accidents. We must also cover before nightfall the distance assigned to each of us.

—ALEXIS CARREL

'Tis God gives skill, But not without men's hands: He could not make Antonio Stradivari's violins without Antonio.

—STRADIVARIUS

ACTION

See also ACCOMPLISHMENT, ACTION SPEAKS LOUDER THAN WORDS, CHOICE, ENERGY, INACTION, RISK

Life consists not in holding good cards but in playing those you hold well.

—JOSH BILLINGS

Things won are done; joy's soul lies in the doing.

—WILLIAM SHAKESPEARE

Go directly—see what she's doing, and tell her she mustn't.

—*PUNCH*

The world is divided into two classes, those who believe the incredible, and those who do the improbable.

—OSCAR WILDE

Always listen to experts. They'll tell you what can't be done and why. Then do it.

—ROBERT HEINLEIN

The great thing in this world is not so much where we are, but in what direction we are moving.

—OLIVER WENDELL HOLMES

People are always blaming their circumstances for what they are. I don't believe in circumstances. The people who get on in this world are the people who get up and look for the circumstances they want, and, if they can't find them, make them.

—GEORGE BERNARD SHAW

Drive thy business, or it will drive thee.

—BENJAMIN FRANKLIN

Look, I really don't want to wax philosophic, but I will say that if you're alive, you got to flap your arms and legs, you got to jump around a lot, you got to make a lot of noise, because life is the very opposite of death. And therefore, as I see it, if you're quiet, you're not living. You've got to be noisy, or at least your *thoughts* should be noisy and colorful and lively.

—MEL BROOKS

Let us, then, be up and doing, With a heart for any fate; Still achieving, still pursuing, Learn to labor and to wait.

—HENRY WADSWORTH LONGFELLOW

It does not matter how slowly you go so long as you do not stop.

—CONFUCIUS

In Endymion, I leaped headlong into the sea, and thereby have become, better acquainted with the soundings, the quicksands, and the rocks, than if I had stayed upon the green shore, and piped a silly pipe, and took tea and comfortable advice.

—JOHN KEATS

To keep a lamp burning we have to keep putting oil in it.

—MOTHER TERESA

The profit on a good action is to have done it.

—SENECA

If you love Jesus work for justice. Anybody can honk.

—BUMPER STICKER

It is better to light a candle than to curse the darkness.

—CHINESE PROVERB
motto of the Christophers

The essential conditions of everything you do must be choice, love, passion.

—NADIA BOULANGER

If you have built castles in the air, your work need not be lost; that is where they should be. Now put the foundations under them.

—HENRY DAVID THOREAU

The hand is the cutting edge of the mind.

—JACOB BRONOWSKI

Our main business is not to see what lies dimly in the distance, but to do what lies clearly at hand.

—THOMAS CARLYLE

I'm very organized. I have this very elaborate schedule. Sure sign of mental health, huh?

—ELAINE NARDO
TAXI

Genius is an infinite capacity for taking pains.

—JANICE ELICE HOPKINS

Just Do It!

—ADVERTISEMENT FOR RUNNING SHOES

It's not the having, it's the getting.

—NEEDLEPOINT PILLOW IN
ELIZABETH TAYLOR'S LIVING ROOM

Getting an idea should be like sitting down on a pin; it should make you jump up and do something.

—E. L. SIMPSON

He flung himself upon his horse and rode madly off in all directions.

—STEPHEN LEACOCK

It is wonderful how much may be done if we are always doing.

—THOMAS JEFFERSON

For anything worth having one must pay the price; and the price is always work, patience, love, self-sacrifice.

—JOHN BURROUGHS

We should be taught not to wait for inspiration to start a thing. Action always generates inspiration. Inspiration seldom generates action.

—FRANK TIBOLT

It is common sense to take a method and try it. If it fails, admit it frankly and try another. But above all, try something.

—FRANKLIN D. ROOSEVELT

Do what you can, with what you have, with where you are.

—THEODORE ROOSEVELT

We must cultivate our garden.

—VOLTAIRE

He who has begun has half done. Dare to be wise; begin!

—HORACE

If we really want to live, we'd better start at once to try; If we don't it doesn't matter, we'd better start to die.

—W. H. AUDEN

It is not enough to have a good mind. The main thing is to use it well.

—RENÉ DESCARTES

Action is the antidote to despair.

—JOAN BAEZ

Do, be, do, be, do.

—FRANCIS ALBERT SINATRA

Take it easy, but take it.

—WOODY GUTHRIE

Anything that's worth having is worth asking for. Some say yes and some say no.

—DR. MELBA COLGROVE

Every human mind is a great slumbering power until awakened by a keen desire and by definite resolution to do.

—EDGAR F. ROBERTS

An idea isn't worth much until a man is found who has the energy and ability to make it work.

—WILLIAM FEATHER

The reward of a thing well done is to have done it.

—RALPH WALDO EMERSON

ACTION SPEAKS LOUDER THAN WORDS

Men are all alike in their promises. It is only in their deeds that they differ.

—MOLIÈRE

The smallest good deed is better than the grandest good intention.

—DUGUET

All worthwhile men have good thoughts, good ideas and good intentions, but precious few of them ever translate those into action.

—JOHN HANCOCK FIELD

All the beautiful sentiments in the world weigh less than a single lovely action.

—JAMES RUSSELL LOWELL

I will not steep my speech in lies; the test of any man lies in action.

—PINDAR

"Do-so" is more important than "say-so."

—PETE SEEGER

The shortest answer is doing.

—LORD HERBERT

You can't build a reputation on what you're GOING to do.

—HENRY FORD

ADULTERY

Adultery is a meanness and a stealing, a taking away from someone what should be theirs, a great selfishness, and surrounded and guarded by lies lest it should be found out. And out of meanness and selfishness and lying flow love and joy and peace beyond anything that can be imagined.

—DAME ROSE MACAULY

A Code of Honor: Never approach a friend's girlfriend or wife with mischief as your goal. There are just too many women in the world to justify that sort of dishonorable behavior. Unless she's *really* attractive.

—BRUCE JAY FRIEDMAN

I said to the wife, "Guess what I heard in the pub? They reckon the milkman has made love to every woman in this road except one." And she said, "I'll bet it's that stuck-up Phyllis at number 23."

—MAX KAUFFMANN

When a Roman was returning from a trip, he used to send someone ahead to let his wife know, so as not to surprise her in the act.

—MICHEL DE MONTAIGNE

The psychology of adultery has been falsified by conventional morals, which assume, in monogamous countries, that attraction to one person cannot coexist with affection for another. Everybody knows that this is untrue.

—BERTRAND RUSSELL

GEORGE S. KAUFMAN: I like your bald head, Marc. It feels just like my wife's behind. *MARC CONNOLLY [feeling his head]:* So it does, George, so it does.

'Tis the established custom (in Vienna) for every lady to have two husbands, one that bears the name and another that performs the duties.

—MARY WORTLEY MONTAGU

I think a man can have two, maybe three affairs while he is married. But three is the absolute maximum. After that, you are cheating.

—YVES MONTAND

I don't think there are any men who are faithful to their wives.

—JACQUELINE KENNEDY ONASSIS

Husbands are chiefly good lovers when they are betraying their wives.

—MARILYN MONROE

ADVERSITY

A man is insensible to the relish of prosperity till he has tasted adversity.

—SA'ID

When times are good, be happy, but when times are bad, consider: God has made the one as well as the other.

—ECCLESIASTES 7:14

The good things which belong to prosperity are to be wished, but good things that belong to adversity are to be admired.

—SENECA

A reasonable amount of fleas is good for a dog; it keeps him from brooding over being a dog.

—EDWARD WESTCOTT

Well-washed and well-combed domestic pets grow dull; they miss the stimulus of fleas.

—FRANCIS GALTON

If we had no winter, the spring would not be so pleasant: if we did not sometimes taste of adversity, prosperity would not be so welcome.

—ANNE BRADSTREET

In the depth of winter, I finally learned that within me there lay an invincible summer.

—ALBERT CAMUS

Oh, isn't life a terrible thing, thank God?

—DYLAN THOMAS

Oh don't the days seem lank and long, when all goes right and nothing goes wrong. And isn't your life extremely flat, with nothing whatever to grumble at!

—W. S. GILBERT

The school of hard knocks is an accelerated curriculum.

—ANONYMOUS

Nobody, as long as he moves about among the chaotic currents of life, is without trouble.

—CARL JUNG

If I had a formula for bypassing trouble, I would not pass it round. Trouble creates a capacity to handle it. I don't embrace trouble; that's as bad as treating it as an enemy. But I do say meet it as a friend, for you'll see a lot of it and had better be on speaking terms with it.

—OLIVER WENDELL HOLMES

God gave burdens, also shoulders.

—YIDDISH PROVERB

One of the best ways to properly evaluate and adapt to the many environmental stresses of life is to simply view them as normal. The adversity and failures in our lives, if adapted to and viewed as normal corrective feedback to use to get back on target, serve to develop in us an immunity against anxiety, depression, and the adverse responses to stress. Instead of tackling the most important priorities that would make us successful and effective in life, we prefer the path of least resistance and do things simply that will relieve our tension, such as shuffling papers and majoring in minors.

—DENIS WAITLEY

That which doesn't destroy us makes us stronger.

—OLD SAYING

Life is mostly froth and bubble, Two things stand like stone, Kindness in another's trouble, Courage in your own.

—ADAM LINDSAY GORDON

ADVICE

I have found the best way to give advice to your children is to find out what they want and then advise them to do it.

—HARRY S. TRUMAN

In matters of religion and matrimony I never give advice; because I will have no man's torments in this world or the next laid to my charge.

—LORD CHESTERFIELD

Please give me some good advice in your next letter. I promise not to follow it.

—EDNA ST. VINCENT MILLAY

I owe my success to having listened respectfully to the very best advice, and then going away and doing the exact opposite.

—G. K. CHESTERTON

Advice to expectant mothers: you must remember that when you are pregnant, you are eating for two. But you must remember that the other one of you is about the size of a golf ball, so let's not go overboard with it. I mean, a lot of pregnant women eat as though the other person they're eating for is Orson Welles.

—DAVE BARRY

Advice is what we ask for when we already know the answer but wish we didn't.

—ERICA JONG

Father told me that if I ever met a lady in a dress like yours, I must look her straight in the eyes.

—CHARLES, PRINCE OF WALES
(on Susan Hampshire's decolletagé)

Quit now, you'll never make it. If you disregard this advice, you'll be halfway there.

—DAVID ZUCKER

There is no human problem which could not be solved if people would simply do as I advise.

—GORE VIDAL

KEVIN KLINE [meeting his hero, Sir John Gielgud]: Mr. Gielgud, do you have any advice for a young actor about to make his first film in London? *GIELGUD [after pondering the question for some time]:* The really good restaurants are in Chelsea and the outlying regions—you want to avoid the restaurants in the big hotels.

If you want to please the critics, don't play too loud, too soft, too fast, too slow.

—ARTURO TOSCANINI
advise for pianist Vladimir Horowitz

Meet the sun every morning as if it could cast a ballot.

—HENRY CABOT LODGE, JR.
to novice political campaigner Dwight D. Eisenhower

Put your ass into the ball, Mr. President!

—SAM SNEAD
advising President Eisenhower on his golf swing

AFFIRMATIONS

If you want a quality, act as if you already had it. Try the "as if" technique.

—WILLIAM JAMES

Affirmation of life is the spiritual act by which man ceases to live unreflectively and begins to devote himself to his life with reverence in order to raise it to its true value. To affirm life is to deepen, to make more inward, and to exalt the will to live.

—ALBERT SCHWEITZER

The words "I am . . ." are potent words; be careful what you hitch them to. The thing you're claiming has a way of reaching back and claiming you.

—A. L. KITSELMAN

I am the state!

—LOUIS XIV

I am that I am.

—GOD

I am by temperament a conquistador.

—SIGMUND FREUD

I know that I am an artist.

—LUDWIG VAN BEETHOVEN

I am the resurrection and the life.

—JESUS OF NAZARETH

I am not a member of any organized political party. I am a Democrat.

—WILL ROGERS

ANALYSIS

You can analyze a glass of water and you're left with a lot of chemical components, but nothing you can drink.

—J. B. S. HALDANE

You think too much, that is your trouble. Clever people and grocers, they weigh everything.

—ZORBA THE GREEK

ANGER

I'll moider de bum.

—TONY TWO-TON GALENTO

Anger is one of the sinews of the soul; he that wants it hath a maimed mind.

—THOMAS FULLER

His huff arrived, and he departed in it.

—ALEXANDER WOOLLCOTT

I suppose I overdo it, but when I'm mad at a man I want to climb right up his chest.

— THEODORE ROOSEVELT

He owned and operated a ferocious temper.

—THOMAS YBARRA

Anybody can become angry—that is easy; but to be angry with the right person, and to the right degree, and at the right time, and for the right purpose, and in the right way—that is not within everybody's power and is not easy.

—ARISTOTLE

If you do not wish to be prone to anger, do not feed the habit; give it nothing which may tend to its increase. At first, keep quiet and count the days when you were not angry: "I used to be angry every day, then every other day: next, every two, then every three days!" and if you succeed in passing thirty days, sacrifice to the gods in thanksgiving.

—EPICTETUS

ANXIETY
Also See FEAR, WORRY

This is, I think, very much the Age of Anxiety.

—LOUIS KRONENBERGER (1954)

Anxiety is the space between the "now" and the "then."

—FRITZ PERLS

Every little yielding to anxiety is a step away from the natural heart of man.

—JAPANESE PROVERB

APPEARANCE

Twenty-four years ago I was strangely handsome; in San Francisco in the rainy season I was often mistaken for fair weather.

—MARK TWAIN

Most human beings use their public life like a visiting card. They show it to others and say, This is me. The others take the card and think to themselves, If you say so. But most human beings have another life too, a gray one, lurking in the darkness, torturing us, a life we try to hide like an ugly sin.

—FEDERICO GARCÍA LORCA

I don't say we all ought to misbehave, but we ought to look as if we could.

—ORSON WELLES

My problem is intense vanity and narcissism. I've always had such a good physique and such intense charm that it's difficult to be true to myself.

—LAWRENCE DURRELL

A full bosom is actually a millstone around a woman's neck; it endears her to the men who want to make their mammet of her, but she is never allowed to think that their popping eyes actually see her.

—GERMAINE GREER

One popular new plastic surgery technique is called lip-grafting, or "fat recycling," wherein fat cells are removed from one part of your body that is too large, such as your buttocks, and injected into your lips; people will then be literally kissing your ass.

—DAVE BARRY

While you're saving your face, you're losing your ass.

—LYNDON B. JOHNSON

A narcissist is someone better looking than you are.

—GORE VIDAL

Only the really plain people know about love. The very fascinating ones try so hard to create an impression that they soon exhaust their talents.

—KATHARINE HEPBURN

The genitals themselves have not undergone the development of the rest of the human form in the direction of beauty.

—SIGMUND FREUD

Almost every man wastes part of his life in attempts to display qualities which he does not possess.

—SAMUEL JOHNSON

Our greatest pretenses are built up not to hide the evil and the ugly in us, but our emptiness. The hardest thing to hide is something that is not there.

—ERIC HOFFER

When you get through all the phony tinsel of Hollywood, you find the genuine tinsel underneath.

—FRED ALLEN

Excuse me, I have to use the toilet. Actually, I have to use the telephone, but I'm too embarrassed to say so.

—DOROTHY PARKER

Be smart, but never show it.

—LOUIS B. MAYER

APPRECIATION
Also See GRATITUDE, WONDER

Today, this hour, this minute is the day, the hour, the minute for each of us to sense the fact that life is good, with all its trials and troubles, and perhaps more interesting because of them.

—ROBERT UPDEGRAFF

That must be wonderful; I don't understand it at all.

—MOLIÉRE

To the dull mind all of nature is leaden. To the illumined mind the whole world sparkles with light.

—RALPH WALDO EMERSON

I would rather be able to appreciate things I can not have than to have things I am not able to appreciate.

— ELBERT HUBBARD

Next to excellence is the appreciation of it.

—WILLIAM MAKEPEACE THACKERAY

Wise men appreciate all men, for they see the good in each and know how hard it is to make anything good.

—BALTASAR GRACIÁN

Why, the greatest invention in history is the safety pin. The second greatest is perforated toilet paper.

—TINY TIM

JED CLAMPETT: Pearl, what d'ya think? Think I oughta move? *COUSIN PEARL:* Jed, how can ya even ask? Look around ya. You're eight miles from yore nearest neighbor. Yore overrun with skunks, possums, coyotes, bobcats. You use kerosene lamps fer light and you cook on a wood stove summer and winter. Yore drinkin' homemade moonshine and washin' with homemade lye soap. And yore bathroom is fifty feet from the house and you ask "should I move?" *JED:* I reckon yore right. A man'd be a dang fool to leave all this!

—*THE BEVERLY HILLBILLIES*

The sheer beauty of our planet surprised me. It was a huge pearl, set in spangled ebony. It was nacreous, it was opal. No, it was far more lovely than any jewel. Its patterned coloring was more subtle, more ethereal. It displayed the delicacy and brilliance, the intricacy and harmony of a live thing.

—OLAF STAPLEDON

Statistically, the probability of any one of us being here is so small that you'd think the mere fact of existing would keep us all in a contented dazzlement of surprise.

—LEWIS THOMAS

All is a miracle. The order of nature, the revolution of a hundred million of worlds around a million of suns, the activity of light, the life of animals, all are grand and perpetual miracles.

—VOLTAIRE

Next to of course God america I love you land of the pilgrims' and so forth.

—E. E. CUMMINGS

We don't know how to celebrate because we don't know what to celebrate.

—PETER BROOK

The primary object of a student of literature is to be delighted. His duty is to enjoy himself: his efforts should be directed to developing his faculty of appreciation.

—LORD DAVID CECIL

A man should always consider how much he has more than he wants, and how much more unhappy he might be than he really is.

—JOSEPH ADDISON

Over the piano was printed a notice: Please do not shoot the pianist. He is doing his best.

—OSCAR WILDE

Father, each of your sermons is better than the next.

—ANONYMOUS CHURCH GOER

ART

Art is a collaboration between God and the artist, and the less the artist does the better.

—ANDRÉ GIDE

A first rate soup is better than a second rate painting.

—ABRAHAM MASLOW

The great joy of the artist is to become aware of a higher order of things, to recognize by the compulsive and spontaneous manipulation of his own impulses the resemblance between human creation and what is called "divine" creation.

—HENRY MILLER

Art is a jealous mistress, and if a man has a genius for painting, poetry, music, architecture or philosophy, he makes a bad husband and an ill provider.

—RALPH WALDO EMERSON

The artist who aims at perfection in everything achieves it in nothing.

—EUGÈNE DELACROIX

Very few people possess true artistic ability. It is therefore both unseemly and unproductive to irritate the situation by making an effort. If you have a burning, restless urge to write or paint, simply eat something sweet and the feeling will pass.

—FRAN LEBOWITZ

ARTISTS

He always did have that "Touch of Madness" that marks the true artist and breaks the hearts of the young girls from fine homes.

—ROBERT CRUMB

It is a mistake for a sculptor or a painter to speak or write very often about his job. It releases tension needed for his work.

—HENRY MOORE

ATOMS

A physicist is an atom's way of knowing about atoms.

—GEORGE WALD

Sooner or later every one of us breathes an atom that has been breathed before by anyone you can think of who has lived before us—Michelangelo or George Washington or Moses.

—JACOB BRONOWSKI

In atomic physics, we can never speak of nature without, at the same time, speaking of ourselves.

—FRITJOF CAPRA

BACHELORHOOD

Being a bachelor is the first requisite of the man who wishes to form an ideal home.

—BEVERLY NICHOLS

I belong to Bridegrooms Anonymous. Whenever I feel like getting married, they send over a lady in a housecoat and hair curlers to burn my toast for me.

—DICK MARTIN

BALANCE

Fortunate, indeed, is the man who takes exactly the right measure of himself, and holds a just balance between what he can acquire and what he can use.

—PETER MERE LATHAM

Man always travels along precipices. His truest obligation is to keep his balance.

—JOSÉ ORTEGA Y GASSET

Food is an important part of a balanced diet.

—FRAN LEBOWITZ

What I dream of is an art of balance, of purity and serenity devoid of troubling or depressing subject matter . . . a soothing, calming influence on the mind, something like a good armchair which provides relaxation from physical fatigue.

—HENRI MATISSE

BEAUTY

She had that indefinable beauty that comes from happiness, enthusiasm, success—a beauty that is nothing more or less than a harmony of temperament and circumstances.

—GUSTAVE FLAUBERT

Beauty is an omnipresence of death and loveliness, a smiling sadness that we discern in nature and all things, a mystic communion that the poet feels.

—CHARLIE CHAPLIN

Beauty is the gift of God.

—ARISTOTLE

BLAME

Lots of folks confuse bad management with destiny.

—KIN HUBBARD

It is no use to blame the looking glass if your face is awry.

—NIKOLAI GOGOL

There is luxury in self-reproach. When we blame ourselves we feel no one else has the right to blame us.

—OSCAR WILDE

People are always blaming their circumstances for what they are. I don't believe in circumstances. The people who get on in this world are the people who get up and look for the circumstances they want, and, if they can't find them, make them.

—GEORGE BERNARD SHAW

When a man blames others for his failures, it's a good idea to credit others with his successes.

—HOWARD W. NEWTON

BLESSINGS

God, give us grace to accept with serenity the things that cannot be changed, courage to change the things which should be changed, and the wisdom to distinguish the one from the other.

—REINHOLD NIEBUHR

Every misery I miss is a new blessing.

—IZAAK WALTON

I came to the conclusion that one of the reasons why I'm so blessed, I think, is because I reach so many people, and you never know whose life you are touching or affecting. And so, because your blessings come back to you based upon how you give them out . . . that's why I'm so . . . You know what I'm saying? You get it? OK, good.

—OPRAH WINFREY

THE BODY

I have bad reflexes. I was once run over by a car being pushed by two guys.

—WOODY ALLEN

The body is a community made up of its innumerable cells or inhabitants.

—THOMAS ALVA EDISON

The body never lies.

—MARTHA GRAHAM

I travel light; as light, That is, as a man can travel who will Still carry his body around because Of its sentimental value.

—CHRISTOPHER FRY*

BOOKS

Properly, we should read for power. Man reading should be man intensely alive. The book should be a ball of light in one's hand.

—EZRA POUND

---

* Uppercased words appearing in the middle of sentences generally signify the beginning of a new line of poetry.

Having your book turned into a movie is like seeing your oxen turned into bouillon cubes.

—JOHN LECARRE

The multitude of books is a great evil. There is no limit to this fever for writing.

—MARTIN LUTHER

To sit alone in the lamplight with a book spread out before you, and hold intimate converse with men of unseen generations—such is a pleasure beyond compare.

—KENKO YOSHIDA

Consider what you have in the smallest chosen library: a company of the wisest and wittiest men that could be picked out of all civil countries in a thousand years. The thought which they did not uncover to their bosom friend is here written out in transparent words to us, the strangers of another age.

—RALPH WALDO EMERSON

When you read a book, you hold another's mind in your hands.

—JAMES BURKE

This book is not to be tossed lightly aside, but to be hurled with great force.

—DOROTHY PARKER

For I bless God in the libraries of the learned and for all the booksellers in the world.

—CHRISTOPHER SMART

CARING FOR YOURSELF
Also See SELF-HELP

I don't do anything that's bad for me. I don't like to be made nervous or angry. Any time you get upset it tears down your nervous system.

—MAE WEST

MACBETH: Canst thou not minister to a mind diseased, pluck from the memory a rooted sorrow, Raze out the written troubles of the brain, and with some sweet oblivious antidote Cleanse the stuffed bosom of that perilous stuff Which weighs upon the heart? *DOCTOR:* Therein the patient Must minister to himself.

—WILLIAM SHAKESPEARE

But how shall we expect charity towards others, when we are uncharitable to ourselves? Charity begins at home, is the voice of the world; yet is every man his greatest enemy, and, as it were, his own executioner.

—THOMAS BROWNE

Compassion for myself is the most powerful healer of them all.

—THEODORE ISAAC RUBIN, M.D.

An occasional compliment is necessary, to keep up one's self-respect. When you cannot get a compliment any other way, pay yourself one.

—MARK TWAIN

. . . to superintend the sick to make them well, to care for the healthy to keep them well, also to care for one's own self.

—PART OF THE HIPPOCRATIC OATH

Be careful, and you will save many men from the sin of robbing you.

—ED HOWE

Only Irish coffee provides in a single glass all four essential food groups: alcohol, caffeine, sugar, and fat.

— ALEX LEVINE

CHALLENGE

If you're not playing a big enough game, you'll screw up the game you're playing just to give yourself something to do.

—ANONYMOUS

CHANCE

Life is like a game of whist, some time ago. From unseen sources the cards are shuffled, and the hands are dealt.

—EUGENE HARE

Life consists not in holding good cards but in playing those you hold well.

—JOSH BILLINGS

CHANGE

You cannot step twice into the same river; for other waters are always flowing on to you.

—HERACLITUS

Nothing endures but change.

—HERACLITUS

Without deviation progress is not possible.

—FRANK ZAPPA

CHARITY
Also See GIVING, GOOD DEEDS, SERVICE, PHILANTROPY

Charity creates a multitude of sins.

—OSCAR WILDE

Charity degrades those who receive it and hardens those who dispense it.

—GEORGE SAND

Charity, as if it didn't have enough trouble in this day and age, will always be suspected of morbidity—sado-masochism, perversity of some sort. All higher or moral tendencies lie under suspicion of being rackets. Things we simply honor with old words, but betray or deny in our very nerves.

— SAUL BELLOW

The Eight Grades of Charity:

1. To give reluctantly
2. To give cheerfully but not adequately
3. To give cheerfully and adequately, but only after being asked
4. To give cheerfully, adequately, and of your own free will, but to put it in the recipient's hand in such a way as to make him feel lesser
5. To let the recipient know who the donor is, but not the reverse
6. To know who is receiving your charity but remain anonymous to him
7. To have neither the donor nor the recipient be aware of the other's identity
8. To dispense with charity altogether, by enabling your fellow humans to have the wherewithal to earn their own living

—MAIMONIDES

For those who are not hungry, it is easy to palaver about the degradation of charity.

— CHARLOTTE BRONTË

Don't use the impudence of a beggar as an excuse for not helping him.

—RABBI SCHMELKE OF NICOLSBURG

Anticipate charity by preventing poverty; assist the reduced fellowman, either by a considerable gift, or a sum of money, or by teaching him a trade, or by putting him in the way of business, so that he may earn an honest livelihood, and not be forced to the dreadful alternative of holding out his hand for charity. This is the highest step and the summit of charity's golden ladder.

—MAIMONIDES

The highest exercise of charity is charity towards the uncharitable.

— J. S. BUCKMINSTER

The contents of Sitting Bull's pockets were often emptied into the hands of small, ragged little boys, nor could he understand how so much wealth should go brushing by, unmindful of the poor.

—ANNIE OAKLEY

The white man knows how to make everything, but he does not know how to distribute it.

—SITTING BULL

Every charitable act is a stepping stone towards heaven.

—HENRY WARD BEECHER

A disciple having asked for a definition of charity, the Master said: Love One Another.

—CONFUCIUS

Every good act is charity. Your smiling in your brother's face, is charity; an exhortation of your fellowman to virtuous deeds, is equal to alms-giving; your putting a wanderer in the right road, is charity; your assisting the blind, is charity; your removing stones, and thorns, and other obstructions from the road, is charity; your giving water to the thirsty, is charity. A man's true wealth hereafter, is the good he does in this world to his fellow-man. When he dies, people will say, "What property has he left behind him?" But the angels will ask, "What good deeds has he sent before him?"

—MOHAMMED

Be charitable in your thoughts, in your speech and in your actions. Be charitable in your judgments, in your attitudes and in your prayers. Think charitably of your friends, your neighbors, your relatives and even your enemies. And if there be those whom you can help in a material way, do so in a quiet, friendly, neighborly way, as if it were the most common and everyday experience for you. Tongues of men and angels, gifts of prophecy and all mysteries and all knowledge are as nothing without charity.

—CARDINAL HAYES

Charity sees the need, not the cause.

—GERMAN PROVERB

Charity begins at home, but should not end there.

—THOMAS FULLER, M.D.

Charity begins at home, and generally dies from lack of outdoor exercise.

—ANONYMOUS

If you haven't got any charity in your heart, you have the worst kind of heart trouble.

—BOB HOPE

Charity is that which opens in each heart a little Heaven.

—MATTHEW PRIOR

CHILDREN

Never lend your car to anyone to whom you have given birth.

—ERMA BOMBECK

I take my children everywhere, but they always find their way back home.

—ROBERT ORBEN

Children today are tyrants. They contradict their parents, gobble their food, and tyrannize their teachers.

—SOCRATES

The childhood shows the man, As morning shows the day.

—JOHN MILTON

Few parents nowadays pay any regard to what their children say to them. The old-fashioned respect for the young is fast dying out.

—OSCAR WILDE

Know you what it is to be a child? It is to be something very different from the man of today. It is to have a spirit yet streaming from the waters of baptism; it is to believe in love, to believe in loveliness, to believe in belief; it is to be so little that the elves can reach to whisper in your ear; it is to turn pumpkins into coaches, and mice into horses, lowness into loftiness, and nothing into everything, for each child has its fairy godmother in its soul.

—FRANCIS THOMPSON SHELLEY

My heart leaps up when I behold A rainbow in the sky: So was it when my life began; So is it now I am a man; So be it when I shall grow old, Or let me die! The child is father of the man; And I could wish my days to be Bound each to each by natural piety.

—WILLIAM WORDSWORTH

The denunciation of the young is a necessary part of the hygiene of older people, and greatly assists the circulation of the blood.

—LOGAN PEARSALL SMITH

Before I was married I had three theories about raising children. Now I have three children and no theories.

—JOHN WILMOT, EARL OF ROCHESTER

BLANCHE: I'm reading this Spock book on baby care, and he says it's very important for a young child to have a male role model around during its formative years. Now what are we gonna do? . . . *ROSE:* Oh, Blanche, we don't have anything to worry about. If we give that baby love and attention and understanding, it'll turn out fine. *DOROTHY:* That's beautiful. *ROSE:* Besides, what does Spock know about raising babies? On Vulcan, all the kids are born in pods.

—*GOLDEN GIRLS*

We are always too busy for our children; we never give them the time or interest they deserve. We lavish gifts upon them; but the most precious gift—our personal association, which means so much to them—we give grudgingly.

—MARK TWAIN

I teach my child to look at life in a thoroughly materialistic fashion. If he escapes and becomes the sort of person I hope he will become, it will be because he sees through the hokum that I hand out.

—E. B. WHITE

If children grew up according to early indications, we should have nothing but geniuses.

—JOHANN WOLFGANG VON GOETHE

CHOICE
Also See ACTION, INACTION, RISK

The last of the human freedoms—to choose one's attitude in any given set of circumstances, to choose one's own way.

—VIKTOR FRANKL

More than any time in history mankind faces a crossroads. One path leads to despair and utter hopelessness, the other to total extinction. Let us pray that we have the wisdom to choose correctly.

—WOODY ALLEN

Decide what you want, decide what you are willing to exchange for it. Establish your priorities and go to work.

—H. L. HUNT

I'd rather have roses on my table than diamonds on my neck.

—EMMA GOLDMAN

If you don't like what you're doing, you can always pick up your needle and move to another groove.

—TIMOTHY LEARY

Liberty, taking the word in its concrete sense, consists in the ability to choose.

—SIMONE WEIL

A man is too apt to forget that in this world he cannot have everything. A choice is all that is left him.

—H. MATHEWS

Destiny is not a matter of chance, it is a matter of choice; it is not a thing to be waited for, it is a thing to be achieved.

—WILLIAM JENNINGS BRYAN

Love thy neighbor as thyself, but choose your neighborhood.

—LOUISE BEAL

Tell him to live by yes and no—yes to everything good, no to everything bad.

—WILLIAM JAMES

I chose and my world was shaken. So what? The choice may have been mistaken, the choosing was not. You have to move on.

—STEPHEN SONDHEIM

Destiny is not a matter of chance; it is a matter of choice. It is not a thing to be waited for; it is a thing to be achieved.

—WILLIAM JENNINGS BRYAN

The way you activate the seeds of your creation is by making choices about the results you want to create. When you make a choice, you mobilize vast human energies and resources which otherwise go untapped. All too often people fail to focus their choices upon results and therefore their choices are ineffective. If you limit your choices only to what seems possible or reasonable, you disconnect yourself from what you truly want and all that is left is a compromise.

—ROBERT FRITZ

As to marriage or celibacy, let a man take which course he will—he will be sure to repent it.

—SOCRATES

If you are distressed by anything external, the pain is not due to the thing itself, but to your estimate of it; and this you have the power to revoke at any moment.

—MARCUS ANTONINUS

CIVILIZATION

I believe that order is better than chaos, creation better than destruction. I prefer gentleness to violence, forgiveness to vendetta . . . I think knowledge is preferable to ignorance and I am sure that human sympathy is more valuable than ideology . . . And I think we should remember we are part of a great whole, which for convenience we call nature. All living things are our brothers and sisters. Above all I believe in the God-given genius of certain individuals, and I value a society that makes their existence possible.

—KENNETH CLARK

Turning and turning in the widening gyre The falcon cannot hear the falconer; Things fall apart; the centre cannot hold; Mere anarchy is loosed upon the world, The blood-dimmed tide is loosed, and everywhere The ceremony of innocence is drowned; The best lack all conviction, while the worst Are full of passionate intensity.

—WILLIAM BUTLER YEATS

COMFORT

We act as though comfort and luxury were the chief requirements of life, when all that we need to make us happy is something to be enthusiastic about.

—CHARLES KINGSLEY

The point on the thermostat in which neither heating nor cooling must operate—around 72 degrees—is called "The Comfort Zone." It's also known as "The Dead Zone."

—HEATING AIR CONDITIONING LORE

No woman has ever so comforted the distressed—or distressed the comfortable.

—CLARE BOOTHE LUCE
describing Eleanor Roosevelt

The superior man thinks always of virtue; the common man thinks of comfort.

—CONFUCIUS

Minds, like bodies, will often fall into a pimpled, ill-conditioned state from mere excess of comfort.

—CHARLES DICKENS

Quotations are comfortable.

—THE AUTHOR

COMMITMENT

I could never think well of a man's intellectual or moral character, if he was habitually unfaithful to his appointments.

—NATHANIEL EMMONS

Never esteem anything as of advantage to you that will make you break your word or lose your self-respect.

—MARCUS ANTONINUS

Never take a solemn oath. People think you mean it.

—NORMAN DOUGLAS

The best way to keep your word is not to give it.

—NAPOLÉON BONAPARTE

If you never want to see a man again, say, "I love you, I want to marry you. I want to have children . . ." —they leave skid marks.

—RITA RUDNER

Until one is committed, there is hesitancy, the chance to draw back, always ineffectiveness. Concerning all acts of initiative (and creation) there is one elementary truth, the ignorance of which kills countless ideas and splendid plans: That the moment one definitely commits oneself, then Providence moves too. All sorts of things occur to help one that would never otherwise have occurred. A whole stream of events issues from the decision, raising in one's favor all manner of unforeseen incidents and meetings and material assistance, which no man could have dreamed would have come his way. I have learned a deep respect for one of Goethe's couplets: "Whatever you can do, or dream you can, begin it. Boldness has genius, power and magic in it."

—W. H. MURRAY
THE SCOTTISH HIMALAYAN EXPEDITION

Always do sober what you said you'd do drunk. That will teach you to keep your mouth shut.

—ERNEST HEMINGWAY

One person with belief is equal to a force of ninety-nine who have only interests.

—JOHN STUART MILL

COMMON SENSE

Common sense is not so common.

—VOLTAIRE

COMMUNICATION

Most conversations are simply monologues delivered in the presence of a witness.

—MARGARET MILLAR

The opposite of talking isn't listening. The opposite of talking is waiting.

—FRAN LEBOWITZ

MOTHER: Do you love me, Albert? *ALBERT:* Yes. *MOTHER:* Yes—what? *ALBERT:* Yes, please.

—TOM STOPPARD

"What Ho!" I said, "What Ho!" said Motty. "What Ho! What Ho!" "What Ho! What Ho! What Ho!" After that it seemed rather difficult to go on with the conversation.

—P. G. WODEHOUSE

When the eagles are silent the parrots begin to jabber.

—WINSTON CHURCHILL

When I was born I was so surprised I didn't talk for a year and a half.

—GRACIE ALLEN

If you have an important point to make, don't try to be subtle or clever. Use a pile driver. Hit the point once. Then come back and hit it again. Then a third time—a tremendous whack!

—WINSTON CHURCHILL

Drawing on my fine command of the English language, I said nothing.

—ROBERT BENCHLEY

The journey of ten thousand miles begins with a single phone call.

—CONFUCIUS BELL

My idea of an agreeable person is a person who agrees with me.

—BENJAMIN DISRAELI

I speak Spanish to God, Italian to women, French to men, and German to my horse.

—CHARLES V

COMPASSION
Also See EMPHATHY

By compassion we make others' misery our own, and so, by relieving them, we relieve ourselves also.

— THOMAS BROWNE

Spiritual energy brings compassion into the real world. With compassion, we see benevolently our own human condition and the condition of our fellow beings. We drop prejudice. We withhold judgment.

—CHRISTINA BALDWIN

COMPETITION

I've always thought that the stereotype of the dirty old man is really the creation of a dirty young man who wants the field to himself.

—HUGH DOWNS

Competition brings out the best in products, and the worst in people.

—DAVID SARNOFF

Do your work with your whole heart, and you will succeed—there's so little competition.

—ELBERT HUBBARD

The first time I saw her perform she was so good I wanted to run up to the stage, put my arms around her—and wring her neck. She just has too much talent!

—JUDY GARLAND
describing Barbra Streisand

CONFORMITY

We forfeit three-fourths of ourselves to be like other people.

—ARTHUR SCHOPENHAUER

CONFRONTATION

Confront your enemies, avoid them when you can. A gentleman will walk but never run.

—STING
about Quentin Crisp

Now that the scriptures have been fulfilled, I shall proceed to beat the hell out of thee.

—QUAKER
after being slapped on one cheek, turning the other cheek, and being slapped again

If I repent of anything, it is very likely to be my good behavior.

—HENRY DAVID THOREAU

The best way out is always through.

—ROBERT FROST

CONTENTMENT
See also HAPPINESS

The secret of contentment is knowing how to enjoy what you have, and to be able to lose all desire for things beyond your reach.

—LIN YUTANG

He is richest who is content with the least, for content is the wealth of nature.

—SOCRATES

Do not strain to seek increases. What you have, let it suffice you.

—AMENEMOPE

There are some days when I think I'm going to die from an overdose of satisfaction.

—SALVADOR DALI

You never know what is enough, until you know what is more than enough.

—WILLIAM BLAKE

The fountain of content must spring up in the mind; and he who has so little knowledge of human nature as to see his happiness by changing anything but his own disposition, will waste his life in fruitless efforts, and multiply the griefs which he proposes to remove.

—SAMUEL JOHNSON

COOPERATION

When bad men combine, the good must associate; else they will fall one by one, an unpitied sacrifice in a contemptible struggle.

—EDMUND BURKE

COURAGE
Also See FEAR, RISK

Everyone has talent. What is rare is the courage to follow the talent to the dark place where it leads.

—ERICA JONG

Courage is the price that life exacts for granting peace. The soul that knows it not, knows no release From little things; Knows not the livid loneliness of fear, Nor mountain heights where bitter joy can hear The sound of wings.

—AMELIA EARHART

Courage is doing what you're afraid to do. There can be no courage unless you're scared.

—EDDIE RICKENBACKER

Be bold—and mighty forces will come to your aid.

—BASIL KING

Courage is mastery of fear—not absence of fear.

—MARK TWAIN

Life shrinks or expands in proportion to one's courage.

—ANAIS NIN

CREATIVITY

The whole difference between construction and creation is exactly this: that a thing constructed can only be loved after it is constructed; but a thing created is loved before it exists.

—G. K. CHESTERTON

Want to be a composer? If you can *think design*, you can *execute design*—it's only a bunch of air molecules, who's gonna check up on you? Just follow these simple instructions:

1. Declare your *intention* to create a "composition."
2. *Start* a piece at *some time.*
3. Cause *something to happen over a period of time*
   (it doesn't matter what happens in your "time hole"—
   we have critics to tell us whether it's any good or
   not, so we won't worry about that part).
4. *End the piece at some time* (or keep it going, telling
   the audience it is a "work in progress").
5. Get a part-time job so you can continue to do stuff
   like this.

—FRANK ZAPPA

Creative activity could be described as a type of learning
process where teacher and pupil are located in the same
individual.

—ARTHUR KOESTLER

Creativity is merely a plus name for regular activity . . .
any activity becomes creative when the doer cares about
doing it right, or better.

—JOHN UPDIKE

Creativity is a drug I cannot live without.

—CECIL B. DEMILLE

Creativity can solve almost any problem. The creative
act, the defeat of habit by originality, overcomes everything.

—GEORGE LOIS

Creativity represents a miraculous coming together of
the uninhibited energy of the child with its apparent
opposite and enemy, the sense of order imposed on the
disciplined adult intelligence.

—NORMAN PODHORETZ

Every creator painfully experiences the chasm between
his inner vision and its ultimate expression.

—ISAAC BASHEVIS SINGER

Passion is in all great searches and is necessary to all creative endeavors.

—W. EUGENE SMITH

When in doubt, make a fool of yourself. There is a microscopically thin line between being brilliantly creative and acting like the most gigantic idiot on earth. So what the hell, leap.

—CYNTHIA HEIMEL

CRITICISM

Self criticism must be my guide to action, and the first rule for its employment is that in itself it is not a virtue, only a procedure.

—KINGSLEY AMIS

I can take any amount of criticism, so long as it is unqualified praise.

—NOËL COWARD

Criticism, as it was first instituted by Aristotle, was meant as a standard of judging well.

—SAMUEL JOHNSON

Do not fear when your enemies criticize you. Beware when they applaud.

—VO DONG GIANG

To avoid criticism, do nothing, say nothing, be nothing.

—ELBERT HUBBARD

Honest criticism is hard to take, particularly from a relative, a friend, an acquaintance, or a stranger.

—FRANKLIN P. JONES

CURES

Also See HEALTH

The music that can deepest reach, And cure all ill, is cordial speech.

—RALPH WALDO EMERSON

We should always presume the disease to be curable, until its own nature prove it otherwise.

—PETER MERE LATHAM

CURIOSITY

What we have to do is to be forever curiously testing new opinions and courting new impressions.

—WALTER PATER

The important thing is not to stop questioning. Curiosity has its own reason for existing. One cannot help but be in awe when he contemplates the mysteries of eternity, of life, of the marvelous structure of reality. It is enough if one tries merely to comprehend a little of this mystery every day. Never lose a holy curiosity.

—ALBERT EINSTEIN

The first and simplest emotion which we discover in the human mind, is curiosity.

—EDMUND BURKE

DARK AGES

Perhaps in time the so-called Dark Ages will be thought of as including our own.

—G. C. LICHTENBERG

DEATH
Also See ETERNITY

The fear of death is more to be dreaded than death itself.

—PUBLILIUS SYRUS

One who longs for death is miserable, but more miserable is he who fears it.

—JULIUS WILHELM ZINCGREF

If I could drop dead right now, I'd be the happiest man alive!

—SAMUEL GOLDWYN

Once you accept your own death, all of a sudden you're free to live. You no longer care about your reputation. You no longer care except so far as your life can be used tactically—to promote a cause you believe in.

—SAUL ALINSKY

I'm not afraid to die. I just don't want to be there when it happens. It is impossible to experience one's death objectively and still carry a tune.

—WOODY ALLEN

Life does not cease to be funny when people die any more than it ceases to be serious when people laugh.

—GEORGE BERNARD SHAW

People living deeply have no fear of death.

—ANAIS NIN

For certain is death for the born And certain is birth for the dead; Therefore over the inevitable Thou shouldst not grieve.

—BHAGAVAD GITA 2:27

Death and taxes and childbirth! There's never any convenient time for any of them.

—SCARLETT O'HARA

Death is nothing to us, since when we are, death has not come, and when death has come, we are not.

—EPICURUS

O death, where is thy sting? O grave, where is thy victory?

—I CORINTHIANS 15:55

Either death is a state of nothingness and utter unconsciousness, or, as men say, there is a change and migration of the soul from this world to another. Now if death be of such a nature, I say that to die is to gain; for eternity is then only a single night.

—PLATO

Nothing can happen more beautiful than death.

—WALT WHITMAN

To be, or not to be: that is the question: Whether 'tis nobler in the mind to suffer The slings and arrows of outrageous fortune, Or to take arms against a sea of troubles, And by opposing end them? To die: to sleep; No more; and, by a sleep to say we end The heartache and the thousand natural shocks That flesh is heir to, 'tis a consummation Devoutly to be wished. To die, to sleep; To sleep: perchance to dream: ay, there's the rub; For in that sleep of death what dreams may come, When we have shuffled off this mortal coil, Must give us pause. There's the respect That makes calamity of so long life; For who would bear the whips and scorns of time, The oppressor's wrong, the proud man's contumely, The pangs of disprized love, the law's delay, The insolence of office, and the spurns That patient merit of the unworthy takes, When he himself might his quietus make With a bare bodkin? who would fardels bear, To grunt and sweat under a weary life, But that the dread of something after death, The undiscovered country from whose bourn No traveler returns, puzzles the will, And makes us rather bear those ills we have Than fly to others that we know not of?

—WILLIAM SHAKESPEARE
HAMLET

Death is no more than passing from one room into another. But there's a difference for me, you know. Because in that other room I shall be able to see.

—HELEN KELLER

Beware! To touch these wires is instant death. Anyone found doing so will be prosecuted.

—SIGN AT A RAILROAD STATION

I must leave all that! Farewell, dear paintings that I have loved so much and which have cost me so much.

—CARDINAL JULES MAZARIN

If you don't go to other men's funerals they won't go to yours.

—CLARENCE DAY

On no subject are our ideas more warped and pitiable than on death. Let children walk with nature, let them see the beautiful blendings and communions of life and death, their joyous inseparable unity, as taught in woods and meadows, plains and mountains and streams of our blessed star, and they will learn that death is stingless indeed, and as beautiful as life, and that the grave has no victory, for it never fights. All is divine harmony.

—JOHN MUIR

Warm summer sun, shine kindly here; Warm northern wind, blow softly here; Green sod above, lie light, lie light Good-night, dear heart, good-night, good-night.

—MARK TWAIN
epitaph for his daughter

Death is not the greatest loss in life. The greatest loss is what dies inside us while we live.

—NORMAN COUSINS

Die, my dear doctor, that's the last thing I shall do.

—LORD PALMERSTON

Death is a friend of ours; and he that is not ready to entertain him is not at home.

—FRANCIS BACON

Thus, thus, it is joy to pass to the world below.

—VIRGIL

One of the situations in which everybody seems to fear loneliness is death. In tones drenched with pity, people say of someone, "He died alone." I have never understood this point of view. Who wants to have to die and be polite at the same time?

—QUENTIN CRISP

Men fear death as children fear to go in the dark; and as that natural fear in children is increased with tales, so is the other.

—FRANCIS BACON

Death is just nature's way of telling you, "Hey, you're not alive anymore."

—BULL
NIGHT COURT

Death is nature's way of saying, "Your table is ready."

— ROBIN WILLIAMS

Sleep after toil, port after stormy seas, Ease after war, death after life does greatly please.

—EDMUND SPENSER

As a well-spent day brings happy sleep, so life well used brings happy death.

—LEONARDO DA VINCI

Death is a low chemical trick played on everybody except sequoia trees.

—J. J. FURNAS

Death is, to us here, the most terrible word we know. But when we have tasted its reality, it will mean to us birth, deliverance, a new creation of ourselves.

—GEORGE MERRIMAN

When you don't have any money, the problem is food. When you have money it's sex. When you have both it's health. If everything is simply jake, then you're frightened of death.

—J. P. DONLEAVY

Death is one of the few things that can be done as easily lying down. The difference between sex and death is that with death you can do it alone and no one is going to make fun of you.

—WOODY ALLEN

The only religious way to think of death is as part and parcel of life; to regard it, with the understanding and the emotions, as the inviolable condition of life.

—THOMAS MANN

Death, the only immortal who treats us all alike, whose pity and whose peace and whose refuge are for all—the soiled and the pure, the rich and the poor, the loved and the unloved.

—MARK TWAIN
near death in 1910

Life is a great surprise. I do not see why death should not be an even greater one.

—VLADIMIR NABOKOV

I have two luxuries to brood over in my walks, your loveliness and the hour of my death. O that I could have possession of them both in the same minute.

—JOHN KEATS
Wooing Fanny Brawne

Whoever has lived long enough to find out what life is, knows how deep a debt of gratitude we owe to Adam, the first great benefactor of our race. He brought death into the world.

—MARK TWAIN

The fear of death is the most unjustified of all fears, for there is no risk of accident to someone who's dead.

—ALBERT EINSTEIN

Drawing near her death, she sent most pious thoughts as harbingers to heaven; and her soul saw a glimpse of happiness—through the chinks of her sickness-broken body.

—THOMAS FULLER
on the death of St. Monica

My candle burns at both ends; It on the death of St. Monica will not last the night; But, ah, my foes, and, oh, my friends—It gives a lovely light.

—EDNA ST. VINCENT MILLAY

Well, Norton, I guess there'll be no more bus rides for me. I've come to the end of the line. I'm going to that big bus depot in the sky. It's a one-way trip with no transfers

—RALPH KRAMDEN
THE HONEYMOONERS

The bus bringeth and the bus taketh away. You know, that's a lot like life.

—FLOYD LAWSON
THE ANDY GRIFFITH SHOW

PETE: Have you ever thought about death? Do you realize that we each must die? *DUD:* Of course we must die, but not yet. It's only half past four of a Wednesday afternoon. *PETE:* No one knows when God in His Almighty Wisdom will choose to vouch-safe His precious gift of Death. *DUD:* Granted. But chances are He won't be making a pounce at this time of day.

—PETER COOK & DUDLEY MOORE

The late F. W. H. Myers used to tell how he asked a man at a dinner table what he thought would happen to him when he died. The man tried to ignore the question, but, on being pressed, replied: "Oh well, I suppose I shall inherit eternal bliss, but I wish you wouldn't talk about such unpleasant subjects."

—BERTRAND RUSSELL

I detest life insurance agents. They always argue that I shall some day die, which is not so.

—STEPHEN LEACOCK

I don't fear death because I don't fear anything I don't understand. When I start to think about it, I order a massage and it goes away.

—HEDY LAMARR

One can survive everything nowadays, except death.

—OSCAR WILDE

We should so use the next world, that it should advance us in that which is before it.

—SAMUEL BUTLER

Truman Capote, near death, was asked by a friend, "Are you all right?" His last words were, "No, I'm not. But I soon will be.

Either this man is dead or my watch has stopped.

—GROUCHO MARX

Do not fear death so much, but rather the inadequate life.

—BERTOLT BRECHT

Why do we have to die? As a kid you get nice little white shoes with white laces and a velvet suit with short pants and a nice collar and you go to college, you meet a nice girl and get married, work a few years and then you have to *die!* What is this shit? They never wrote that in the contract!

—MEL BROOKS

In the last analysis it is our conception of death which decides our answers to all the questions that life puts to us.

—DAG HAMMARSKJÖLD

Even very young children need to be informed about dying. Explain the concept of death very carefully to your child. This will make threatening him with it much more effective.

—P. J. O'ROURKE

When you cease to make a contribution you begin to die.

—ELEANOR ROOSEVELT

How could they tell?

—DOROTHY PARKER
when told of "Silent" Calvin Coolidge's death

Life is not lost by dying; life is lost minute by minute, day by dragging day, in all the thousand small uncaring ways.

—STEPHEN VINCENT BENÉT

DEBT

If it isn't the sheriff, it's the finance company; I've got more attachments on me than a vacuum cleaner.

—JOHN BARRYMORE

DEPENDENCE

Independence? That's middle-class blasphemy. We are all dependent on one another, every soul of us on earth.

—GEORGE BERNARD SHAW

DEPRESSION

Self-love depressed becomes self-loathing.

—SALLY KEMPTON

When water covers the head, a hundred fathoms are as one.

—PERSIAN PROVERB

The problems of alcoholism and drug addiction have strong links to depression. The search for highs may often begin as a flight from lows.

—NATHAN S. KLINE, M.D.

Physical and social functioning are impaired by depression to a greater degree than by hypertension, diabetes, angina, arthritis, gastrointestinal diseases, lung problems, or back ailments.

—JOSÉ M. SANTIAGO, M.D.
JOURNAL OF CLINICAL PSYCHOLOGY

Mysteriously and in ways that are totally remote from natural experience, the gray drizzle of horror induced by depression takes on the quality of physical pain.

—WILLIAM STYRON

The term clinical depression finds its way into too many conversations these days. One has a sense that a catastrophe has occurred in the psychic landscape.

—LEONARD COHEN

I am now the most miserable man living. If what I feel were equally distributed to the whole human family there would be not one cheerful face on earth. Whether I shall ever be better, I cannot tell. I awfully forebode I shall not. To remain as I am is impossible. I must die or be better it appears to me.

—ABRAHAM LINCOLN
who suffered from depression most of his adult life

I was once thrown out of a mental hospital for depressing the other patients.

—OSCAR LEVANT

A depressed person is someone who, if he is in the bath, will not get out to answer the telephone.

—QUENTIN CRISP

DESIRE

All human activity is prompted by desire.

—BERTRAND RUSSELL

Desire (Continued)

I'd love to see Christ come back to crush the spirit of hate and make men put down their guns. I'd also like just one more hit single.

—TINY TIM

It seems to me we can never give up longing and wishing while we are thoroughly alive. There are certain things we feel to be beautiful and good, and we must hunger after them.

—GEORGE ELIOT

Our necessities are few but our wants are endless.

—JOSH BILLINGS

I want a man who's kind and understanding. Is that too much to ask of a millionaire?

—ZSA ZSA GABOR

Bring me my bow of burning gold, Bring me my arrows of desire, Bring me my spear O clouds, unfold! Bring me my chariot of fire!

—WILLIAM BLAKE

We lived for days on nothing but food and water.

—W. C. FIELDS

There are two tragedies in life. One is to lose your heart's desire. The other is to gain it.

—GEORGE BERNARD SHAW

If you desire many things, many things will seem few.

—BEN FRANKLIN

Some desire is necessary to keep life in motion.

—SAMUEL JOHNSON

The stoical scheme of supplying our wants by lopping off our desires, is like cutting off our feet, when we want shoes.

—JONATHAN SWIFT

How few our real wants! and how easy it is to satisfy them! Our imaginary ones are boundless and insatiable.

—JULIUS & AUGUSTUS HARE
GUESSES AT TRUTH

Follow your desire as long as you live . . . When riches are gained, follow desire, for riches will not profit if one is sluggish.

—PTAHHOTEP

If you refuse to accept anything but the best, you very often get it.

—W. SOMERSET MAUGHAM

We need some imaginative stimulus, some not impossible ideal such as may shape vague hope, and transform it into effective desire, to carry us year after year, without disgust, through the routine work which is so large a part of life.

—WALTER PATER

If a man could have half his wishes, he would double his troubles.

—BENJAMIN FRANKLIN

There are a million things in this universe you can have, and there are a million things you can't have. It's no fun facing that, but that's the way things are.

—CAPTAIN KIRK
STAR TREK

RICKY RICARDO: There you go again, wanting something that you haven't got. *LUCY RICARDO:* I do not. I just want to see what I haven't got that I don't want.

—*I LOVE LUCY*

NOTICE TO OUR GUESTS: If there is anything you need and don't see, please let us know, and we will show you how to do without it.

—MARY TOARMINA MC WILLIAMS FADDEN

I got up on my feet and went over to the bowl in the corner and threw cold water on my face. After a while I felt a little better, but very little. I needed a drink, I needed a lot of life insurance, I needed a vacation, I needed a home in the country. What I had was a coat, a hat and a gun. I put them on and went out of the room.

—RAYMOND CHANDLER'S DETECTIVE PHILIP MARLOWE

A "Bay Area Bisexual" told me I didn't quite coincide with either of her desires.

—WOODY ALLEN

You can have anything you want if you want it desperately enough. You must want it with an inner exuberance that erupts through the skin and joins the energy that created the world.

—SHEILA GRAHAM

The one thing I do not want to be called is First Lady. It sounds like a saddle horse.

—JACQUELINE KENNEDY

I don't want the cheese, I just want to get out of the trap.

—SPANISH PROVERB

One must not lose desires. They are mighty stimulants to creativeness, to love, and to long life.

—ALEXANDER BOGOMOLETZ

I'd like a bird for an old lady of ninety-four. She had one, but it died and she doesn't realize it. She keeps it in a cage, talks to it, and takes it out and kisses its head.

—CONTESTANT
QUEEN FOR A DAY

My motto is "contented with little, yet wishing for more."

—CHARLES LAMB

DETACHMENT

The sun will set without thy assistance.

—THE TALMUD

Attachment is the great fabricator of illusions; reality can be attained only by someone who is detached.

—SIMONE WEIL

Most people are *on* the world, not in it—having no conscious sympathy or relationship to anything about them—undiffused, separate, and rigidly alone like marbles of polished stone, touching but separate.

—JOHN MUIR

DETERMINATION
Also See PERSEVERANCE

Nothing in the world can take the place of persistence. Talent will not; nothing is more common than unsuccessful men with talent. Genius will not; unrewarded genius is almost a proverb. Education alone will not; the world is full of educated derelicts. Persistence and determination alone are omnipotent.

—CALVIN COOLIDGE

Let me tell you the secret that has led to my goal. My strength lies solely in my tenacity.

—LOUIS PASTEUR

Never retreat. Never explain. Get it done and let them howl.

—BENJAMIN JOWETT

I am in earnest; I will not equivocate; I will not excuse; I will not retreat a single inch; and I will be heard.

—WILLIAM LLOYD GARRISON

DISCIPLINE

A prince should therefore have no other aim or thought but war and discipline, for that is the only art that is necessary to one who commands.

—MACHIAVELLI

You never will be the person you can be if pressure, tension, and discipline are taken out of your life.

—JAMES G. BILKEY

DISCOMFORT
Also See COMFORT

An Englishman thinks he is moral when he is only uncomfortable.

—GEORGE BERNARD SHAW

The only thing I can't stand is discomfort.

—GLORIA STEINEM

My boat sleeps four comfortably, but five is three too many.

—WILLIAM F. BUCKLEY, JR.

DISSATISFACTION
Also See INGRATITUDE

It is not irritating to be where one is. It is only irritating to think one would like to be somewhere else.

—JOHN CAGE

Isn't there any other part of the matzo you can eat?

—MARILYN MONROE
when served matzo ball
soup three times in a row

If this is coffee, please bring me some tea; but if this is tea, please bring me some coffee.

—ABRAHAM LINCOLN

In Rome you long for the country; in the country—oh inconstant!—you praise the distant city to the stars.

—HORACE

He worked like hell in the country so he could live in the city, where he worked like hell so he could live in the country.

—DON MARQUIS

You're really letting me down as a boyfriend, not being able to control the weather and all.

—STEPHANIE VANDERKELLAN
NEWHART

She not only expects the worst, but makes the worst of it when it happens.

—MICHAEL ARLEN

Life is a hospital, in which every patient is possessed by the desire to change his bed.

—CHARLES BAUDELAIRE

There was never a banquet so sumptuous, but someone dined poorly at it.

—FRENCH PROVERB

BEAVER: Gee, there's something wrong with just about everything, isn't there Dad? *WARD:* Just about, Beav.

—*LEAVE IT TO BEAVER*

DIVERSITY

If we are to achieve a richer culture, rich in contrasting values, we must recognize the whole gamut of human potentialities, and so weave a less arbitrary social fabric, one in which each diverse human gift will find a fitting place.

—MARGARET MEAD

DIVINITY
See also GOD

If you have anything really valuable to contribute to the world it will come through the expression of your own personality, that single spark of divinity that sets you off and makes you different from every other living creature.

—BRUCE BARTON

There is surely a piece of divinity in us, something that was before the elements, and owes no homage unto the sun.

—THOMAS BROWNE

The currents of the Universal Being circulate through me; I am part and parcel of God.

—RALPH WALDO EMERSON

In no other period of history were the learned so mistrustful of the divine possibilities in man as they are now.

—GOPI KRISHNA

To see a world in a grain of sand And heaven in a wild flower, To hold Infinity in the palm of your hand, And Eternity in an hour.

—WILLIAM BLAKE

There is surely a piece of divinity in us, something that was before the elements, and owes no homage unto the sun.

—THOMAS BROWNE

DIVORCE

She cried—and the judge wiped her tears with my checkbook.

—TOMMY MANVILLE
thirteen-times-divorced millionaire

When a couple decide to divorce, they should inform both sets of parents before having a party and telling all their friends. This is not only courteous but practical. Parents may be very willing to pitch in with comments, criticism and malicious gossip of their own to help the divorce along.

—P. J. O'ROURKE

I don't think I'll get married again. I'll just find a woman I don't like and give her a house.

—LEWIS GRIZZARD

I am a marvelous housekeeper. Every time I leave a man I keep his house.

—ZSA ZSA GABOR

The happiest time in any man's life is just after the first divorce.

—JOHN KENNETH GALBRAITH

DO AS I SAY . . .

I have been a selfish being all my life, in practice, though not in principle.

—JANE AUSTEN

For what I do is not the good I want to do; no, the evil I do not want to do—this I keep on doing.

—ROMANS 7:19

I have, all my life long, been lying till noon; yet I tell all young men, and tell them with great sincerity, that nobody who does not rise early will ever do any good.

—SAMUEL JOHNSON

It is easier to fight for one's principles than to live up to them.

—ALFRED ADLER

DREAMS
See also GOALS, PUPOSE

Use your weaknesses; aspire to the strength.

—LAURENCE OLIVIER

Saddle your dreams afore you ride 'em.

—MARY WEBB

I used to work at the International House of Pancakes. It was a dream, and I made it happen.

—PAULA POUNDSTONE

You've got to create a dream. You've got to uphold the dream. If you can't, go back to the factory or go back to the desk.

—ERIC BURDON

It is said that a man's life can be measured by the dreams he fulfills.

—MR. ROARKE
FANTASY ISLAND

Dreams are the soul's pantry. Keep it well stocked and your soul will never hunger.

—SHIRLEY FEENEY
LAVERNE & SHIRLEY

The phone rings. I am not amused. This is not my favorite way to wake up. My favorite way to wake up is to have a certain French movie star whisper to me softly at two thirty in the afternoon that if I want to get to Sweden in time to pick up my Nobel Prize for Literature I had better ring for breakfast. This occurs rather less often than one might wish.

—FRAN LEBOWITZ

Ah, but a man's reach should exceed his grasp, Or what's a heaven for?

—ROBERT BROWNING

You see things; and you say, "Why?" But I dream things that never were; and I say, "Why not?"

—GEORGE BERNARD SHAW

Back of the job—the dreamer who's making the dream come true!

—BERTON BRADLEY

The only thing I ever dream is that I just won every beauty contest in the world and all the people I don't like are forced to build me a castle in France.

—STEPHANIE VANDERKELLAN
NEWHART

EARTH

The earth is like a spaceship that didn't come with an operating manual.

—R. BUCKMINSTER FULLER

EDUCATION
See also FAMILY VALUES, LEARNING

The first idea that the child must acquire, in order to be actively disciplined, is that of the difference between good and evil; and the task of the educator lies in seeing that the child does not confound good with immobility, and evil with activity.

—MARIA MONTESSORI

Enlighten the people generally, and tyranny and oppressions of body and mind will vanish like evil spirits at the dawn of day.

—THOMAS JEFFERSON

Universities should be safe havens where ruthless examination of realities will not be distorted by the aim to please or inhibited by the risk of displeasure.

—KINGMAN BREWSTER

The most important function of education at any level is to develop the personality of the individual and the significance of his life to himself and to others. This is the basic architecture of a life; the rest is ornamentation and decoration of the structure.

—GRAYSON KIRK

We learn simply by the exposure of living. Much that passes for education is not education at all but ritual. The fact is that we are being educated when we know it least.

—DAVID P. GARDNER

I was thrown out of college for cheating on the metaphysics exam; I looked into the soul of the boy next to me.

—WOODY ALLEN

I'm not a very good advertisement for the American school system.

—DAVID BRINKLEY

The important thing in science is not so much to obtain new facts as to discover new ways of thinking about them.

—WILLIAM BRAGG

I was thrown out of NYU for cheating—with the dean's wife.

—WOODY ALLEN

Education is the ability to listen to almost anything without losing your temper or your self-confidence.

—ROBERT FROST

Perhaps the most valuable result of all education is the ability to make yourself do the thing you have to do when it ought to be done, whether you like it or not; it is the first lesson that ought to be learned; and however early a man's training begins, it is probably the last lesson that he learns thoroughly.

—T. H. HUXLEY

The great aim of education is not knowledge but action.

—HERBERT SPENCER

One looks back with appreciation to the brilliant teachers, but with gratitude to those who touched our human feelings. The curriculum is so much necessary raw material, but warmth is the vital element for the growing plant and for the soul of the child.

—CARL JUNG

Education is what survives when what has been learned has been forgotten.

—B. F. SKINNER

BOY: Teach me what you know, Jim. *REVEREND JIM:* That would take hours, Terry. Ah, what the heck! We've all got a little Obi Wan Kenobie in us.

—TAXI

She knows what is the best purpose of education: not to be frightened by the best but to treat it as part of daily life.

—JOHN MASON BROWN

If you feel you have both feet planted on level ground, then the university has failed you.

—ROBERT F. GOHEEN

The whole art of teaching is only the art of awakening the natural curiosity of young minds for the purpose of satisfying it afterwards.

—ANATOLE FRANCE

If you're taking an essay exam on geography, and the exam could be on any of the countries in the world, study one country, and know it well. Let's say you choose China. When it comes time for the exam, and the question is, "Write one thousand words on Nigeria," you begin your essay, "Nigeria is nothing like China . . ." and proceed to write everything you know about China.

—QUENTIN CRISP

Creative minds always have been known to survive any kind of bad training.

—ANNA FREUD

He was not made for climbing the tree of knowledge.

—SIGRID UNDSET

SCHOOL PRINCIPAL: I'm sure your children will be very happy here. *GOMEZ:* If we'd wanted them to be happy, we would've let them stay at home.

—*THE ADDAMS FAMILY*

Educational television should be absolutely forbidden. It can only lead to unreasonable expectations and eventual disappointment when your child discovers that the letters of the alphabet do not leap out of books and dance around the room with royal-blue chickens.

—FRAN LEBOWITZ

Of what question is the following the answer: "Washington Irving"? The question: "Who was the first President of the United States, Max?"

—ANONYMOUS
(and with good reason)

I learned the way a monkey learns—by watching its parents.

—QUEEN ELIZABETH II

It is the supreme art of the teacher to awaken joy in creative expression and knowledge.

—ALBERT EINSTEIN

It is no profit to have learned well, if you neglect to do well.

—PUBLILIUS SYRUS

Give a man a fish, and you feed him for a day. Teach a man to fish, and you feed him for a lifetime.

— CHINESE PROVERB

EMPATHY
See also COMPASSION

If we could read the secret history of our enemies, we should find in each man's life sorrow and suffering enough to disarm all hostility.

—HENRY WADSWORTH LONGFELLOW

The love of our neighbor in all its fullness simply means being able to say to him, "What are you going through?"

—SIMONE WEIL

In the sick room, ten cents' worth of human understanding equals ten dollars' worth of medical science.

—MARTIN H. FISCHER

ENDURANCE

In the darkest hour the soul is replenished and given strength to continue and endure.

—HEART WARRIOR CHOSA

In spite of illness, in spite even of the archenemy sorrow, one can remain alive long past the usual date of disintegration if one is unafraid of change, insatiable in intellectual curiosity, interested in big things, and happy in small ways.

—EDITH WHARTON

The more the marble wastes, the more the statue grows.

—MICHELANGELO

Yes, as my swift days near their goal, 'Tis all that I implore: In life and death a chainless soul, With courage to endure.

—EMILY BRONTË

ENERGY
Also See ACTION

If an unusual necessity forces us onward, a surprising thing occurs. The fatigue gets worse up to a certain point, when, gradually or suddenly, it passes away and we are fresher than before! We have evidently tapped a new level of energy. There may be layer after layer of this experience, a third and fourth "wind." We find amounts of ease and power that we never dreamed ourselves to own, sources of strength habitually not taxed, because habitually we never push through the obstruction of fatigue.

—WILLIAM JAMES

One may go a long way after one is tired.

—FRENCH PROVERB

An effort impelled by desire must also have an automatic or subconscious energy to aid its realization.

—MAN RAY

Energy flowing through a system acts to organize that system.

—*WHOLE EARTH CATALOG*

This art of resting the mind and the power of dismissing from it all care and worry is probably one of the secrets of energy in our great men.

—CAPTAIN J. A. HADFIELD

ENJOYMENT
See also FUN, JOY

In those vernal seasons of the year, when the air is calm and pleasant, it were an injury and sullenness against Nature not to go out, and see her riches, and partake in her rejoicing with heaven and earth.

—JOHN MILTON

The entire object of true education, is to make people not merely do the right thing, but to enjoy right things; not merely industrious, but to love industry; not merely learned, but to love knowledge.

—JOHN RUSKIN

There are two things to aim at in life: first, to get what you want; and, after that, to enjoy it. Only the wisest of mankind achieve the second.

—LOGAN PEARSALL SMITH

Wealth is not his that has it, but his that enjoys it.

—BENJAMIN FRANKLIN

If your capacity to acquire has outstripped your capacity to enjoy, you are on the way to the scrap-heap.

—GLEN BUCK

We may lay in a stock of pleasures, as we would lay in a stock of wine, but if we defer tasting them too long, we shall find that both are soured with age.

—CHARLES COLTON

Enjoyment is *not* a goal; it is a feeling that accompanies important ongoing activity.

—PAUL GOODMAN

All of the animals except man know that the principal business of life is to enjoy it.

—SAMUEL BUTLER

There is no time like the pleasant.

—OLIVER HERFORD

I like long walks, especially when they are taken by people who annoy me.

—FRED ALLEN

The New England conscience doesn't keep you from doing what you shouldn't—it just keeps you from enjoying it.

—CLEVELAND AMORY

If you're going to do something wrong, at least enjoy it.

—LEO ROSTEN

There is no cure for birth and death save to enjoy the interval.

—GEORGE SANTAYANA

Don't expect to enjoy life if you keep your milk of human kindness all bottled up.

—ANONYMOUS

Seek not, my soul, the life of the immortals; but enjoy to the full the resources that are within thy reach.

—PINDAR.

ENTHUSIASM

Nothing great was ever achieved without enthusiasm.

—RALPH WALDO EMERSON

I rate enthusiasm even above professional skill.

—EDWARD APPLETON

Every production of genius must be the production of enthusiasm.

—BENJAMIN DISRAELI

If you're not fired with enthusiasm, you will be fired with enthusiasm.

— VINCE LOMBARDI

ETERNITY

Eternity is a terrible thought. I mean, where's it going to end?

—TOM STOPPARD

It is eternity now. I am in the midst of it. It is about me in the sunshine; I am in it, as the butterfly in the light-laden air. Nothing has to come; it is now. Now is eternity; now is the immortal life.

—RICHARD JEFFRIES

Life is eternal; and love is immortal; and death is only a horizon; and a horizon is nothing save the limit of our sight.

—ROSSITER RAYMOND
COMMENDATORY PRAYER

EVIL
See also SIN

When choosing between two evils, I always like to try the one I've never tried before.

—MAE WEST

If you resist evil, as soon as it's gone, you'll fold.

—KEN KESEY

Lack of money is the root of all evil.

—GEORGE BERNARD SHAW

"EVIL" is "LIVE" spelled backwards.

—ANONYMOUS

The only thing necessary for the triumph of evil is for good men to do nothing.

—EDMUND BURKE

Let us not paralyze our capacity for good by brooding over man's capacity for evil.

— DAVID SARNOFF

EXCELLENCE

If you don't do it excellently, don't do it at all. Because if it's not excellent, it won't be profitable or fun, and if you're not in business for fun or profit, what the hell are you doing there?

—ROBERT TOWNSEND

Come, give us a taste of your quality.

—WILLIAM SHAKESPEARE

The best things and best people rise out of their separateness. I'm against a homogenized society because I want the cream to rise.

—ROBERT FROST

EXPECTATIONS

Not as bad as you might have imagined.

—CALVIN TRILLIN
motto suggested for New Jersey

Your request for no MSG was ignored.

—FORTUNE COOKIE

Don't go around saying the world owes you a living; the world owes you nothing; it was here first.

—MARK TWAIN

The thing always happens that you really believe in; and the belief in a thing makes it happen.

—FRANK LLOYD WRIGHT

JEAN-PAUL SARTRE [arriving in heaven]: It's not what I expected. *GOD:* What did you expect? *SARTRE:* Nothing.

—SCTV

If you think you can do a thing or think you can't do a thing, you're right.

—HENRY FORD

The world has a way of giving what is demanded of it. If you are frightened and look for failure and poverty, you will get them, no matter how hard you may try to succeed. Lack of faith in yourself, in what life will do for you, cuts you off from the good things of the world. Expect victory and you make victory.

—PRESTON BRADLEY

THE EXPERTS SPEAK

The talking picture will not supplant the regular silent motion picture.

—THOMAS EDISON

Women may be said to be an inferior man.

—ARISTOTLE

The phonograph is not of any commercial value.

—THOMAS EDISON

With over 50 foreign cars already on sale here, the Japanese auto industry isn't likely to carve out a big slice of the U.S. market for itself.

—*BUSINESS WEEK*, 1968

The radio craze will soon die out.

—THOMAS EDISON

FAILURE
See also RISK, SUCCESS

If at first you don't succeed, find out if the loser gets anything.

—BILL LYON

The man who tried his best and failed is superior to the man who never tried.

—BUD WILKINSON

Far better it is to dare mighty things, to win glorious triumphs even though checkered by failure, than to rank with those poor spirits who neither enjoy nor suffer much because they live in the gray twilight that knows neither victory nor defeat.

—THEODORE ROOSEVELT

There is the greatest practical benefit in making a few failures early in life.

—T. H. HUXLEY

Many of life's failures are people who did not realize how close they were to success when they gave up.

—THOMAS EDISON

No matter how cynical you get, it is impossible to keep up.

—LILY TOMLIN

Good people are good because they've come to wisdom through failure.

—WILLIAM SAROYAN

Zeus does not bring all men's plans to fulfillment.

—HOMER

You said, "but." I've put my finger on the whole trouble. You're a "but" man. Don't say, "but." That little word "but" is the difference between success and failure. Henry Ford said, "I'm going to invent the automobile," and Arthur T. Flanken said, "But . . ."

—SGT. ERNIE BILKO
THE PHIL SILVERS SHOW

I cannot give you the formula for success, but I can give you the formula for failure which is: Try to please everybody.

—HERBERT BAYARD SWOPE

There is no failure except in no longer trying.

—ELBERT HUBBARD

Give me the young man who has brains enough to make a fool of himself.

—ROBERT LOUIS STEVENSON

We are all of us failures—at least, the best of us are.

—JAMES BARRIE

Flops are a part of life's menu and I've never been a girl to miss out on any of the courses.

—ROSALIND RUSSELL

FAME
Also See SUCCESS

Fame is only good for one thing—they will cash your check in a small town.

—TRUMAN CAPOTE

FAMILY
See also FAMILY VALUES

I have known more men destroyed by the desire to have wife and child and to keep them in comfort than I have seen destroyed by drink and harlots.

—W. B. YEATS

Far from being the basis of the good society, the family, with its narrow privacy and tawdry secrets, is the source of all our discontents.

—EDMUND LEACH

The Family! Home of all social evils, a charitable institution for indolent women, a prison workshop for the slaving breadwinner, and a hell for children.

—AUGUST STRINDBERG

Perhaps the greatest social service that can be rendered by anybody to the country and to mankind is to bring up a family.

—GEORGE BERNARD SHAW

FAMILY VALUES
See also FAMILY, MARRIAGE

When I can no longer bear to think of the victims of broken homes, I begin to think of the victims of intact ones.

—PETER DE VRIES

My parents have been visiting me for a few days. I just dropped them off at the airport. They leave tomorrow.

—MARGARET SMITH

Basically my wife was immature. I'd be at home in the bath and she'd come in and sink my boats.

—WOODY ALLEN

My grandmother started walking five miles a day when she was sixty. She's ninety-five now, and we don't know where the hell she is.

—ELLEN DEGENERES

FRED SANFORD: Didn't you learn anything being my son? Who do you think I'm doing this all for? *LAMONT SANFORD:* Yourself. *FRED:* Yeah, you learned something.

Happiness is having a large, loving, caring, close-knit family in another city.

—GEORGE BURNS

Dear United States Army: My husband asked me to write a recommend that he supports his family. He cannot read, so don't tell him. Just take him. He ain't no good to me. He ain't done nothing but raise hell and drink lemon essence since I married him eight years ago, and I got to feed seven kids of his. Maybe you can get him to carry a gun. He's good on squirrels and eating. Take him and welcome. I need the grub and his bed for the kids. Don't tell him this, but just take him.

—HAND-DELIVERED IN 1943
BY AN ARKANSAS MAN
TO HIS DRAFT BOARD

Wallpaper design for the marital bedroom:

EXCUSE ME COULD YOU PLEASE SAY THAT AGAIN I DON'T BELIEVE I HEARD YOU CORRECTLY LISTEN JUST WHO THE HELL DO YOU THINK YOU ARE FOR GOD'S SAKE WHAT AM I SUPPOSED TO BE YOUR SERVANT DON'T YOU DARE TALK TO ME IN THAT TONE OF VOICE I GUESS WE JUST AREN'T MEANT TO BE TOGETHER THAT'S ALL I'VE HAD IT UP TO HERE WITH YOU THAT'S RIGHT YOU HEARD ME THAT'S NOT MEANT TO BE A THREAT WE'RE JUST IN DIFFERENT TIMES IN OUR LIFE OK GO AHEAD THEN LEAVE I'LL HELP YOU PACK YOUR BAGS I GUESS WE DON'T NEED TO BE TOGETHER OH THAT'S CUTE REAL CUTE I DON'T HAVE TO STAND FOR.

—DAN GREENBURG & SUZANNE O'MALLEY

My wife was in labor with our first child for thirty-two hours and I was faithful to her the whole time.

—JONATHAN KATZ

Your responsibility as a parent is not as great as you might imagine. You need not supply the world with the next conqueror of disease or major motion picture star. If your child simply grows up to be someone who does not use the word "collectible" as a noun, you can consider yourself an unqualified success.

—FRAN LEBOWITZ

Dad worked hard for us, he provided for us, and he certainly didn't want to have to talk to us on top of that.

—KEVIN ARNOLD
THE WONDER YEARS

GRANNY: Why don' y' just shoot me like an ol' horse an' sell m' body fer glue? *JED CLAMPETT:* Now, Granny, that's ridiculous. *JETHRO BODINE:* Yeah, you wouldn't make enough glue fer a — *JED:* Don't help me, boy!

—*THE BEVERLY HILLBILLIES*

I wish I knew how customs like this get started; it would make them easier to stamp out.

—MARTIN LANE
THE PATTY DUKE SHOW

BEN CARTWRIGHT: I'm not in the habit of giving lectures, and if I do, it's because they're needed. Might have been a good idea if your father had given you a few. *CANDY CANADAY:* Oh, he did. *BEN:* Obviously they didn't have much effect. *CANDY:* Oh, yes they did; I left home.

—*BONANZA*

I think our parents got together in 1946 and said, "Let's have lots of kids and give them everything they want, so that they can grow up and be totally messed up and unable to cope with life."

—HOPE STEADMAN
THIRTYSOMETHING

My father worked for the same firm for twelve years. They fired him. They replaced him with a tiny gadget this big. It does everything that my father does, only it does it much better. The depressing thing is my mother ran out and bought one.

—WOODY ALLEN

FAITH

Faith is the bird that feels the light and sings when the dawn is still dark.

—RABINDRANATH TAGORE

FEAR
See also ANXIETY, WORRY

Do not be too timid and squeamish about your actions. All life is an experiment.

—RALPH WALDO EMERSON

Fear is the main source of superstition, and one of the main sources of cruelty. To conquer fear is the beginning of wisdom.

—BERTRAND RUSSELL

Fear is that little darkroom where negatives are developed.

—MICHAEL PRITCHARD

Of all base passions, fear is the most accursed.

—WILLIAM SHAKESPEARE

Fear is pain arising from the anticipation of evil.

—ARISTOTLE

For as children tremble and fear everything in the blind darkness, so we in the light sometimes fear what is no more to be feared than the things children in the dark hold in terror and imagine will come true.

—LUCRETIUS

To him who is in fear, everything rustles.

—SOPHOCLES

I'm a paranoiac, baby, so I hope you don't make the mistake of laboring under the false impression that you are talking to a sane person.

—TENNESSEE WILLIAMS

Fear of death has been the greatest ally of tyranny past and present.

—SYDNEY HOOK

It is better to be a coward for a minute than to be dead the rest of your life.

—PROVERB

You gain strength, courage and confidence by every experience in which you really stop to look fear in the face. You are able to say to yourself, "I've lived through this horror. I can take the next thing that comes along." You must do the thing you think you cannot do.

—ELEANOR ROOSEVELT

Our doubts are traitors, and make us lose the good we oft might win by fearing to attempt.

—WILLIAM SHAKESPEARE

Show me a guy who's afraid to look bad, and I'll show you a guy you can beat every time.

—RENE AUBERJONOIS

Do the thing you fear, and the death of fear is certain.

—RALPH WALDO EMERSON

Aim for success, not perfection. Never give up your right to be wrong, because then you will lose the ability to learn new things and move forward with your life. Remember that fear always lurks behind perfectionism. Confronting your fears and allowing yourself the right to be human can, paradoxically, make you a far happier and more productive person.

—DR. DAVID M. BURNS

A coward dies a hundred deaths, a brave man only once . . . But then, once is enough, isn't it?

—JUDGE HARRY STONE
NIGHT COURT

I believe that anyone can conquer fear by doing the things he fears to do, provided he keeps doing them until he gets a record of successful experiences behind him.

—ELEANOR ROOSEVELT

All through the five acts he played the King as though under momentary apprehension that someone else was about to play the Ace.

—EUGENE FIELD

FEAR OF FEAR

The thing I fear most is fear.

—MICHEL DE MONTAIGNE

Nothing is terrible except fear itself.

—FRANCIS BACON

The only thing I am afraid of is fear.

—DUKE OF WELLINGTON

Nothing is so much to be feared as fear.

—HENRY DAVID THOREAU

FICKLENESS

That sir which serves and seeks for gain, And follows but for form, Will pack when it begins to rain, And leave thee in the storm.

—WILLIAM SHAKESPEARE

FORGETTING

Necessary, forever necessary, to burn out false shames and smelt the heaviest ore of the body into purity.

—D. H. LAWRENCE

To be wronged is nothing unless you continue to remember it.

—CONFUCIUS

A retentive memory may be a good thing, but the ability to forget is the true token of greatness.

—ELBERT HUBBARD

To err is human To forgive takes restraint; To forget you forgave Is the mark of a saint.

—SUZANNE DOUGLASS

FORGIVING

She got even in a way that was almost cruel. She forgave them.

—RALPH McGILL
on Eleanor Roosevelt

One should forgive one's enemies, but not before they are hanged.

—HEINRICH HEINE

If I owe Smith ten dollars, and God forgives me, that doesn't pay Smith.

—ROBERT G. INGERSOLL

Since nothing we intend is ever faultless, and nothing we attempt ever without error, and nothing we achieve without some measure of finitude and fallibility we call humanness, we are saved by forgiveness.

—DAVID AUGSBURGER

God may forgive you, but I never can.

—QUENN ELIZABETH I

Of course God will forgive me; that's his business.

—HEINRICH HEINE
last words

The American public would forgive me anything except running off with Eddie Fisher.

—JACQUELINE KENNEDY

Love is an act of endless forgiveness.

—PETER USTINOV

The weak can never forgive. Forgiveness is the attribute of the strong.

—MAHATMA GANDHI

Here is a mental treatment guaranteed to cure every ill that flesh is heir to: sit for half an hour every night and mentally forgive everyone against whom you have any ill will or antipathy.

—CHARLES FILLMORE

Always forgive your enemies—nothing annoys them so much.

—OSCAR WILDE

Forgiveness is the key to action and freedom.

—HANNAH ARENDT

FREEDOM

The only man who is really free is the one who can turn down an invitation to dinner without giving an excuse.

—JULES RENARD

In the last analysis, our only freedom is the freedom to discipline ourselves.

—BERNARD BARUCH

You have everything but one thing, madness. A man needs a little madness or else—he never dares cut the rope and be free.

—ZORBA THE GREEK

I call that mind free which jealously guards its intellectual rights and powers, which calls no man master, which does not content itself with a passive or hereditary faith, which opens itself to light whencesoever it may come, which receives new truth as an angel from Heaven.

—WILLIAM ELLERY CHANNING

Liberty is a beloved discipline.

—GEORGE C. HOMANS

As soon as man apprehends himself as free and wishes to use his freedom, his activity is play.

—JEAN-PAUL SARTRE

To be free is to have achieved your life.

—TENNESSEE WILLIAMS

Free your mind and your ass will follow.

—GEORGE CLINTON

Man must choose whether to be rich in things or in the freedom to use them.

—IVAN ILLICH

FRIENDSHIP

The best mirror is an old friend.

—GEORGE HERBERT

A friend is a gift you give yourself.

—ROBERT LOUIS STEVENSON

It isn't so much what's on the table that matters, as what's on the chairs.

—W. S. GILBERT
on dining with friends

A friend, I am told, is worth more than pure gold.

— POPEYE

Wealth brings many friends, but a poor man's friend deserts him.

—PROVERBS 19:4

Friendship is like money, easier made than kept.

—SAMUEL BUTLER

To whom can I speak today? I am heavy-laden with trouble Through lack of an intimate friend.

—THE MAN WHO WAS TIRED OF LIFE, 1990 B.C.

A faithful friend is the medicine of life.

—ECCLESIASTICUS 6:16

One's friends are that part of the human race with which one can be human.

—GEORGE SANTAYANA

Each friend represents a world in us, a world possibly not born until they arrive, and it is only by this meeting that a new world is born.

—ANAIS NIN

Elysium is as far as to The very nearest Room If in that Room a Friend await Felicity or Doom—what Fortitude the Soul contains, That it can so endure The accent of a coming Foot—The opening of a Door.

—EMILY DICKINSON

For memory has painted this perfect day with colors that never fade, and we find at the end of a perfect day the soul of a friend we've made.

—CARRIE JACOBS BOND

We cherish our friends not for their ability to amuse us, but for ours to amuse them.

—EVELYN WAUGH

The only service a friend can really render is to keep up your courage by holding up to you a mirror in which you can see a noble image of yourself.

—GEORGE BERNARD SHAW

If you want to make a friend, let someone do you a favor.

—BENJAMIN FRANKLIN

Given the choice of friendship or success, I'd probably choose success.

—STING, 1980

Friendship's much more important to me [now] than what I thought success was.

—STING, 1990

FUN
See also ENJOYMENT

Getting there isn't half the fun—it's all the fun.

—ROBERT TOWNSEND

The world is a stage, the stage is a world of entertainment!

—HOWARD DIETZ

If all the year were playing holidays To sport would be as tedious as to work.

—WILLIAM SHAKESPEARE

Leisure time is the five or six hours when you sleep at night.

—GEORGE ALLEN

The parties all reminded me of the Gay Nineties—all the men are gay and the women are in their nineties.

— ALICE-LEONE MOATS
describing Philadelphia society

Baseball is fun for you & me. There is batting and fielding and making an out, There is doubles & triples and even home runs, But what I like about baseball is for the fun.

—MATT BOHN
at age 11

A good and wholesome thing is a little harmless fun in this world; it tones a body up and keeps him human and prevents him from souring.

—MARK TWAIN

The superfluous, a very necessary thing.

—VOLTAIRE

There is nothing I love as much as a good fight.

—FRANKLIN D. ROOSEVELT
January 22, 1911

GENETICS

She's descended from a long line her mother listened to.

—GYPSY ROSE LEE

With me, it's just a genetic dissatisfaction with everything.

—WOODY ALLEN

We are all omnibuses in which our ancestors ride, and every now and then one of them sticks his head out and embarrasses us.

—OLIVER WENDELL HOLMES

Breed is stronger than pasture.

—GEORGE ELIOT

GIVING
See also CHARITY, GOOD DEEDS, SERVICE, SHARING, STINGINESS

Money-giving is a very good criterion of a person's mental health. Generous people are rarely mentally ill people.

—DR. KARL A. MENNINGER

The Sea of Galilee and the Dead Sea are made of the same water. It flows down, clear and cool, from the heights of Hermon and the roots of the cedars of Lebanon. The Sea of Galilee makes beauty of it, for the Sea of Galilee has an outlet. It gets to give. It gathers in its riches that it may pour them out again to fertilize the Jordan plain. But the Dead Sea with the same water makes horror. For the Dead Sea has no outlet. It gets to keep.

—HARRY EMERSON FOSDICK
THE MEANING OF SERVICE

Let the season of giving be yours and not that of your inheritors.

—KHALIL GIBRAN
THE PROPHET

We are rich only through what we give, and poor only through what we refuse.

—ANNE-SOPHIE SWETCHINE

We are better pleased to see those on whom we confer benefits than those from whom we receive them.

—FRANÇOIS LA ROCHEFOUCAULD

The giving of money, time, support, and encouragement to worthy causes can never be detrimental to the giver. The laws of nature are structured so that acts of charity will open an individual to an unbounded reservoir of riches.

—JEFFREY MOSES

"I have got to take a few pints of soup to the deserving poor," said Myrtle. "I'd better set about it. Amazing the way these bimbos absorb soup. Like sponges."

—P. G. WODEHOUSE

For every action there is an equal and opposite reaction. If you want to receive a great deal, you first have to give a great deal. If each individual will give of himself to whomever he can, wherever he can, in any way that he can, in the long run he will be compensated in the exact proportion that he gives.

—R. A. HAYWARD

They who give have all things; they who withhold have nothing.

—HINDU PROVERB

The house which is not opened for charity, will be opened to the physician.

—THE TALMUD

The spirit in which a thing is given determines that in which the debt is acknowledged; it's the intention, not the face-value of the gift, that's weighed.

—SENECA

Give light and the people will find their own way.

—MOTTO OF THE SCRIPPS-HOWARD NEWSPAPERS

The first great gift we can bestow on others is a good example.

—THOMAS MORELL

Give what you have. To someone, it may be better than you dare to think.

—HENRY WADSWORTH LONGFELLOW

Avarice hoards itself poor; charity gives itself rich.

—GERMAN PROVERB

Riches may enable us to confer favours, but to confer them with propriety and grace requires a something that riches cannot give.

—CHARLES CALEB COLTON

So when you give to the needy, do not announce it with trumpets, as the hypocrites do in the synagogues and on the streets, to be honored by men. I tell you the truth, they have received their reward in full. But when you give to the needy, do not let your left hand know what your right hand is doing, so that your giving may be in secret. Then your Father, who sees what is done in secret, will reward you.

—JESUS OF NAZARETH
Matthew 6:2–4

It hurteth not the tongue to give fair words.

—JOHN HEYWOOD

The most difficult part is to give. Then why not add a smile?

—JEAN DE LA BRUYÈRE

We should give as we would receive, cheerfully, quickly, and without hesitation; for there is no grace in a benefit that sticks to the fingers.

—SENECA

Let him that desires to see others happy, make haste to give while his gift can be enjoyed, and remember that every moment of delay takes away something from the value of his benefaction.

—SAMUEL JOHNSON

Do not give dogs what is sacred; do not throw your pearls to pigs. If you do, they may trample them under their feet, and then turn and tear you to pieces.

—JESUS OF NAZARETH
Matthew 7:6

Jesus sat down opposite the place where the offerings were put and watched the crowd putting their money into the temple treasury. Many rich people threw in large amounts. But a poor widow came and put in two very small copper coins [mites], worth only a fraction of a penny. Calling his disciples to him, Jesus said, "I tell you the truth, this poor widow has put more into the treasury than all the others. They all gave out of their wealth; but she, out of her poverty, put in everything— all she had to live on."

—MARK 12:41–44

Let your hand feel for the afflictions and distresses of everyone, and let your hand give in proportion to your purse; remembering always the estimation of the widow's mite.

—GEORGE WASHINGTON

Man discovers his own wealth when God comes to ask gifts of him.

—RABINDRANATH TAGORE

As you go, preach this message: "The kingdom of heaven is near." Heal the sick, raise the dead, cleanse those who have leprosy, drive out demons. Freely you have received, freely give.

—JESUS OF NAZARETH
Matthew 10:7–8

By Jove the stranger and the poor are sent, And what to those we give, to Jove is lent.

—HOMER

God loveth a cheerful giver.

—PAUL
2 Corinthians 9:7

The Lord loveth a cheerful giver. He also accepteth from a grouch.

—NOTICE IN A CHURCH BULLETIN

It is more blessed to give than to receive.

—JESUS OF NAZARETH
Acts 20:35

'Tis always more blessed to give than to receive; for example, wedding presents.

—H. L. MENCKEN

If riches increase, let thy mind hold pace with them; and think it not enough to be liberal, but munificent.

—THOMAS BROWNE

If you have much give of your wealth, if you have little give of your heart.

—ARAB PROVERB

Da da da (that is) Be subdued, Give, Be merciful.

—BRIHADARANYAKA UPANISHAD

Not he who has much is rich, but he who gives much.

—ERICH FROMM

Then Peter said, "Silver or gold I do not have, but what I have I give you."

— ACTS 3:6

Behold, I do not give lectures or a little charity, When I give I give myself.

—WALT WHITMAN

You give but little when you give of your possessions. It is when you give of yourself that you truly give.

—KHALIL GIBRAN

No person was ever honored for what he received. Honor has been the reward for what he gave.

—CALVIN COOLIDGE

When we grow old, there can only be one regret—not to have given enough of ourselves.

— ELEONORA DUSE

Many people give a tenth to the Lord—a tenth of what they ought to give.

—ANONYMOUS

Prayer carries us half way to God, fasting brings us to the door of His palace, and alms-giving procures us admission.

—KORAN

There are those who give with joy, and that joy is their reward. And there are those who give with pain, and that pain is their baptism. And there are those who give and know not pain in giving, nor do they seek joy, nor give with mindfulness of virtue; They give as in yonder valley the myrtle breathes its fragrance into space. Through the hands of such as these God speaks, and from behind their eyes He smiles upon the earth.

—KHALIL GIBRAN

As the purse is emptied, the heart is filled.

—VICTOR HUGO

He who cannot give anything away cannot feel anything either.

—FRIEDRICH NIETZSCHE

A cheerful giver does not count the cost of what he gives. His heart is set on pleasing and cheering him to whom the gift is given.

—JULIAN OF NORWICH

Don't give till it hurts—give till it feels good.

—ANONYMOUS

The fragrance always remains in the hand that gives the rose.

—HEDA BEJAR

See first that you yourself deserve to be a giver, and an instrument of giving. For in truth it is life that gives unto life—while you, who deem yourself a giver, are but a witness.

—KHALIL GIBRAN

Man discovers his own wealth when God comes to ask gifts of him.

—RABINDRANATH TAGORE

Or what man is there of you, whom if his son ask bread, will he give him a stone? Or if he ask a fish, will he give him a serpent? If ye then, being evil, know how to give good gifts unto your children, how much more shall your Father which is in heaven give good things to them that ask him?

—MATTHEW 7:9–11

For too many giving is occasional, spasmodic, ill-proportioned. It depends on what is left over when other things have had their full share. Sometimes what it means is that only the small change lying in their pockets goes to the support of good and worthy causes.

—ROBERT J. MC CRACKEN, D.D.

In this world it is not what we take up, but what we give up, that makes us rich.

—HENRY WARD BEECHER

GIVING UP

I phoned my dad to tell him I had stopped smoking. He called me a quitter.

—STEVEN PEARL

GOALS
See also DREAMS, PURPOSE

Men cannot for long live hopefully unless they are embarked upon some great unifying enterprise—one for which they may pledge their lives, their fortunes and their honor.

—C. A. DYKSTRA

Since the mind is a specific biocomputer, it needs specific instructions and directions. The reason most people never reach their goals is that they don't define them, or ever seriously consider them as believable or achievable. Winners can tell you where they are going, what they plan to do along the way, and who will be sharing the adventure with them.

—DENIS WAITLEY

I'm not a little girl from a little town planning to make it in the big town. I'm a big girl from a big town, and I have every intention of making it in this small town.

—MAE WEST
A year later, she was the biggest star in Hollywood.

The highest good; towards this all government, all social conventions, all art, literature, and science should directly or indirectly tend. Holy men and holy women are those who keep this unconsciously in view at all times whether of work or pastime.

—SAMUEL BUTLER

Forget goals. Value the process.

—JIM BOUTON

GOD

See also DIVINITY, PRAYER, RELIGION, WORSHIP

I know God will not give me anything I can't handle. I just wish that He didn't trust me so much.

—MOTHER TERESA

I am ready to meet my Maker. Whether my Maker is prepared for the ordeal of meeting me is another matter.

—WINSTON CHURCHILL

Oh God, in the name of Thine only beloved Son, Jesus Christ, Our Lord, let him phone me *now*.

—DOROTHY PARKER

God is love, but get it in writing.

—GYPSY ROSE LEE

I love God, and when you get to know Him, you find He's a Livin' Doll.

—JANE RUSSELL

Many a time we've been down to our last piece of fatback. And I'd say, "Should we eat it, or render it down for soap?" Your Uncle Jed would say, "Render it down. God will provide food for us poor folks, but we gotta do our own washin'."

—GRANNY
THE BEVERLY HILLBILLIES

Men talk of "finding God," but no wonder it is difficult; He is hidden in that darkest hiding-place, your heart. You yourself are a part of him.

—CHRISTOPHER MORLEY

Einstein was a man who could ask immensely simple questions. And what his work showed is that when the answers are simple too, then you can hear God thinking.

—JACOB BRONOWSKI

I am a disciplined comedian; of course I take direction. From God, that is.

—SPIKE MILLIGAN

God enters by a private door into every individual.

—RALPH WALDO EMERSON

The best way to know God is to love many things.

—VINCENT VAN GOGH

What is God? Everything.

—PINDAR

Even God lends a hand to honest boldness.

—MENANDER

When God wounds from on high he will follow with the remedy.

—FERNANDO DE ROJAS

I treated him, God cured him.

—AMBROISE PAR

God is usually on the side of the big squadrons and against the small ones.

—ROGER DE BUSSY-RABUTIN

If God were not a necessary Being of Himself, He might almost seem to be made for the use and benefit of men.

—JOHN TILLOTSON

Live innocently; God is here.

—LINNAEUS

The universe is the language of God.

—LORENZ OKEN

In the faces of men and women I see God.

—WALT WHITMAN

VISITOR: Henry, have you made your peace with God?
THOREAU: We have never quarreled.

God hid the fossils in the rocks in order to tempt geologists into infidelity.

—EDMUND GOSSE

The Lord God is subtle, but malicious he is not.

—ALBERT EINSTEIN

God is a verb.

—R. BUCKMINSTER FULLER

Isn't God special?

—CHURCH LADY

If only God would give me some clear sign! Like making a large deposit in my name at a Swiss bank.

—WOODY ALLEN

I simply haven't the nerve to imagine a being, a force, a cause which keeps the planets revolving in their orbits, and then suddenly stops in order to give me a bicycle with three speeds.

—QUENTIN CRISP

GOOD DEEDS
See also CHARITY, GIVING, SERVICE

We are here on earth to do good to others. What the others are here for, I don't know.

—W. H. AUDEN

The last temptation is the greatest treason: To do the right deed for the wrong reason.

—T. S. ELIOT

Do right *for your own sake*, and be happy in knowing that your *neighbor* will certainly share in the benefits resulting.

—MARK TWAIN

I'm no angel, but I've spread my wings a bit.

—MAE WEST

Such tendency toward doing good as is in men's hearts would not be diminished by the removal of the delusion that good deeds are primarily for the sake of No. 2 instead of for the sake of No. 1.

—MARK TWAIN

Do all the good you can, By all the means you can, In all the ways you can, In all the places you can, At all the times you can, To all the people you can, As long as ever you can.

—JOHN WESLEY

Avoid what is evil; do what is good; purify the mind—this is the teaching of the Awakened One.

—PALI CANON

BELINDA: Ay, but you know we must return good for evil. *LADY BRUTE:* That may be a mistake in the translation.

—JOHN VANBRUGH

The deed is all, not the glory.

—JOHANN WOLFGANG VON GOETHE

Noble deeds are most estimable when hidden.

—BLAISE PASCAL

Isn't it better to have men being ungrateful than to miss a chance to do good?

—DENIS DIDEROT

He that returns a good for evil obtains the victory.

—THOMAS FULLER, M.D.

How far that little candle throws his beams! So shines a good deed in a naughty world.

—WILLIAM SHAKESPEARE

I expect to pass through life but once. If, therefore, there be any kindness I can show, or any good thing I can do to any fellow being, let me do it now, and not defer or neglect it, as I shall not pass this way again.

—WILLIAM PENN

Neither do people light a lamp and put it under a bowl. Instead they put it on its stand, and it gives light to everyone in the house. In the same way, let your light shine before men, that they may see your good deeds and praise your Father in heaven.

—JESUS OF NAZARETH
Matthew 5:15–16

It's so much easier to do good than to be good.

—B. C. FORBES

A man makes no noise over a good deed, but passes on to another as a vine to bear grapes again in season.

—MARCUS ANTONINUS

Command them to do good, to be rich in good deeds, and to be generous and willing to share. In this way they will lay up treasure for themselves as a firm foundation for the coming age, so that they may take hold of the life that is truly life.

—PAUL
I Timothy 6:18–19

A man does not have to be an angel in order to be a saint.

—ALBERT SCHWEITZER

Noble deeds and hot baths are the best cures for depression.

—DODIE SMITH

GOODNESS

Hail to you gods, On that day of the great reckoning. Behold me, I have come to you, Without sin, without guilt, without evil, Without a witness against me, Without one whom I have wronged. I am one pure of mouth, pure of hands.

—THE BOOK OF THE DEAD
address to the gods 1700-1000 B.C.
(not used in many centuries—obviously)

See golden days, fruitful of golden deeds, With Joy and Love triumphing.

—JOHN MILTON

Good behavior is the last refuge of mediocrity.

—HENRY S. HASKINS

The chief ingredients in the composition of those qualities that gain esteem and praise, are good nature, truth, good sense, and good breeding.

—JOSEPH ADDISON

GRATITUDE
See also APPRECIATION

Rest and be thankful.

—INSCRIPTION ON A STONE SEAT
IN THE SCOTTISH HIGHLANDS

The best thing about the future is that it comes only one day at a time.

—ABRAHAM LINCOLN

Thank God for tea! What would the world do without tea? —how did it exist? I am glad I was not born before tea.

—SYDNEY SMITH

Blessed is he who expects no gratitude, for he shall not be disappointed.

— W. C. BENNETT

Thank God men cannot fly, and lay waste the sky as well as the earth.

—HENRY DAVID THOREAU

Gratitude is not only the greatest of virtues, but the parent of all the others.

—CICERO

Gratitude is the heart's memory.

—FRENCH PROVERB

Thank-you, music-lovers.

—SPIKE JONES

Got no check books, got no banks. Still I'd like to express my thanks—I got the sun in the mornin' and the moon at night.

—IRVING BERLIN

I got the son in the mornin' and the father at night.

—RUSTY WARREN

Gratitude is not only the greatest of virtues, but the parent of all others.

—CICERO

Gratitude is the fruit of great cultivation. You do not find it among gross people.

—SAMUEL JOHNSON

Gratitude is a blessing we give to one another.

—ROBERT RAYNOLDS

Gratitude is to thank God for all His infinite goodness with all our heart.

—OTTOKAR PROHASZKA

I feel a very unusual sensation. If it is not indigestion, I think it must be gratitude.

—BENJAMIN DISRAELI

When eating bamboo sprouts, remember the man who planted them.

—CHINESE PROVERB

Let not thine hand be stretched out to receive and shut when thou shouldst repay.

—APOCRYPHA

Do not refuse a wing to the person who gave you the whole chicken.

—R. G. H. SIU

Don't drown the man who taught you to swim.

—ENGLISH PROVERB

There are minds so impatient of inferiority that their gratitude is a species of revenge, and they return benefits, not because recompense is a pleasure, but because obligation is a pain.

—SAMUEL JOHNSON

There is as much greatness of mind in acknowledging a good turn as in doing it.

—SENECA

I can live for two months on a good compliment.

—MARK TWAIN

Some people pay a compliment as if they expected a receipt.

—ELBERT HUBBARD

In most of mankind gratitude is merely a secret hope for greater favors.

—FRANÇOIS LA ROCHEFOUCAULD

When befriended, remember it. When you befriend, forget it.

—BENJAMIN FRANKLIN

Gratitude is one of the least articulate of the emotions, especially when it is deep.

—FELIX FRANKFURTER

There are two kinds of gratitude: the sudden kind we feel for what we take; and the larger kind we feel for what we give.

—E. A. ROBINSON

Things could be a lot worse.

—JOYCE CAROL OATES

Every time we tell anybody to cheer up, things might be worse, we run away for fear we might be asked to specify how.

—FRANKLIN P. ADAMS

The best medicine I know for rheumatism is to thank the Lord it ain't the gout.

—JOSH BILLINGS

GRIEF

See also PAIN, SUFFERING, UNHAPPINESS

Tears, idle tears, I know not what they mean, Tears from the depth of some divine despair Rise in the heart, and gather to the eyes, In looking on the happy autumn fields, And thinking of the days that are no more.

—LORD ALFRED TENNYSON

The sound of her silk skirt has stopped. On the marble pavement dust grows. Her empty room is cold and still. Fallen leaves are piled against the doors. Longing for that lovely lady, How can I bring my aching heart to rest?

—HAN WU-TI
on the death of his mistress

GUILT

We find the defendants incredibly guilty.

—FOREMAN RETURNING THE VERDICT
ON ZERO MOSTEL AND GENE WILDER
IN MEL BROOKS'S *THE PRODUCERS*

Guilt is never a rational thing; it distorts all the faculties of the human mind, it perverts them, it leaves a man no longer in the free use of his reason, it puts him into confusion.

—EDMUND BURKE

Guilt is the source of sorrows, the avenging fiend that follows us behind with whips and stings.

—NICHOLAS ROWE

Guilt is the mafia of the mind.

—BOB MANDEL

Joe, never feel guilty about having warm human feelings toward anyone.

—BEN CARTWRIGHT
BONANZA

HABITS

First we form habits, then they form us. Conquer your bad habits, or they'll eventually conquer you.

—DR. ROB GILBERT

Have a place for everything and keep the thing somewhere else; this is not a piece of advice, it is merely a custom.

—MARK TWAIN

I'm glad I don't have to explain to a man from Mars why each day I set fire to dozens of little pieces of paper, and then put them in my mouth.

—MIGNON MC LAUGHLIN

Good habits, which bring our lower passions and appetites under automatic control, leave our natures free to explore the larger experiences of life. Too many of us divide and dissipate our energies in debating actions which should be taken for granted.

—RALPH W. SOCKMAN

Cultivate only the habits that you are willing should master you.

—ELBERT HUBBARD

Custom is the plague of wise men and the idol of fools.

—THOMAS FULLER

Habit with him was all the test of truth, "It must be right: I've done it from my youth."

—GEORGE CRABBE

To fall into a habit is to begin to cease to be.

—MIGUEL DE UNAMUNO

I always keep a supply of stimulant handy in case I see a snake—which I also keep handy.

—W. C. FIELDS

Faced with the choice between changing one's mind and proving there is no need to do so, almost everyone gets busy on the proof.

—JOHN KENNETH GALBRAITH

Life is made up, not of great sacrifices or duties, but of little things, in which smiles and kindness, and small obligations given habitually, are what preserve the heart and secure comfort.

—WILLIAM DAVY

HAPPINESS
Also See ENJOYMENT, JOY

The only true happiness comes from squandering ourselves for a purpose.

—WILLIAM COWPER

Happiness? A good cigar, a good meal, and a good woman—or a bad woman. It depends on how much happiness you can handle.

—GEORGE BURNS

The only way to avoid being miserable is not to have enough leisure to wonder whether you are happy or not.

—GEORGE BERNARD SHAW

My creed is that: Happiness is the only good. The place to be happy is here. The time to be happy is now. The way to be happy is to make others so.

—ROBERT G. INGERSOLL

What more felicity can fall to creature, Than to enjoy delight with liberty.

—EDMUND SPENSER
THE FATE OF THE BUTTERFLY

Happiness is always a by-product. It is probably a matter of temperament, and for anything I know it may be glandular.

—ROBERTSON DAVIES

True happiness is of a retired nature, and an enemy to pomp and noise; it arises, in the first place, from the enjoyment of one's self; and, in the next, from the friendship and conversation of a few select companions.

—JOSEPH ADDISON

INTERVIEWER: Ever meet a man that could make you happy? *MAE WEST:* Several times.

Happiness is the most powerful of tonics.

—HERBERT SPENCER

Happiness consists in activity: such is the constitution of our nature: it is a running stream, and not a stagnant pool.

—JOHN M. GOOD

A merry heart doeth good like a medicine.

—PROVERBS 17:22

It is the chiefest point of happiness that a man is willing to be what he is.

—ERASMUS

No man chooses evil because it is evil; he only mistakes it for happiness, the good he seeks.

—MARY WOLLSTONECRAFT SHELLEY

It's good to be just plain happy; it's a little better to know that you're happy; but to understand that you're happy and to know why and how and still be happy, be happy in the being and the knowing, well that is beyond happiness, that is bliss.

—HENRY MILLER

Mirth is like a flash of lightning, that breaks through a gloom of clouds, and glitters for a moment; cheerfulness keeps up a kind of daylight in the mind, and fills it with a steady and perpetual serenity.

—JOSEPH ADDISON

Full of love for all things in the world, practicing virtue in order to benefit others, this man alone is happy.

— BUDDHA

In about the same degree as you are helpful, you will be happy.

—KARL REILAND

Getters generally don't get happiness; givers get it. You simply give to others a bit of yourself—a thoughtful act, a helpful idea, a word of appreciation, a lift over a rough spot, a sense of understanding, a timely suggestion. You take something out of your mind, garnished in kindness out of your heart, and put it into the other fellow's mind and heart.

—CHARLES H. BURR

The roots of happiness grow deepest in the soil of service.

—ANONYMOUS

Happiness lies in good health and a bad memory.

—INGRID BERGMAN

When one door of happiness closes, another opens; but often we look so long at the closed door that we do not see the one that has been opened for us.

—HELEN KELLER

The best advice on the art of being happy is about as easy to follow as advice to be well when one is sick.

—ANNE-SOPHIE SWETCHINE

Happiness depends, as Nature shows, Less on exterior things than most suppose.

—WILLIAM COWPER

Some day people will learn that material things do not bring happiness and are of little use in making people creative and powerful.

—CHARLES STEINMETZ

[We look] for happiness in possession of the external—in money, a good time, somebody to lean on, and so on. We are impatient, hurried and fretful because we do not find happiness where we look for it.

—JOHN DEWEY

Happiness depends upon ourselves.

—ARISTOTLE

The man who makes everything that leads to happiness depend on himself, and not upon other men, has adopted the very best plan for living happily.

—PLATO

He that is of a merry heart hath a continual feast.

—PROVERBS 15:15

Happiness is in the taste, and not in the things.

—FRANÇOIS LA ROCHEFOUCAULD

The happiness of your life depends on the quality of your thoughts.

—MARCUS ANTONINUS

It is not in doing what you like, but in liking what you do that is the secret of happiness.

— JAMES BARRIE

Happiness is not having what you want, but wanting what you have.

—RABBI HYMAN SCHACHTEL

The Constitution of America only guarantees pursuit of happiness—you have to catch up with it yourself. Fortunately, happiness is something that depends not on position but on disposition, and life is what you make it.

—GILL ROBB WILSON

Perfect happiness, I believe, was never intended by the Deity to be the lot of one of his creatures in this world, but that he has very much put in our power the nearness of our approaches to it is what I have steadfastly believed.

—THOMAS JEFFERSON

Happiness seems to require a modicum of external prosperity.

—ARISTOTLE

It is not the rich man you should properly call happy, but him who knows how to use with wisdom the blessings of the gods.

—HORACE

May we never let the things we can't have, or don't have, or shouldn't have, spoil our enjoyment of the things we do have and can have. As we value our happiness let us not forget it, for one of the greatest lessons in life is learning to be happy without the things we cannot or should not have.

—RICHARD EVANS

No enjoyment, however inconsiderable, is confined to the present moment. A man is the happier for life from having made once an agreeable tour, or lived for any length of time with pleasant people, or enjoyed any considerable interval of innocent pleasure.

—SYDNEY SMITH

Happiness is the sense of having worked according to one's capacity and light to make things clear and get rid of cant and shams.

—T. H. HUXLEY

Happiness is itself a kind of gratitude.

—JOSEPH WOOD KRUTCH

We must select the illusion which appeals to our temperament and embrace it with passion if we want to be happy.

—CYRIL CONNOLLY

Happiness lies not in the mere possession of money; it lies in the joy of achievement, in the thrill of creative effort.

—FRANKLIN D. ROOSEVELT

If a man is happy in America it is considered he is doing something wrong.

—CLARENCE DARROW

A great obstacle to happiness is to anticipate too great a happiness.

—BERNARD FONTENELLE

To be without some of the things you want is an indispensable part of happiness.

—BERTRAND RUSSELL

Our greatest happiness does not depend on the condition of life in which chance has placed us, but is always the result of a good conscience, good health, occupation, and freedom in all just pursuits.

—THOMAS JEFFERSON

HATE

I'm not a vegetarian because I love animals; I'm a vegetarian because I hate plants.

—A. WHITNEY BROWN

He loved me absolutely; that's why he hates me absolutely.

—FRIEDA (MRS. D.H.) LAWRENCE

People hate me because I am a multifaceted, talented, wealthy, internationally famous genius.

—JERRY LEWIS

I'm so busy loving everybody, I don't have any time to hate anybody.

—DALE EVANS

It is better to be hated for what you are than loved for what you are not.

—ANDRÉ GIDE

Hate must make a man productive. Otherwise one might as well love.

—KARL KRAUS

Hating people is like burning your own house down to get rid of a rat.

—HARRY EMERSON FOSDICK

I never hated a man enough to give him his diamonds back.

—ZSA ZSA GABOR

HEALING

See also CURE, ILLNESS, MEDICINE, PHYSICIANS

When an emotional injury takes place, the body begins a process as natural as the healing of a physical wound. Let the process happen. Trust that nature will do the healing. Know that the pain will pass and, when it passes, you will be stronger, happier, more sensitive and aware.

—HOW TO SURVIVE THE LOSS OF A LOVE

Pleasant words are a honeycomb sweet to the soul and healing to the bones.

—PROVERBS 16:24

Happiness, grief, gaiety, sadness, are by nature contagious. Bring your health and your strength to the weak and sickly, and so you will be of use to them. Give them, not your weakness, but your energy, so you will revive and lift them up. Life alone can rekindle life.

—HENRI-FRÉDÉRIC AMIEL

HEALTH

Health is the state about which medicine has nothing to say.

—W. H. AUDEN

Positive attitudes—optimism, high self-esteem, an outgoing nature, joyousness, and the ability to cope with stress—may be the most important bases for continued good health.

—HELEN HAYES

The first wealth is health.

—RALPH WALDO EMERSON

Without health, life is not life; it is only a state of languor and suffering.

—FRANÇOIS RABELAIS

A healthy body is a guest-chamber for the soul; a sick body is a prison.

—FRANCIS BACON

Look to your health; and if you have it, praise God, and value it next to a good conscience, for health is the second blessing that we mortals are capable of; a blessing that money cannot buy.

—IZAAK WALTON

O, health! health! The blessings of the rich! the riches of the poor! Who can buy thee at too dear a rate, since there is no enjoying the world without thee?

—BEN JOHNSON

Measure your health by your sympathy with morning and Spring. If there is no response in you to the awakening of nature, if the prospect of an early morning walk does not banish sleep, if the warble of the first bluebird does not thrill you, know that the morning and spring of your life are past. Thus may you feel your pulse.

—HENRY DAVID THOREAU

There's lots of people in this world who spend so much time watching their health, that they haven't the time to enjoy it.

—JOSH BILLINGS

I've never met a healthy person who worried much about his health, or a good person who worried much about his soul.

—JOHN HALDANE

Long life to you! Good health to you and your household! And good health to all that is yours!

—I SAMUEL 25:6

HEAVEN

God forbid that I should go to any heaven in which there are no horses.

—ROBERT BONTINE

My idea of heaven is eating *pâtés de foie gras* to the sound of trumpets.

—SYDNEY SMITH

HOMOSEXUALITY

Dear Miss Manners, What am I supposed to say when I am introduced to a homosexual couple? Gentle Reader, "How do you do?" "How do you do?"

—JUDITH MARTIN

HOPE

Hope is a good breakfast, but it is a bad supper.

—FRANCIS BACON

A gentleman who had been very unhappy in marriage, married immediately after his wife died: Johnson said, it was the triumph of hope over experience.

—JAMES BOSWELL

There is nothing so well known as that we should not expect something for nothing—but we all do and call it Hope.

—EDGAR WATSON HOWE

Hope is the feeling you have that the feeling you have isn't permanent.

—JEAN KERR

It is natural to man to indulge in the illusion of hope. We are apt to shut our eyes against a painful truth, and listen to the song of that siren, till she transforms us into beasts.

—PATRICK HENRY

In the factory we make cosmetics; in the store we sell hope.

—CHARLES REVSON

Hope is the most treacherous of human fancies.

—JAMES FENIMORE COOPER

Just as dumb animals are snared by food, human beings would not be caught unless they had a nibble of hope.

—PETRONIUS

Hope in reality is the worst of all evils, because it prolongs the torments of man.

—FRIEDRICH NIETZSCHE

I suppose it can be truthfully said that Hope is the only universal liar who never loses his reputation for veracity.

—ROBERT G. INGERSOLL

A man will sometimes devote all his life to the development of one part of his body—the wishbone.

—ROBERT FROST

Many of us spend half of our time wishing for things we could have if we didn't spend half our time wishing.

—ALEXANDER WOOLLCOTT

Hope springs eternal in the human breast. Man never is, but always to be blest.

—ALEXANDER POPE

This wonder we find in hope, that she is both a flatterer and a true friend. How many would die did not hope sustain them; how many have died by hoping too much!

—OWEN FELTHAM

The man who lives only by hope, will die with despair.

—ITALIAN PROVERB

He that lives upon hope, dies fasting.

—BENJAMIN FRANKLIN

The prestigious *Harper Book of American Quotations* had one of the most amusing typos we've discovered. It quoted Mr. Franklin as saying, "He that lives upon Hope, dies farting."

Abandon hope, all ye who enter here.

—MOTTO ON GATES OF HELL,
ACCORDING TO DANTE

HUMAN POTENTIAL

Most people live, whether physically, intellectually or morally, in a very restricted circle of their potential being. They make use of a very small portion of their possible consciousness, and of their soul's resources in general, much like a man who, out of his whole bodily organism, should get into a habit of using and moving only his little finger. Great emergencies and crises show us how much greater our vital resources are than we had supposed.

—WILLIAM JAMES

What one has to do, usually can be done.

—ELEANOR ROOSEVELT

The truth is that all of us attain the greatest success and happiness possible in this life whenever we use our native capacities to their greatest extent.

—DR. SMILEY BLANTON

When people say to me: "How do you do so many things?" I often answer them, without meaning to be cruel: "How do you do so little?" It seems to me that people have vast potential. Most people can do extraordinary things if they have the confidence or take the risks. Yet most people don't. They sit in front of the telly and treat life as if it goes on forever.

—PHILIP ADAMS

HUMANITY

Human beings yield in many situations, even important and spiritual and central ones, as long as it prolongs one's well-being.

—ALEXANDER SOLZHENITSYN

Man is slightly nearer to the atom than to the star. From his central position man can survey the grandest works of Nature with the astronomer, or the minutest works with the physicist.

—ARTHUR STANLEY

Man is his own star, and the soul that can Render an honest and a perfect man Commands all light, all influence, all fate.

—JOHN FLETCHER

Men are not against you; they are merely for themselves.

—GENE FOWLER

We are made out of oppositions; we live between two poles—you don't reconcile the poles, you just recognize them.

—ORSON WELLES

We are the products of editing, rather than authorship.

—GEORGE WALD

Give them great meals of beef and iron and steel, they will eat like wolves and fight like devils.

—WILLIAM SHAKESPEARE

He was a poor weak human being like themselves, a human soul, weak and helpless in suffering, shivering in the toils of the eternal struggle of the human soul with pain.

—LIAM O'FLAHERTY

It is possible that our race may be an accident, in a meaningless universe, living its brief life uncared for, on this dark, cooling star: but even so—and all the more—what marvelous creatures we are! What fairy story, what tale from the Arabian Nights of the Jinns, is a hundredth part as wonderful as this true fairy story of simians! It is so much more heartening, too, than the tales we invent. A universe capable of giving birth to many such accidents is—blind or not—a good world to live in, a promising universe. We once thought we lived on God's footstool; it may be a throne.

—CLARENCE DAY

The tendency of man's nature to good is like the tendency of water to flow downwards.

—MENCIUS

From a distance the earth looks blue and green and the snow-capped mountains white. From a distance the ocean meets the stream and the eagle takes to flight. From a distance there is harmony and it echoes through the land. It's the voice of hope. It's the voice of peace. It's the voice of every man.

—JULIE GOLD

I love humanity; it's people I can't stand.

—ANONYMOUS

MR. SPOCK: May I point out that I had an opportunity to observe your counterparts quite closely. They were brutal, savage, unprincipled, uncivilized, treacherous—in every way, splendid examples of Homo sapiens. The very flower of humanity. I found them quite refreshing. *CAPTAIN KIRK [To Dr. McCoy]:* I'm not sure, but I think we've been insulted.

—*STAR TREK*

Adam was human; he didn't want the apple for the apple's sake; he wanted it because it was forbidden.

—MARK TWAIN

Is not man himself the most unsettled of all the creatures of the earth? What is this trembling sensation that is intensified with each ascending step in the natural order?

—UGO BETTI

Joy, interrupted now and again by pain and terminated ultimately by death, seems the normal course of life in Nature. Anxiety and distress, interrupted occasionally by pleasure, is the normal course of man's existence.

—JOSEPH KRUTCH

The deepest principle in human nature, is the craving to be appreciated.

—WILLIAM JAMES

Consider that people are like tea bags. They don't know their own strength until they get into hot water.

—DAN MC KINNON

People become who they are. Even Beethoven became Beethoven.

—RANDY NEWMAN

The only normal people are the ones we haven't gotten to know yet.

—HAROLD H. BLOOMFIELD, M.D.

HUMILITY

Only the untalented can afford to be humble.

—SYLVIA MILES

What the world needs is more geniuses with humility. There are so few of us left.

—OSCAR LEVANT

HUMOR

He deserves Paradise who makes his companions laugh.

— KORAN

Among those whom I like or admire, I can find no common denominator, but among those whom I love, I can: all of them make me laugh.

—W. H. AUDEN

Humor is something that thrives between man's aspirations and his limitations. There is more logic in humor than in anything else. Because, you see, humor is truth.

—VICTOR BORGE

One is healthy when one can laugh at the earnestness and zeal with which one has been hypnotized by any single detail in one's life.

—FRIEDRICH NIETZSCHE

Humor is emotional chaos, remembered in emotional tranquility.

—JAMES THURBER

Humor is an affirmation of dignity, a declaration of man's superiority to all that befalls him.

—ROMAIN GARY

I am *sincere* about life, but I'm not *serious* about it.

—ALAN WATTS

Shall I crack any of those old jokes, master, at which the audience never fail to laugh?

—ARISTOPHANES

Nothing shortens a journey so pleasantly as an account of misfortunes at which the hearer is permitted to laugh.

—QUENTIN CRISP

Laughter is inner jogging.

—NORMAN COUSINS

Not a shred of evidence exists in favor of the idea that life is serious.

—BRENDAN GILL

Imagination is a quality given a man to compensate him for what he is not, and a sense of humor was provided to console him for what he is.

—OSCAR WILDE

The one important thing I have learned over the years is the difference between taking one's work seriously and taking one's self seriously. The first is imperative and the second is disastrous.

—MARGOT FONTEYN

Laughter is an orgasm triggered by the intercourse of reason with unreason.

—JACK KROLL

Humor is vague, runaway stuff that hisses around the fissures and crevices of the mind, like some sort of loose physic gas.

—JONATHAN MILLER

Laughter is man's most distinctive emotional expression. Man shares the capacity for love and hate, anger and fear, loyalty and grief, with other living creatures. But humor, which has an intellectual as well as an emotional element, belongs to man.

—MARGARET MEAD

Life's more amusing than we thought.

—ANDREW LONG

Don't take yourself too seriously. And don't be too serious about not taking yourself too seriously.

—HOWARD OGDEN

A difference of taste in jokes is a great strain on the affections.

—GEORGE ELIOT

Seriousness is the only refuge of the shallow.

—OSCAR WILDE

Humor must be one of the chief attributes of God. Plants and animals that are distinctly humorous in form and characteristics are God's jokes.

—MARK TWAIN

For some of the large indignities of life, the best remedy is direct action. For the small indignities, the best remedy is a Charlie Chaplin movie.

—CAROL TAVRIS

Laughter is the tonic, the relief, the surcease for pain.

—CHARLIE CHAPLIN

Humor is laughing at what you haven't got when you ought to have it.

—LANGSTON HUGHES

Humor, in all its many-splendored varieties, can be simply defined as a type of stimulation which tends to elicit the laughter reflex.

—ARTHUR KOESTLER

If an idea is important enough it is worth laughing at.

—ALAN PLATER

Do not take life too seriously. You will never get out of it alive.

—ELBERT HUBBARD

Humor is a prelude to faith and Laughter is the beginning of prayer.

— REINHOLD NIEBUHR

Angels fly because they take themselves lightly.

—G. K. CHESTERTON

HYPOCRISY

Why do you look at the speck of sawdust in your brother's eye and pay no attention to the plank in your own eye? How can you say to your brother, "Let me take the speck out of your eye," when all the time there is a plank in your own eye? You hypocrite, first take the plank out of your own eye, and then you will see clearly to remove the speck from your brother's eye.

—JESUS OF NAZARETH
Matthew 7:3–5

IDEALS

Men would like to learn to love themselves, but they usually find they cannot. That is because they have built an ideal image of themselves which puts their real self in the shade.

—GERALD BRENAN

We do not know whether it is good to live or to die. Therefore, we should not take delight in living nor should we tremble at the thought of death. We should be equiminded towards both. This is the ideal.

—MAHATMA GANDHI

The "what should be" never did exist, but people keep trying to live up to it. There is no "what should be," there is only what is.

—LENNY BRUCE

It doesn't matter who gives them as long as you never wear anything second-rate. Wait for the first-class jewels, Gigi. Hold on to your ideals.

—COLETTE

Men would like to love themselves but they usually find that they cannot. That is because they have built an ideal image of themselves which puts their real self in the shade.

—GERALD BRENAN

Castles in the air cost a vast deal to keep up.

—BARON LYTTON

American women expect to find in their husbands a perfection that English women only hope to find in their butlers.

—SOMERSET MAUGHAM

It is not materialism that is the chief curse of the world, but idealism. Men get into trouble by taking their visions and hallucinations too seriously.

—H. L. MENCKEN

The poet, described in ideal perfection, brings the whole soul of man into activity, with the subordination of its faculties to each other, according to their relative worth and dignity. He diffuses a tone and spirit of unity, that blends, and (as it were) fuses, each into each, by that synthetic and magical power . . . imagination.

—SAMUEL COLERIDGE

Don't use that foreign word "ideals." We have that excellent native word "lies."

—HENRIK IBSEN

What we need most, is not so much to realize the ideal as to idealize the real.

—H. F. HEDGE

The true ideal is not opposed to the real, but lies in it; and blessed are the eyes that find it.

—JAMES RUSSELL LOWELL

ILLNESS
See also HEALTH

To hate and to fear is to be psychologically ill. It is, in fact, the consuming illness of our time.

—H. A. OVERSTREET

All interest in disease and death is only another expression of interest in life.

—THOMAS MANN

The more serious the illness, the more important it is for you to fight back, mobilizing all your resources—spiritual, emotional, intellectual, physical.

—NORMAN COUSINS

If the essential core of the person is denied or suppressed, he gets sick sometimes in obvious ways, sometimes in subtle ways, sometimes immediately, sometimes later.

—ABRAHAM MASLOW

It's been troubling me. Now, why is it that most of us can talk openly about the illnesses of our bodies, but when it comes to our brain and illnesses of the mind we clam up and because we clam up, people with emotional disorders feel ashamed, stigmatized and don't seek the help that can make the difference.

—KIRK DOUGLAS

The past few years have seen a steady increase in the number of people playing music in the streets. The past few years have also seen a steady increase in the number of malignant diseases. Are these two facts related?

—FRAN LEBOWITZ

A wise man should consider that health is the greatest of human blessings, and learn how by his own thought to derive benefit from his illnesses.

—HIPPOCRATES

We forget ourselves and our destinies in health, and the chief use of temporary sickness is to remind us of these concerns.

—RALPH WALDO EMERSON

ILLUSION

The greatest obstacle to discovery is not ignorance—it is the illusion of knowledge.

—DANIEL J. BOORSTIN

Illusion is the first of all pleasures.

—OSCAR WILDE

The most fatal illusion is the settled point of view. Since life is growth and motion, a fixed point of view kills anybody who has one.

—BROOKS ATKINSON

What if everything is an illusion and nothing exists? In that case, I definitely overpaid for my carpet.

—WOODY ALLEN

IMAGINATION
See also THINKING

It is the spirit of the age to believe that any fact, however suspect, is superior to any imaginative exercise, no matter how true.

—GORE VIDAL

Never lose in your imagination. Never. Never. Never. Never.

—WINSTON CHURCHILL
paraphrased

To be one's self, and unafraid whether right or wrong, is more admirable than the easy cowardice of surrender to conformity.

—IRVING WALLACE

Imagination is more important than knowledge.

—ALBERT EINSTEIN

There is only one admirable form of the imagination: the imagination that is so intense that it creates a new reality, that it makes things happen, whether it be a political thing, or a social thing or a work of art.

—SEAN O'FAOLAIN

We must reserve a back shop all our own, entirely free, in which to establish our real liberty and our principal retreat and solitude.

—MICHEL DE MONTAIGNE

No man that does not see visions will ever realize any high hope or undertake any high enterprise.

—WOODROW WILSON

Love doesn't grow on the trees like apples in Eden— it's something you have to make. And you must use your imagination to make it too, just like anything else.

—JOYCE CARY

Without this playing with fantasy no creative work has ever yet come to birth. The debt we owe to the play of imagination is incalculable.

—CARL JUNG

His imagination resembled the wings of an ostrich. It enabled him to run, though not to soar.

—MACAULAY
on John Dryden

The imagination may be compared to Adam's dream— he awoke and found it truth.

—JOHN KEATS

Imagination is very rapid; it jumps from admiration to love, from love to matrimony in a moment.

—JANE AUSTEN

IMMORTALITY
See also ETERNITY

I don't want to achieve immortality through my work. I want to achieve it through not dying.

—WOODY ALLEN

Immortality consists largely of boredom.

—COCHRANE
STAR TREK

For God so loved the world, that he gave his only begotten Son, that whosoever believeth in him should not perish, but have everlasting life. For God sent not his son into the world to condemn the world; but that the world through him might be saved.

—JOHN 3:16–17

INACTION
See also ACTION, BLAME, CHOICE, PROCRASTINATION, RISK

"Let's go." "Yes, let's go." *STAGE DIRECTION:* They do not move.

—LAST LINES OF *WAITING FOR GODOT*
SAMUEL BECKETT

Life is to be lived. If you have to support yourself, you had bloody well better find some way that is going to be interesting. And you don't do that by sitting around wondering about yourself.

—KATHARINE HEPBURN

Why should we take up farming when there are so many mongongo nuts in the world?

—AFRICAN BUSHMAN

Help! I'm being held prisoner by my heredity and environment!

—DENNIS ALLEN

He not busy being born is busy dying.

—BOB DYLAN

There are hazards in anything one does, but there are greater hazards in doing nothing.

—SHIRLEY WILLIAMS

Even if you're on the right track, you'll get run over if you just sit there.

—WILL ROGERS

When you have to make a choice and don't make it, that is in itself a choice.

—WILLIAM JAMES

INDIVIDUALITY
See also SELF

I once complained to my father that I didn't seem to be able to do things the same way other people did. Dad's advice? "Margo, don't be a sheep. People hate sheep. They eat sheep."

—MARGO KAUFMAN

There are many who are living far below their possibilities because they are continually handing over their individualities to others. Do you want to be a power in the world? Then be yourself. Be true to the highest within your soul and then allow yourself to be governed by no customs or conventionalities or arbitrary man-made rules that are not founded on principle.

—RALPH WALDO TRINE

As President Nixon says, presidents can do almost anything, and President Nixon has done many things that nobody would have thought of doing.

—GOLDA MEIR

In order to be irreplaceable one must always be different.

—COCO CHANEL

Who is it that says most? Which can say more than this rich praise—that you alone are you?

—WILLIAM SHAKESPEARE

INGRATITUDE
See also DISSATISFACTION

Why is it no one ever sent me yet one perfect limousine, do you suppose? Ah no, it's always just my luck to get one perfect rose.

—DOROTHY PARKER

Blow, blow, thou winter wind, Thou art not so unkind As man's ingratitude.

—WILLIAM SHAKESPEARE
AS YOU LIKE IT

I hate ingratitude more in a man Than lying, vainness, babbling, drunkenness, Or any taint of vice whose strong corruption Inhabits our frail blood.

—WILLIAM SHAKESPEARE
TWELFTH NIGHT

INSPIRATION

Have I ever told you you're my hero? You're everything I would like to be. I can climb higher than an eagle. You are the wind beneath my wings.

—LARRY HENLEY & JEFF SILBAR

The one thing I do not want to be called is First Lady. It sounds like a saddle horse.

—JACQUELINE KENNEDY

I wish I was Donna Reed— she'd have something wonderful to say. Or Shirley Jones—she'd have something wonderful to say, too, and maybe even some fresh-baked cookies. Or Loretta Young; of course, she wouldn't have anything wonderful to say, but she would make a stunning entrance.

—JESSICA TATE

INTEGRITY

Some persons are likeable in spite of their unswerving integrity.

—DON MARQUIS

INTOLERANCE

There are some people that if they don't know, you can't tell 'em.

—LOUIS ARMSTRONG

Anybody who sees and paints a sky green and pastures blue ought to be sterilized.

—ADOLF HILTER

The mind of a bigot is like the pupil of an eye, the more light you pour upon it, the more it will contract.

—OLIVER WENDELL HOLMES, JR.

THE INVISIBLE

We look at it and do not see it; Its name is The Invisible. We listen to it and do not hear it; Its name is The Inaudible. We touch it and do not find it; Its name is The Formless.

—LAO-TZU

The power of the visible is the invisible.

—MARIANNE MOORE

JOY
See also ENJOYMENT, HAPPINESS

With coarse rice to eat, with water to drink, and my bended arm for a pillow—I still have joy in the midst of these things.

—CONFUCIUS

With an eye made quiet by the power of harmony, and the deep power of joy, we see into the life of things.

—WILLIAM WORDSWORTH

The eye sees the open heaven, The heart is intoxicated with bliss.

—FRIEDRICH VON SCHILLER

How good is man's life, the mere living! How fit to employ all the heart and the soul and the senses forever in joy!

—ROBERT BROWNING

Gladness of the heart is the life of a man, and the joyfulness of a man prolongeth his days.

—ECCLESIASTICUS 30:22

Mirth is the sweet wine of human life. It should be offered sparkling with zestful life unto God.

—HENRY WARD BEECHER

Since Time is not a person we can overtake when he is gone, let us honor him with mirth and cheerfulness of heart while he is passing.

—JOHANN WOLFGANG VON GOETHE

Joy is the sweet voice, Joy the luminous cloud—We in ourselves rejoice! And thence flows all that charms or ear or sight, All melodies the echoes of that voice, All colors a suffusion from that light.

—SAMUEL COLERIDGE

His lord said unto him, Well done, thou good and faithful servant: thou hast been faithful over a few things, I will make thee ruler over many things: enter thou into the joy of thy lord.

— JESUS OF NAZARETH
Matthew 25:21

"On with the dance, let the joy be unconfined!" is my motto, whether there's any dance to dance or any joy to unconfine.

—MARK TWAIN

Joy is the feeling of grinning inside.

—DR. MELBA COLGROVE

There is no such thing as the pursuit of happiness, but there is the discovery of joy.

—JOYCE GRENFELL

One joy scatters a hundred griefs.

—CHINESE PROVERB

The very society of joy redoubles it, so that, while it lights upon my friend, it rebounds upon myself, and the brighter his candle burns, the more easily will it light mine.

—ROBERT SOUTH

To love what you do and feel that it matters—how could anything be more fun?

—KATHERINE GRAHAM

We may allow ourselves a brief period of rejoicing.

—WINSTON CHURCHILL
on the day World War II ended

Gude nicht, and joy be wi' you a'.

—CAROLINA OLIPHANT

KINDNESS

When I played pro football, I never set out to hurt anybody deliberately—unless it was, you know, important, like a league game or something.

—DICK BUTKUS

Kindness can become its own motive. We are made kind by being kind.

—ERIC HOFFER

One of the most difficult things to give away is kindness; it usually comes back to you.

—ANONYMOUS

Kindness is loving people more than they deserve.

—JOSEPH JOUBERT

Kind looks, kind words, kind acts, and warm handshakes—these are secondary means of grace when men are in trouble and are fighting their unseen battles.

—JOHN HALL

Kindness is gladdening the hearts of those who are traveling the dark journey with us.

—HENRI-FRÉDÉRIC AMIEL

Kind words do not cost much. They never blister the tongue or lips. Mental trouble was never known to arise from such quarters. Though they do not cost much yet they accomplish much. They make other people good natured. They also produce their own image on men's souls, and a beautiful image it is.

—BLAISE PASCAL

If you can't be kind, at least be vague.

—MISS MANNERS

You cannot do a kindness too soon, for you never know how soon it will be too late.

—RALPH WALDO EMERSON

When kindness has left people, even for a few moments, we become afraid of them as if their reason has left them.

—WILLA CATHER

Do not ask me to be kind; just ask me to act as though I were.

—JULES RENARD

Kindness is the insignia of a loving heart.

—ANONYMOUS

Be kind and considerate to others, depending somewhat upon who they are.

—DON HEROLD

Kindness is never wasted. If it has no effect on the recipient, at least it benefits the bestower.

—ANONYMOUS

KNOWLEDGE
See also EDUCATION, LEARNING

Pleasure is a shadow, wealth is vanity, and power is a pageant; but knowledge is ecstatic in enjoyment, perennial in frame, unlimited in space and infinite in duration.

—DE WITT CLINTON

We are here and it is now. Further than that, all knowledge is moonshine.

—H. L. MENCKEN

Knowledge, in truth, is the great sun in the firmament. Life and power are scattered with all its beams.

—DANIEL WEBSTER

You are free to eat from any tree of the garden, but you must not eat from the tree of the knowledge of good and evil, for when you eat of it you will surely die.

—GOD, TO ADAM
Genesis 2:16–17

We may eat fruit from the trees in the garden, but God did say, "You must not eat fruit from the tree that is in the middle of the garden, and you must not touch it, or you will die."

—EVE, TO SERPENT
Genesis 3:2–3

The public have an insatiable curiosity to know everything, except what is worth knowing.

—OSCAR WILDE

The things most people want to know about are usually none of their business.

—GEORGE BERNARD SHAW

Most men believe that it would benefit them if they could get a little from those who *have* more. How much more would it benefit them if they would learn a little from those who *know* more.

—WM. J. H. BOETCKER

I know only two tunes; one of them is "Yankee Doodle," and the other isn't.

—U. S. GRANT

LAWYERS

There are three reasons why lawyers are replacing rats as laboratory research animals. One is that they're plentiful, another is that lab assistants don't get attached to them, and the third is that there are some things rats just won't do.

—LAWYER JOKE NO. 3,479,153(c)

They have no lawyers among them, for they consider them as a sort of people whose profession it is to disguise matters.

—THOMAS MORE
describing Utopia

LEADERSHIP

A leader is one who, out of madness or goodness, volunteers to take upon himself the woe of the people. There are few men so foolish, hence the erratic quality of leadership in the world.

—JOHN UPDIKE

True leadership must be for the benefit of the followers, not the enrichment of the leaders.

—ROBERT TOWNSEND
UP THE ORGANIZATION

How far would Moses have gone if he had taken a poll in Egypt?

—HARRY S. TRUMAN

LEARNING
See also EDUCATION, KNOWLEDGE

For the things we have to learn before we can do them, we learn by doing them.

—ARISTOTLE

Learning is not attained by chance, it must be sought for with ardor and attended to with diligence.

—ABIGAIL ADAMS

Wear your learning like your watch, in a private pocket: and do not pull it out and strike it, merely to show that you have one.

—EARL OF CHESTERFIELD

What a wonderful day we've had. You have learned something, and I have learned something. Too bad we didn't learn it sooner. We could have gone to the movies instead.

—BALKI BARTOKOMOUS

I bid him look into the lives of men as though into a mirror, and from others to take an example for himself.

—TERENCE

LIES

I am different from Washington; I have a higher, grander standard of principle. Washington could not lie. I *can* lie, but I won't.

—MARK TWAIN

There's one way to find out if a man is honest—ask him. If he says, "Yes," you know he's a crook.

—GROUCHO MARX

INTERVIEWER: You've been accused of vulgarity. *MEL BROOKS:* Bullshit!

The biggest liar in the world is They Say.

—DOUGLAS MALLOCH

There are three kinds of lies: lies, damn lies, and statistics.

—BENJAMIN DISRAELI

That's not a lie, it's a terminological inexactitude.

—ALEXANDER HAIG

The liar's punishment is not in the least that he is not believed, but that he cannot believe anyone else.

—GEORGE BERNARD SHAW

I can't tell a lie—not even when I hear one.

—JOHN KENDRICK BANGS

LIFE
See also LIFE IS . . .

Life! Can't live with it, can't live without it.

—CYNTHIA NELMA

There is more to life than increasing its speed.

—MAHATMA GANDHI

Some people die at twenty-five and aren't buried until they are seventy-five.

—BENJAMIN FRANKLIN

Life was meant to be lived, and curiosity must be kept alive. One must never, for whatever reason, turn his back on life.

—ELEANOR ROOSEVELT

While alive, he lived.

—MALCOLM FORBES
etched on his tombstone

Life's experiments are great fun. This is but another one.

—RUDYARD KIPLING

A man's life of any worth is a continual allegory.

—JOHN KEATS

Unified, disciplined, armed with the secret powers of the atom and with knowledge as yet beyond dreaming, Life, forever dying to be born afresh, forever young and eager, will presently stand upon this earth as upon a footstool and stretch out its realm amidst the stars.

—H. G. WELLS

There's an old joke: Two elderly women are at a Catskill Mountain resort and one of them says, "Boy, the food at this place is really terrible." The other one says, "Yeah, I know, and such small portions." Well, that's essentially how I feel about life.

—WOODY ALLEN
opening lines to *Annie Hall*

The hardest years in life are those between ten and seventy.

—HELEN HAYES AT AGE 83

Some say life is the thing, but I prefer reading.

—RUTH RENDELL

We cannot be *normal* and *alive* at the same time.

—E. M. CIORAN

Is life not a hundred times too short for us to stifle ourselves?

—FRIEDRICH NIETZSCHE

Who knows? Maybe my life belongs to God. Maybe it belongs to me. But I do know one thing: I'm damned if it belongs to the government.

—ARTHUR HOPPE

I have set before you life and death, blessing and cursing: therefore choose life, that both thou and thy seed may live.

—DEUTERONOMY 30:19

Tom appeared on the sidewalk with a bucket of whitewash and a long-handled brush. He surveyed the fence, and all gladness left him and a deep melancholy settled down upon his spirit. Thirty yards of board fence nine feet high. Life to him seemed hollow, and existence but a burden.

—MARK TWAIN
TOM SAWYER

Life is too short to waste In critical peep or cynic bark, Quarrel or reprimand: 'Twill soon be dark; Up! Mind thine own aim, and God speed the mark!

—RALPH WALDO EMERSON

What a wonderful life I've had! I only wish I'd realized it sooner.

—COLETTE

If I had to define life in a word, it would be: Life is creation.

—CLAUDE BERNARD
The Bulletin of New York Academy of Medicine

Dear friend, all theory is gray, And green the golden tree of life.

—JOHANN WOLFGANG VON GOETHE

There must be more to life than having everything.

—MAURICE SENDAK

There's got to be more to life than sittin' here watchin' *Days of Our Lives* and foldin' your Fruit of the Looms.

—MAMA
MAMA'S FAMILY

Remember that you ought to behave in life as you would at a banquet. As something is being passed around it comes to you; stretch out your hand, take a portion of it politely. It passes on; do not detain it. Or it has not come to you yet; do not project your desire to meet it, but wait until it comes in front of you. So act toward children, so toward a wife, so toward office, so toward wealth.

—EPICTETUS

Grasshopper, look beyond the game, as you look beneath the surface of the pool to see its depths.

—MASTER PO
KUNG FU

Life teaches us to be less harsh with ourselves and with others.

—JOHANN WOLFGANG VON GOETHE

LIFE IS . . .
Also see LIFE

. . . a banquet, and some poor sons-of-bitches are starving to death.

—AUNTIE MAME

. . . working.

—KARL MARX

. . . work.

—HENRY FORD

. . . but play.

—LEON DE MONTENAEKEN

. . . a cabaret.

—LIZA MINNELLI

. . . a play. It's not its length, but its performance that counts.

—SENECA

. . . short. Live it up.

—NIKITA KHRUSCHEV

. . . a tragedy for those who feel, a comedy for those who think.

—JEAN DE LA BRUYERE

. . . a B-picture script.

—KIRK DOUGLAS

. . . like an overlong drama through which we sit being nagged by the vague memories of having read the reviews.

—JOHN UPDIKE

. . . a poor player, that struts and frets his hour upon the stage.

—WILLIAM SHAKESPEARE

. . . a tale told in an idiom, full of unsoundness and fury, signifying nonism.

—JAMES THURBER

. . . no brief candle to me. It is sort of a splendid torch that I have got hold of for the moment.

—GEORGE BERNARD SHAW

. . . something like a trumpet. If you don't put anything in, you won't get anything out.

—W. C. HANDY

. . . playing a violin solo in public and learning the instrument as one goes on.

—SAMUEL BUTLER

. . . either a daring adventure, or nothing.

—HELEN KELLER

. . . an onion. You peel it off one layer at a time, and sometimes you weep.

—CARL SANDBURG

. . . like eating artichokes. You've got to go through so much to get so little.

—T. A. DORGAN

. . . a scrambled egg.

—DON MARQUIS

. . . far too important a thing ever to talk about.

—OSCAR WILDE

. . . like a dogsled team. If you ain't the lead dog, the scenery never changes.

—LEWIS GRIZZARD

LIGHT

These are the soul cages. These are the soul cages. Swim to the light.

—STING

I'm going to turn on the light, and we'll be two people in a room looking at each other and wondering why on earth we were afraid of the dark.

—GALE WILHELM

His word burned like a lamp.

—ECCLESIASTICUS 48:1

Light, love, life.

—JOHANN GOTTFRIED VON HERDER
epitaph

In the beginning God created the heaven and the earth. And the earth was without form, and void; and darkness was upon the face of the deep. And the Spirit of God moved upon the face of the waters. And God said, "Let there be light, and there was light."

—GENESIS 1:1–3

Ye are the light of the world. A city that is set on a hill cannot be hid. Neither do men light a candle, and put it under a bushel, but on a candlestick; and giveth light unto all that are in the house. Let your light so shine before men, that they may see your good works, and glorify your Father in heaven.

—JESUS OF NAZARETH
Matthew 5:14–16

Beyond plants are animals, Beyond animals is man, Beyond man is the universe. The Big Light, Let the Big Light in!

—JEAN TOOMER

There are two ways of spreading light: to be the candle or the mirror that reflects it.

—EDITH WHARTON

There was a young lady named Bright, Whose speed was far faster than light; She set out one day In a relative way, And returned home the previous night.

—ARTHUR BULLER

Light seeking light doth light of light beguile.

—WILLIAM SHAKESPEARE

And God smiled again, And the rainbow appeared, And curled itself around his shoulder.

—JAMES WELDON JOHNSON

Everything has a crack in it—that's how the light gets in.

—LEONARD COHEN

More light!

—JOHANN WOLFGANG VON GOETHE
last words

[The sun] gives light as soon as he rises.

—BENJAMIN FRANKLIN

The first creature of God, in the works of the days, was the light of the sense: the last was the light of reason.

—FRANCIS BACON

Reason is the light and lamp of life.

—CICERO

Reason is a natural revelation, whereby the eternal Father of light communicates to mankind that portion of truth which he has laid within the reach of their natural faculties.

—JOHN LOCKE

If we would be guided by the light of reason, we must let our minds be bold.

—LOUIS BRANDEIS

Literature is a kind of intellectual light which, like the light of the sun, may sometimes enable us to see what we do not like.

—SAMUEL JOHNSON

There is no object so foul that intense light will not make it beautiful.

—RALPH WALDO EMERSON

There are two kinds of light—the glow that illumines, and the glare that obscures.

—JAMES THURBER

Light is the symbol of truth.

—JAMES RUSSELL LOWELL

Knowledge is nothing but the continually burning up of error to set free the light of truth.

—RABINDRANATH TAGORE

To do right is to be faithful to the light within.

—OLIVER WENDELL HOLMES

A university should be a place of light, of liberty, and of learning.

—BENJAMIN DISRAELI

In life, the thing to do is supply light and not heat.

—WOODROW WILSON

Consciousness is the inner light kindled in the soul; a music, strident or sweet, made by the friction of existence.

—GEORGE SANTAYANA

Dreaming is to think by moonlight by the light of an inner moon.

—JULES RENARD

Everywhere the human soul stands between a hemisphere of light and another of darkness.

—THOMAS CARLYLE

LIVING IN THE FUTURE

I still lived in the future—a habit which is the death of happiness.

—QUENTIN CRISP

Haste, haste, has no blessing.

—SWAHILI PROVERB

If a man carefully examine his thoughts he will be surprised to find how much he lives in the future. His well-being is always ahead. Such a creature is probably immortal.

—RALPH WALDO EMERSON

We are never present with, but always beyond ourselves; fear, desire, hope still push us on toward the future.

—MICHEL DE MONTAIGNE

Ah, the future! That period of time in which our affairs prosper, our friends are true and our happiness is assured.

—AMBROSE BIERCE

LIVING IN THE PAST

Memory, the priestess, kills the present and offers its heart on the shrine of the dead past.

—RABINDRANATH TAGORE

LIVING IN THE PRESENT

I hear that you're building your house deep in the desert. Are you living for nothing now? I hope you're keeping some kind of record.

—LEONARD COHEN
"FAMOUS BLUE RAINCOAT"

Events in the past may be roughly divided into those which probably never happened and those which do not matter.

—WILLIAM INGE, DEAN
St. Paul's, London

They were upon their great theme: "When I get to be a man!" Being human, though boys, they considered their present estate too commonplace to be dwelt upon. So, when the old men gather, they say: "When I was a boy!" It really is the land of nowadays that we never discover.

—BOOTH TARKINGTON

I scarcely remember counting upon happiness—I look not for it if it be not in the present hour—nothing startles me beyond the moment. The setting sun will always set me to rights—or if a sparrow come before my window I will take part in its existence and pick about the gravel.

—JOHN KEATS

"We live in the present, we dream of the future and we learn eternal truths from the past.

—MADAME CHIANG KAI-SHEK

No time like the present.

—MARY DE LA RIVIÈRE MANLEY

Every situation—nay, every moment—is of infinite worth; for it is the representative of a whole eternity.

—JOHANN WOLFGANG VON GOETHE

I am in the present. I cannot know what tomorrow will bring forth. I can know only what the truth is for me today. That is what I am called upon to serve, and I serve it in all lucidity.

—IGOR STRAVINSKY

No mind is much employed upon the present. Recollection and anticipation fill up almost all our moments.

—SAMUEL JOHNSON

The supreme value is not the future but the present. The future is a deceitful time that always says to us, "Not yet," and thus denies us. The future is not the time of love: what man truly wants he wants now. Whoever builds a house for future happiness builds a prison for the present.

—OCTAVIO PAZ

Those who talk about the future are scoundrels. It is the present that matters.

—LOUIS FERDINAND CÉLINE

Trust no Future, howe'er pleasant! Let the dead Past bury its dead! Act,—act in the living Present! Heart within, and God o'erhead!

—HENRY WADSWORTH LONGFELLOW

The word "now" is like a bomb through the window, and it ticks.

—ARTHUR MILLER

Past and to come seem best; things present worst.

—WILLIAM SHAKESPEARE

Philosophy triumphs easily over past evils and future evils, but present evils triumph over it.

—FRANÇOIS LA ROCHEFOUCAULD

It is not the weight of the future or the past that is pressing upon you, but ever that of the present alone. Remember that the sole life which a man can lose is that which he is living at the moment.

—MARCUS ANTONIN

—US

For present joys are more to flesh and blood, than a dull prospect of a distant good.

—JOHN DRYDEN

The present time has one advantage over every other—it is our own.

—CHARLES CALEB COLTON

Look not mournfully into the Past. It comes not back again. Wisely improve the Present. It is thine.

—HENRY WADSWORTH LONGFELLOW

Let anyone try, I will not say to arrest, but to notice or to attend to, the present moment of time. One of the most baffling experiences occurs. Where is it, this present? It has melted in our grasp, fled ere we could touch it, gone in the instant of becoming.

—WILLIAM JAMES

We can see well into the past; we can guess shrewdly into the future; but that which is rolled up and muffled in impenetrable folds is today.

—RALPH WALDO EMERSON

Children enjoy the present because they have neither a past nor a future.

—JEAN DE LA BRUYÈRE

Real generosity toward the future lies in giving all to the present.

—ALBERT CAMUS

There is no moment like the present. The man who will not execute his resolutions when they are fresh upon him can have no hope from them afterwards; they will be dissipated, lost, and perish in the hurry and scurry of the world, or sunk in the slough of indolence.

—MARIE EDGEWORTH

Every tomorrow has two handles. We can take hold of it with the handle of anxiety or the handle of faith. We should live for the future, and yet should find our life in the fidelities of the present; the last is only the method of the first.

—HENRY WARD BEECHER

As for the Future, your task is not to foresee but to enable it.

—ANTOINE DE SAINT-ÉXUPÉRY

The man least dependent upon the morrow, that is, the person living in and enjoying the moment, goes to meet the morrow most cheerfully.

—EPICURUS

AIDS has come upon us with cruel abandon. It has forced us to confront and deal with the frailty of our being and the reality of death. It has forced us into a realization that we must cherish every moment of the glorious experience of this thing we call life. We are learning to value our own lives and the lives of our loved ones as if any moment may be the last.

—ELIZABETH TAYLOR

Capture the moment, whoever you are. None of us is here forever.

—ADRIAN

Be here now.

—RAM DASS

The present is burdened too much with the past. We have not time, in our earthly existence, to appreciate what is warm with life, and immediately around us.

—NATHANIEL HAWTHORNE

LOVE
See also ROMANTIC LOVE

Love your enemies just in case your friends turn out to be a bunch of bastards.

—R. A. DICKSON

Love is but the discovery of ourselves in others, and the delight in the recognition.

—ALEXANDER SMITH

We don't love qualities; we love a person; sometimes by reason of their defects as well as their qualities.

—JACQUES MARITAIN

People think love is an emotion. Love is good sense.

—KEN KESEY

If love is the answer, could you rephrase the question?

—LILY TOMLIN

Love ain't nothing but sex misspelled.

—HARLAN ELLISON

You love me so much, you want to put me in your pocket. And I should die there smothered.

—D. H. LAWRENCE

There is a Law that man should love his neighbor as himself. In a few years it should be as natural to mankind as breathing or the upright gait; but if he does not learn it he must perish.

—ALFRED ADLER

Love is a metaphysical gravity.

—R. BUCKMINSTER FULLER

Now I adore my life With the Bird, the abiding Leaf, With the Fish, the questing Snail, And the Eye altering all; And I dance with William Blake For love, for Love's sake.

—THEODORE ROETHKE

Neither a lofty degree of intelligence nor imagination nor both together go to the making of genius. Love, love, love, that is the soul of genius.

—WOLFGANG AMADÉUS MOZART

I love Mickey Mouse more than any woman I've ever known.

—WALT DISNEY

I never loved another person the way I loved myself.

—MAE WEST

In bed my real love has always been the sleep that rescued me by allowing me to dream.

—LUIGI PIRANDELLO

Love without attachment is light.

—NORMAN O. BROWN

Familiar acts are beautiful through love.

—PERCY BYSSHE SHELLEY

Thousands have lived without love, not one without water.

—W. H. AUDEN

So long as we love we serve; so long as we are loved by others, I would almost say that we are indispensable; and no man is useless while he has a friend.

—ROBERT LOUIS STEVENSON

Man must evolve for all human conflict a method which rejects revenge, aggression and retaliation. The foundation of such a method is love.

—MARTIN LUTHER KING, JR.

If I have the gift of prophecy and can fathom all mysteries and all knowledge, and if I have a faith that can move mountains, but have not love, I am nothing. If I give all I possess to the poor and surrender my body to the flames, but have not love, I gain nothing. Love is patient, love is kind. It does not envy, it does not boast, it is not proud. It is not rude, it is not self-seeking, it is not easily angered, it keeps no record of wrongs. Love does not delight in evil but rejoices with the truth. It always protects, always trusts, always hopes, always perseveres. Love never fails. And now these three remain: faith, hope and love. But the greatest of these is love.

—PAUL
I Corinthians 13

He that gives his heart will not deny his money.

—THOMAS FULLER, M.D.

This is what is hardest: to close the open hand because one loves.

—FRIEDRICH NIETZSCHE

Love sought is good, but giv'n unsought is better.

—WILLIAM SHAKESPEARE

Give all to love; Obey thy heart.

—RALPH WALDO EMERSON

So, the All-Great, were the All-Loving too.

—ROBERT BROWNING

The pleasure of love is in loving. We are happier in the passion we feel than in that we arouse.

—FRANÇOIS LA ROCHEFOUCAULD

I love it, I love it; and who shall dare, to chide me for loving that old armchair?

—ELIZA COOK

To love for the sake of being loved is human, but to love for the sake of loving is angelic.

—ALPHONSE DE LAMARTINE

Large was his wealth, but larger was his heart.

—JOHN DRYDEN

LUXURY

A private railroad car is not an acquired taste. One takes to it immediately.

—ELEANOR R. BELMONT

It's lavish, but I call it home.

—CLIFTON WEBB
(TO DANA ANDREWS)
LAURA

Who serves a good lord lives always in luxury.

—*POEM OF THE CID*

The luxury of doing good surpasses every other personal enjoyment.

—JOHN GAY

His successor will send out a tax collector to maintain the royal splendor.

—DANIEL 11:20
explaining what to do after
inheriting a kingdom

Luxury comes as a guest, to take a slave.

—JONI MITCHELL

MARRIAGE
See also BACHELORHOOD, DIVORCE,
FAMILY VALUES, MEN, WOMEN

My wife and I were happy for twenty years. Then we met.

—RODNEY DANGERFIELD

If you want to sacrifice the admiration of many men for the criticism of one, go ahead, get married.

—KATHARINE HEPBURN

Seldom or never does a marriage develop into an individual relationship smoothly and without crisis. There is no birth of consciousness without pain.

—C. G. JUNG

The trouble with some women is that they get all excited about nothing—and then marry him.

—CHER

In Hollywood, all the marriages are happy. It's trying to live together afterwards that causes all the problems.

—SHELLEY WINTERS

My boyfriend and I broke up. He wanted to get married and I didn't want him to.

—RITA RUDNER

Marriage is based on the theory that when a man discovers a brand of beer exactly to his taste he should at once throw up his job and go to work in a brewery.

—GEORGE JEAN NATHAN

Love is an ideal thing; marriage is a real thing. A confusion of the real with the ideal never goes unpunished.

—JOHANN WOLFGANG VON GOETHE

When two people are under the influence of the most violent, most insane, most delusive, and most transient of passions, they are required to swear that they will remain in that excited, abnormal, and exhausting condition continuously until death do them part.

—GEORGE BERNARD SHAW

In olden times sacrifices were made at the altar—a practice which is still continued.

—HELEN ROWLAND

We declare that love cannot exist between two people who are married to each other. For lovers give to each other freely, under no compulsion; married people are in duty bound to give in to each other's desires.

—MARIE, COUNTESS OF CHAMPAGNE

The whole point of marriage is to stop you getting anywhere near real life. You think it's a great struggle with the mystery of being. It's more like being smothered in warm cocoa. There's sex, but it's not what you think. Marvellous, for the first fortnight. Then every Wednesday. If there isn't a good late-night concert on the Third. Meanwhile you become a biological functionary. An agent of the great female womb, spawning away, dumping its goods in your lap for succour. Daddy, daddy, we're here and we're expensive,

—MALCOM BRADBURY

Pitt the younger was a great British Prime Minister. He saved Europe from Napoleon, he was the pilot who weathered the storm. I don't know whether he'd have done it any better or quicker had he been married.

—EDWARD HEATH

I have sacrificed everything in my life that I consider precious in order to advance the political career of my husband.

—PAT NIXON

Husbands think we should know where everything is— like the uterus is a tracking device. He asks me, "Roseanne, do we have any Chee-tos left?" Like he can't go over to that sofa cushion and lift it himself.

—ROSEANNE

Passion, sexual passion, may lead to marriage, but cannot sustain marriage. The purpose of marriage is the raising of children, for which patience, not passion, is the necessary foundation.

—EDWARD ABBEY

Venus, a beautiful, good-natured lady, was the goddess of love; Juno, a terrible shrew, the goddess of marriage: and they were always mortal enemies.

—JONATHAN SWIFT

A good marriage, if there is such a thing, rejects the company and conditions of love. It tries to imitate those of friendship.

—MICHEL DE MONTAIGNE

I would like to be like my father and all the rest of my ancestors who never married.

—MOLIÈRE

Marriage, in life, is like a duel in the midst of a battle.

—EDMOND ABOUT

There are some good marriages, but practically no delightful ones.

—FRANÇOIS LA ROCHEFOUCAULD

Love is a reciprocity of soul and has a different end and obeys different laws from marriage. Hence one should not take the loved one to wife.

—ALESSANDRO PICCOLOMINI

Passion and marriage are essentially irreconcilable. Their origins and their ends make them mutually exclusive. Their co-existence in our midst constantly raises insoluble problems, and the strife thereby engendered constitutes a persistent danger for every one of our social safeguards.

—DENIS DE ROUGEMONT

Spouses are impediments to great enterprises.

—FRANCIS BACON

Marriage must incessantly contend with a monster that devours everything: familiarity.

—HONORÉ DE BALZAC

A system could not well have been devised more studiously hostile to human happiness than marriage.

—PERCY BYSSHE SHELLEY

It is most unwise for people in love to marry.

—GEORGE BERNARD SHAW

I feel sure that no girl could go to the altar, and would probably *refuse*, if she knew all.

—QUEEN VICTORIA

I would not marry God.

—MAXINE ELLIOTT
telegram denying rumors of her marriage

It destroys one's nerves to be amiable every day to the same human being.

—BENJAMIN DISRAELI

What God hath joined together no man shall put asunder: God will take care of that.

—GEORGE BERNARD SHAW

At the beginning of a marriage ask yourself whether this woman will be interesting to talk to from now until old age. Everything else in marriage is transitory: most of the time is spent in conversation.

—FRIEDRICH NIETZSCHE

I have certainly seen more men destroyed by the desire to have a wife and child and to keep them in comfort than I have seen destroyed by drink or harlots.

—W. B. YEATS

Any intelligent woman who reads the marriage contract, and then goes into it, deserves all the consequences.

—ISADORA DUNCAN

Love is an obsessive delusion that is cured by marriage.

—DR. KARL BOWMAN

A word which should be pronounced "mirage."

—HERBERT SPENCER

If married couples did not live together, happy marriages would be more frequent.

—FRIEDRICH NIETZSCHE

In our part of the world where monogamy is the rule, to marry means to halve one's rights and double one's duties.

—ARTHUR SCHOPENHAUER

He had been building one of those piles of thought, as ramshackle and fantastic as a Chinese pagoda, half from words let fall by gentlemen in gaiters, half from the litter in his own mind, about duck shooting and legal history, about the Roman occupation of Lincoln and the relations of country gentlemen with their wives, when, from all this disconnected rambling, there suddenly formed itself in his mind the idea that he would ask Mary to marry him.

—VIRGINIA WOOLF

Nothing anybody tells you about marriage helps.

—MAX SIEGEL

Not all women give most of their waking thoughts to the problem of pleasing men. Some are married.

—EMMA LEE

I've sometimes thought of marrying, and then I've thought again.

—NOËL COWARD

I cannot see myself as a wife—ugly word.

—GRETA GARBO

I was in rare fettle and the heart had touched a new high. I don't know anything that braces one up like finding you haven't got to get married after all.

—P. G. WODEHOUSE

The difficulty with marriage is that we fall in love with a personality, but must live with a character.

—PETER DEVRIES

INTERVIEWER: Aren't you forgetting you're married?
MAE WEST: Hmmm—I'm doing my best.

I was married by a judge. I should have asked for a jury.

—GEORGE BURNS

Before marriage, a man declares that he would lay down his life to serve you; after marriage, he won't even lay down his newspaper to talk to you.

—HELEN ROWLAND

I should never have married, but I didn't want to live without a man. Brought up to respect the conventions, love had to end in marriage. I'm afraid it did.

—BETTE DAVIS

Marriage is a bribe to make a housekeeper think she's a householder.

—THORNTON WILDER

Take it from me, marriage isn't a word—it's a sentence.

—KING VIDOR

Only choose in marriage a woman whom you would choose as a friend if she were a man.

—JOSEPH JOUBERT

People marry for a variety of reasons, and with varying results; but to marry for love is to invite inevitable tragedy.

—JAMES BRANCH CABELL

Politics doesn't make strange bedfellows—marriage does.

—GROUCHO MARX

Do you know what it means to come home at night to a woman who'll give you a little love, a little affection, a little tenderness? It means you're in the wrong house, that's what it means.

—HENNY YOUNGMAN

We do not squabble, fight or have rows. We collect grudges. We're in an arms race, storing up warheads for the domestic Armageddon.

—HUGH LEONARD

If you want to read about love and marriage you've got to buy two separate books.

—ALAN KING

ERIC: She's a lovely girl . . . I'd like to marry her, but her family objects. *ERNIE:* Her family? *ERIC:* Yes, her husband and four kids.

—ERIC MORECAMBE & ERNIE WISE

Alcestis had exercised a mysterious attraction and then an unmysterious repulsion on two former husbands, the second of whom had to resort to fatal coronary disease to get away from her.

—KINGSLEY AMIS

I'd like to get married because I like the idea of a man being required by law to sleep with me every night.

—CARRIE SNOW

Marriage is really tough because you have to deal with feelings and lawyers.

—RICHARD PRYOR

When a girl marries she exchanges the attentions of many men for the inattention of one.

—HELEN ROWLAND

A man in love is incomplete until he is married. Then he is finished.

—ZSA ZSA GABOR

The act of getting married, stripped of the necessity to have a secure setting to raise children, seems to me no less grim than registering your emotions with the government.

—HARRY SHEARER

I want a man who's kind and understanding. Is that too much to ask of a millionaire?

—ZSA ZSA GABOR

Even under the best of circumstances men are hard creatures to trap. Women who flatter themselves into thinking they've trapped one are like people who believe they can get rid of the cockroaches in their kitchen. They're in for a big surprise late one night when they turn on the light.

—HARRY SHEARER

I love being married. It's so great to find that one special person you want to annoy for the rest of your life.

—RITA RUDNER

Marriage is a great institution, but I'm not ready for an institution yet.

—MAE WEST

I'd marry again if I found a man who had $15 million and would sign over half of it to me before the marriage, and guarantee that he'd be dead within a year.

—BETTE DAVIS

We sleep in separate rooms, we have dinner apart, we take separate vacations—we're doing everything we can to keep our marriage together.

—RODNEY DANGERFIELD

I hate to be a failure. I hate and regret the failure of my marriages. I would gladly give all my millions for just one lasting marital success.

—J. PAUL GETTY

It is ridiculous to think you can spend your entire life with just one person. Three is about the right number. Yes, I imagine three husbands would do it.

—CLARE BOOTHE LUCE

I think every woman is entitled to a middle husband she can forget.

—ADELA ROGERS ST. JOHN

LADY ASTOR: If you were my husband, Winston, I'd put poison in your tea. *WINSTON CHURCHILL:* If I were your husband, Nancy, I'd drink it.

WIFE: Mr. Watt next door blows his wife a kiss every morning as he leaves the house. I wish you'd do that. *HUSBAND:* But I hardly know the woman!

—ALFRED MC FOTE

The chief cause of unhappiness in married life is that people think that marriage is sex attraction, which takes the form of promises and hopes and happiness—a view supported by public opinion and by literature. But marriage cannot cause happiness. Instead, it is always torture, which man has to pay for satisfying his sex urge.

—LEO TOLSTOY

Why do you always, when you mention my name in your diaries, speak so ill of me? Why do you want all future generations and our descendants to hold my name in contempt? Are you afraid that your glory after death will be diminished unless you show me to have been your torment and yourself as a martyr, bearing a cross in the form of your wife?

—SONYA TOLSTOY
in a letter to her husband

In 1910, eighty-two-year-old Leo Tolstoy flees from his wife and dies in a railway station of exposure.

—JON WINOKUR

Men and women, women and men. It will never work.

—ERICA JONG

There's a story about President and Mrs. Coolidge visiting a poultry show. The guide says to Mrs. Coolidge, "You know, ma'am, the rooster here performs his services up to eight or nine times a day," to which the First

Lady replied, "Please see to it that the President is given that information!" A while later the President's party came through the same exhibit and the guide told him, "Sir, Mrs. Coolidge said to be sure to tell you that the rooster there performs his services up to eight or nine times a day." Coolidge thought for a moment and asked, "Same chicken each time?" "No, Mr. President, different chickens each time." "Then see to it that Mrs. Coolidge is given that information!"

—ORSON BEAN

In 453, Attila the Hun died from a nosebleed on his wedding night.

—JON WINOKUR

MASTER

If you call him your Master will hear you. Seven bars on the door will not hold him. Seven fires burning bright only bring him delight. You can live the life you dream.

—JUDY COLLINS

MATURITY

Every human being on this earth is born with a tragedy, and it isn't original sin. He's born with the tragedy that he has to grow up. A lot of people don't have the courage to do it.

—HELEN HAYES

I'm at an age where I think more about food than sex. Last week I put a mirror over my dining room table.

—RODNEY DANGERFIELD

Nobody grows old by merely living a number of years. People grow old only by deserting their ideals. Years wrinkle the face, but to give up enthusiasm wrinkles the soul. Worry, doubt, self-interest, fear, despair— these are the long, long years that bow the head and turn the growing spirit back to dust.

—WATTERSON LOWE

A boy becomes an adult three years before his parents think he does, and about two years after he thinks he does.

—LEWIS B. HERSHEY

I'm an experienced woman; I've been around . . . Well, all right, I might not've been around, but I've been . . . nearby.

—MARY RICHARDS
THE MARY TYLER MOORE SHOW

From birth to age 18, a girl needs good parents, from 18 to 35 she needs good looks, from 35 to 55 she needs a good personality, and from 55 on she needs cash.

—SOPHIE TUCKER

The human race, to which so many of my readers belong, has been playing at children's games from the beginning, which is a nuisance for the few people who grow up.

—G. K. CHESTERTON

The children despise their parents until the age of forty, when they suddenly become just like them—thus preserving the system.

—QUENTIN CREWE

Is life so wretched? Isn't it rather your hands which are too small, your vision which is muddied. You are the one who must grow up.

—DAG HAMMARSKJÖLD

Some of us are becoming the men we wanted to marry.

—GLORIA STEINEM

The lovely thing about being forty is that you can appreciate twenty-five-year-old men more.

—COLLEEN MCCULLOUGH

You grow up the day you have your first real laugh—at yourself.

—ETHEL BARRYMORE

MEDICINE
See also CURE, HEALING, ILLNESS, PHYSICIANS

The principles of Washington's farewell address are still sources of wisdom when cures for social ills are sought. The methods of Washington's physicians, however, are no longer studied.

—THURMAN ARNOLD

The art of medicine consists of amusing the patient while nature cures the disease.

—VOLTAIRE

It is true that I am carrying out various methods of treatment recommended by doctors and dentists in the hope of dying in the remote future in perfect health.

—GEORGE SANTAYANA

MEMORIES

One must have a good memory to be able to keep the promises one makes.

—FRIEDRICH NIETZSCHE

Each man's memory is his private literature.

—ALDOUS HUXLEY

I might repeat to myself, slowly and soothingly, a list of quotations beautiful from minds profound—if I can remember any of the damn things.

—DOROTHY PARKER

By means of an image we are often able to hold on to our lost belongings. But it is the desperateness of losing which picks the flowers of memory, binds the bouquet.

—COLETTE

MRS. MALAPROP: Illiterate him, I say, quite from your memory.

—RICHARD SHERIDAN

Our memories are card indexes consulted, and then put back in disorder by authorities whom we do not control.

—CYRIL CONNOLLY

A good memory is one trained to forget the trivial.

—CLIFTON FADIMAN

MEN

When it comes to women, modern men are idiots. They don't know what they want, and so they never want, permanently, what they get. They want a cream cake that is at the same time ham and eggs and at the same time porridge. They are fools. If only women weren't bound by fate to play up to them.

—D. H. LAWRENCE

I require three things in a man: he must be handsome, ruthless, and stupid.

—DOROTHY PARKER

Men are my hobby; if I ever got married I'd have to give it up.

—MAE WEST

One good Husband is worth two good wives, for the scarcer things are the more they're valued.

—BENJAMIN FRANKLIN

Before marriage, a man declares that he would lay down his life to serve you; after marriage, he won't even lay down his newspaper to talk to you.

—HELEN ROWLAND

His mother should have thrown him away and kept the stork.

—MAE WEST

I have a big flaw in that I am attracted to thin, tall, good-looking men who have one common denominator. They must be lurking bastards.

—EDNA O'BRIEN

He speaks to me as if I were a public meeting.

—QUEEN VICTORIA
about Gladstone

I have had my belly full of great men (forgive the expression). I quite like to read about them in the pages of Plutarch, where they don't outrage my humanity. Let us see them carved in marble or cast in bronze, and hear no more about them. In real life they are nasty creatures, persecutors, temperamental, despotic, bitter and suspicious.

—GEORGE SAND

All men are frauds. The only difference between them is that some admit it. I myself deny it.

—H. L. MENCKEN

THE MIND
See also IMAGINATION, MEMORY, NEGATIVE THINKING,
THINKING, THOUGHTS

It is hard to fight an enemy who has outposts in your head.

—SALLY KEMPTON

The voice of the intellect is a soft one, but it does not rest until it has gained a hearing. Ultimately, after endlessly repeated rebuffs, it succeeds. This is one of the few points in which one may be optimistic about the future of mankind, but in itself it signifies not a little.

—SIGMUND FREUD

What the inner voice says Will not disappoint the hoping soul.

—FRIEDRICH VON SCHILLER

We contain an internal world which is just as active and complicated as the one we live in.

—JONATHAN MILLER, M.D.

CRYSTAL: Do you realize that most people use two percent of their mind's potential? *ROSEANNE:* That much, huh?

—*ROSEANNE*

Your mind must always go, even while you're shaking hands and going through all the maneuvers. I developed the ability long ago to do one thing while thinking another.

—RICHARD M. NIXON

Where is the love, beauty and truth we seek, But in our mind?

—PERCY BYSSHE SHELLEY

Sit in reverie and watch the changing color of the waves that break upon the idle seashore of the mind.

—HENRY WADSWORTH LONGFELLOW

Quiet minds cannot be perplexed or frightened but go on in fortune or misfortune at their own private pace, like a clock during a thunderstorm.

—ROBERT LOUIS STEVENSON

That inward eye which is the bliss of solitude.

—WILLIAM WORDSWORTH

When the mind's eye turns inward, it blazes upon the dearly beloved image of oneself.

—FANNIE HURST

And we are here as on a darkling plain Swept with confused alarms of struggle and flight, Where ignorant armies clash by night.

—MATTHEW ARNOLD

The growth of the human mind is still high adventure, in many ways the highest adventure on earth.

—NORMAN COUSINS

The mind is its own place, and in itself can make heaven of Hell, a hell of Heaven.

—JOHN MILTON

Most of the time we think we're sick, it's all in the mind.

—THOMAS WOLFE

All that is comes from the mind; it is based on the mind, it is fashioned by the mind.

—PALI CANON

The mind, in proportion as it is cut off from free communication with nature, with revelation, with God, with itself, loses its life, just as the body droops when debarred from the air and the cheering light from heaven.

—WILLIAM ELLERY CHANNING

MISTAKES

I've got to keep breathing. It'll be my worst business mistake if I don't.

—NATHAN MEYER ROTHSCHILD

LARRY APPLETON: This must have been how Eisenhower felt just before D-Day. All around him the troops sleeping; not Ike! He knew that one single mistake could change the course of world history. *BALKI BARTOUKOMOUS:* Was this before or after Ike met Tina Turner?

The higher up you go, the more mistakes you're allowed. Right at the top, if you make enough of them, it's considered to be your style.

—FRED ASTAIRE

You will make all kinds of mistakes; but as long as you are generous and true, and also fierce, you cannot hurt the world or even seriously distress her.

—WINSTON CHURCHILL

The only way to even *approach* doing something perfectly is through experience, and experience is the name everyone gives to their mistakes.

—OSCAR WILDE

I have learned more from my mistakes than from my successes.

—HUMPHREY DAVY

The Athenians, alarmed at the internal decay of their Republic, asked Demosthenes what to do. His reply: "Do not do what you are doing now."

—JOSEPH RAY

Do not look where you fell, but where you slipped.

—AFRICAN PROVERB

When you make a mistake, admit it. If you don't, you only make matters worse.

—WARD CLEAVER
LEAVE IT TO BEAVER

The doctor can bury his mistakes but an architect can only advise his client to plant vines.

—FRANK LLOYD WRIGHT

Experience is the name everyone gives to their mistakes.

—OSCAR WILDE

Mistakes are the portals of discovery.

—JAMES JOYCE

Every great mistake has a halfway moment, a split second when it can be recalled and perhaps remedied.

—PEARL S. BUCK

While one person hesitates because he feels inferior, the other is busy making mistakes and becoming superior.

—HENRY C. LINK

Love truth, but pardon error.

—VOLTAIRE

CRIMINAL: You made a mistake, and I'm not going to pay for it. *SGT. JOE FRIDAY:* You going to use a credit card?

—*DRAGNET*

Only the hand that erases can write the true thing.

—MEISTER ECKHART

MODESTY

With people of only moderate ability modesty is mere honesty; but with those who possess great talent it is hypocrisy.

—ARTHUR SCHOPENHAUER

The legs aren't so beautiful, I just know what to do with them.

—MARLENE DIETRICH

MONEY
See also SPENDING, WEALTH

One and one is two, two and two are four, and five'll get you ten if you know how to work it.

—MAE WEST

This is the way God would do it if He only had money.

—GEORGE S. KAUFMAN
describing Moss Hart's home

Money is a sweet balm.

—ARABIAN PROVERB

Money is a guarantee that we may have what we want in the future. Though we need nothing at the moment, it insures the possibility of satisfying a necessary desire when it arises.

—ARISTOTLE

Money is the sovereign queen of all delights—for her, the lawyer pleads, the soldier fights.

—RICHARD BARNFIELD

Money is the symbol of everything that is necessary for man's well-being and happiness. Money means freedom, independence, liberty.

—EDWARD E. BEALS

Money is the sinews of art and literature.

—SAMUEL BUTLER

Money is Aladdin's lamp.

—LORD BYRON

Money is like an arm or a leg—use it or lose it.

—HENRY FORD

Money is the representative of a certain quantity of corn or other commodity. Its value is in the necessities of the animal man. It is so much warmth, so much bread.

—RALPH WALDO EMERSON

Money is health, and liberty, and strength.

—CHARLES LAMB

Money is the sixth sense which enables you to enjoy the other five.

—W. SOMERSET MAUGHAM

Money is that which brings honor, friends, conquest, and realms.

—JOHN MILTON

Money is the only substance which can keep a cold world from nicknaming a citizen "Hey, you!"

—WILSON MIZNER

Money is the cause of good things to a good man, of evil things to a bad man.

—PHILO

Money is human happiness in the abstract.

—ARTHUR SCHOPENHAUER

Money is the most important thing in the world.

—GEORGE BERNARD SHAW

Money is an article which may be used as a universal passport to everywhere except heaven, and as a universal provider for everything except happiness.

—*WALL STREET JOURNAL*

Money is the root of all good.

—RUDOLF WANDERONE

Money is better than poverty, if only for financial reasons.

—WOODY ALLEN

I don't like money, actually, but it quiets my nerves.

—JOE LOUIS

Those who have some means think that the most important thing in the world is love. The poor know that it is money.

—GERALD BRENAN

You mean you can actually spend $70,000 at Woolworth's?

—BOB KRASNO
after seeing Ike and Tina Turner's house

No one would remember the Good Samaritan if he only had good intentions. He had money as well.

— MARGARET THATCHER

A lot of people are willing to give God the credit, but not too many are willing to give him the cash.

—I don't know where this one came
from, but my bet is on *Laugh-In*

There are people who have money and people who are rich.

—COCO CHANEL

Money, it turned out, was exactly like sex, you thought of nothing else if you didn't have it and thought of other things if you did.

—JAMES BALDWIN

My friends, money is not all. It is not money that will mend a broken heart or reassemble the fragments of a dream. Money cannot brighten the hearth nor repair the portals of a shattered home. I refer, of course, to Confederate money.

—ARTEMUS WARD

The chief value of money lies in the fact that one lives in a world in which it is overestimated.

—H. L. MENCKEN

My life is a bubble; but how much solid cash it costs to keep that bubble floating!

—LOGAN PEARSALL SMITH

Money doesn't always bring happiness. People with ten million dollars are no happier than people with nine million dollars.

—HOBART BROWN

Actually, I have no regard for money. Aside from its purchasing power, it's completely useless as far as I'm concerned.

—ALFRED HITCHCOCK

Much work is merely a way to make money; much leisure is merely a way to spend it.

—C. WRIGHT MILLS

It is not a custom with me to keep money to look at.

—GEORGE WASHINGTON

I don't care too much for money, money can't buy me love.

—PAUL MC CARTNEY

Gold will buy the highest honors; and gold will purchase love.

—OVID
THE ART OF LOVE

Money brings you food, but not appetite; medicine, but not health; acquaintances, but not friends.

—HENRIK IBSEN

I'm tired of love, I'm tired of rhyme, but money gives me pleasure all the time.

—HILAIRE BELLOC

Money is like love, it kills slowly and painfully the one who withholds it, and it enlivens the other who turns it upon his fellow man.

—KHALIL GIBRAN

With money in your pocket, you are wise and you are handsome and you sing well too.

—YIDDISH PROVERB

The love of money is the root of all evil.

— I TIMOTHY 6:10

A feast is made for laughter, and wine maketh merry: but money answereth all things.

—ECCLESIASTES 10:19

Money is not required to buy one necessity of the soul.

—HENRY DAVID THOREAU

It's a kind of spiritual snobbery that makes people think they can be happy without money.

—ALBERT CAMUS

Money, which represents the prose of life, and which is hardly spoken of in parlors without an apology, is, in its effects and laws, as beautiful as roses.

—RALPH WALDO EMERSON

Money often costs too much.

—RALPH WALDO EMERSON

Money wasn't that important. Money doesn't help you sleep. Money doesn't help your mother be well, money doesn't help your brother stay interested in his studies. Money don't help nothing. Money is only good when you've got something else to do with it. A man can lose everything, family, all your dreams, and still have a pocketful of money.

—GEORGE FOREMAN

Money is indeed the most important thing in the world, and all sound and successful personal and national morality should have this fact for its basis.

—GEORGE BERNARD SHAW

A good reputation is more valuable than money.

—PUBLILIUS SYRUS

Money alone sets all the world in motion.

—MAXIM FROM 425 B.C.

Money's the wise man's religion.

—EURIPIDES

Only our characters are steadfast, not our gold.

—EURIPIDES
twelve years later

The love of money as a possession—as distinguished from the love of money as a means to the enjoyments and realities of life—will be recognized for what it is, a somewhat disgusting morbidity, one of those semi-criminal, semi-pathological propensities which one hands over with a shudder to the specialists in mental disease.

—JOHN MAYNARD KEYNES

The only point in making money is, you can tell some big shot where to go.

—HUMPHREY BOGART

I find all this money a considerable burden.

—J. PAUL GETTY

Money never made a fool of anybody; it only shows 'em up.

—ELBERT HUBBARD

The urbane activity with which a man receives money is really marvelous, considering that we so earnestly believe money to be the root of all earthly ills, and that on no account can a monied man enter heaven. Ah! how cheerfully we consign ourselves to perdition!

—HERMAN MELVILLE

Lack of money is the root of all evil.

—GEORGE BERNARD SHAW

Money alone can't bring you happiness, but money alone has not brought me unhappiness. I won't say my previous husbands thought only of my money, but it had a certain fascination for them.

—BARBARA HUTTON

Money doesn't buy happiness, but that's not the reason so many people are poor.

—LAURENCE J. PETERS

Study: concentration of the mind on whatever will ultimately put something in the pocket.

—ELBERT HUBBARD

Money is the symbol of duty, it is the sacrament of having done for mankind that which mankind wanted.

—SAMUEL BUTLER

If you can actually count your money then you are not really a rich man.

—J. PAUL GETTY

I bless God I do find that I am worth more than ever I yet was, which is £6,200, for which the Holy Name of God be praised!

—SAMUEL PEPYS

Money is God in action.

—FREDERICK J. EIKERENKOETTER II
REVEREND IKE

After a certain point money is meaningless. It ceases to be the goal. The game is what counts.

—ARISTOTLE ONASSIS

Hello, good evening and welcome to *Blackmail.* And to start tonight's program, we go north to Preston in Lancashire and Mrs. Betty Teal. Hello Mrs. Teal! Now Mrs. Teal, this is for fifteen pounds and it's to stop us revealing the name of your lover in Bolton. So, Mrs. Teal, send us fifteen pounds by return of post please and your husband Trevor and your lovely children, Diane, Janice and Juliet, need never know the name of your lover in Bolton.

—*MONTY PYTHON*

If thou wouldst keep money, save money; If thou wouldst reap money, sow money.

—THOMAS FULLER

Money is the seed of money.

—JEAN-JACQUES ROUSSEAU

If a little does not go, much cash will not come.

—CHINESE PROVERB

A lot of people will also urge you to put some money in a bank, and in fact—within reason—this is very good advice. But don't go overboard. Remember, what you are doing is giving your money to somebody else to hold on to, and I think that it is worth keeping in mind that the businessmen who run banks are so worried about holding on to things that they put little chains on all their pens.

—MISS PIGGY

I cannot easily buy a blankbook to write thoughts in; they are commonly ruled for dollars and cents.

—HENRY DAVID THOREAU

Money isn't everything as long as you have enough.

—MALCOLM FORBES

MORALITY

The only good is knowledge and the only evil is ignorance.

—SOCRATES

We can act *as if* there were a God; feel *as if* we were free; consider Nature *as if* she were full of special designs; lay plans *as if* we were to be immortal; and we find then that these words do make a genuine difference in our moral life.

—WILLIAM JAMES

We must learn to distinguish morality from moralizing.

—HENRY KISSINGER

Any preoccupation with ideas of what is right or wrong in conduct shows an arrested intellectual development.

—OSCAR WILDE

MUSIC

Take a music bath once or twice a week for a few seasons, and you will find that it is to the soul what the
water-bath is to the body.

—OLIVER WENDELL HOLMES

Music is my mistress, and she plays second fiddle to no one.

—DUKE ELLINGTON

NARROW MINDEDNESS

Like all weak men, he laid an exaggerated stress on not
changing one's mind.

—SOMERSET MAUGHAM

I am firm; *you* are obstinate; *he* is a pig-headed fool.

—BERTRAND RUSSELL

NATURE

Cats are intended to teach us that not everything in
nature has a function.

—GARRISON KEILLOR

We are a spectacular, splendid manifestation of life. We
have language . . . We have affection. We have genes for
usefulness, and usefulness is about as close to a "common goal" of nature as I can guess at.

—LEWIS THOMAS

At twilight nature becomes a wonderfully suggestive effect, and is not without loveliness, though perhaps its
chief use is to illustrate quotations from the poets.

—OSCAR WILDE

Nature is an infinite sphere whose center is everywhere and whose circumference is nowhere.

—BLAISE PASCAL

The most common trait of all primitive peoples is a reverence for the lifegiving earth, and the native American shared this elemental ethic: the land was alive to his loving touch, and he, its son, was brother to all creatures. His feelings were made visible in medicine bundles and dance rhythms for rain, and all of his religious rites and land attitudes savored the inseparable world of nature and God, the master of Life. During the long Indian tenure the land remained undefiled save for scars no deeper than the scratches of cornfield clearings or the farming canals of the Hohokams on the Arizona desert.

—STEWART LEE UDALL

NEGATIVE THINKING

A pessimist is one who builds dungeons in the air.

—WALTER WINCHELL

I was going to buy a copy of *The Power of Positive Thinking*, and then I thought: What the hell good would that do?

—RONNIE SHAKES

The strangest and most fantastic fact about negative emotions is that people actually worship them.

—P. D. OUSPENSKY

If you can't say anything good about someone, sit right here by me.

—ALICE ROOSEVELT LONGWORTH

MARY RICHARDS: I quit. I'm going to Africa to work with Schweitzer. *LOU GRANT:* Mary, Albert Schweitzer is dead. *MARY:* You see what I mean, Mr. Grant? It's a lousy, lousy world.

—*THE MARY TYLER MOORE SHOW*

Many of our cares are but a morbid way of looking at our privileges.

—WALTER SCOTT

God made everything out of nothing, but the nothingness shows through.

—PAUL VALÉRY

OBSERVATION

You do not need to leave your room. Remain sitting at your table and listen. Do not even listen, simply wait. Do not even wait, be quite still and solitary. The world will freely offer itself to you to be unmasked, it has no choice, it will roll in ecstasy at your feet.

—FRANZ KAFKA

To be conscious that we are perceiving or thinking is to be conscious of our own existence.

—ARISTOTLE

To become the spectator of one's own life is to escape the suffering of life.

—OSCAR WILDE

I am a camera with its shutter open, quite passive, recording, not thinking. Recording the man shaving at the window opposite and the woman in the kimono washing her hair.

—CHRISTOPHER ISHERWOOD

OPPORTUNITY
See also RECEPTIVITY

If someone says "can't," that shows you what to do.

—JOHN CAGE

Opportunity is missed by most people because it is dressed in overalls and looks like work.

—THOMAS EDISON

Problems are only opportunities in work clothes.

—HENRY J. KAISER

Breaks balance out. The sun don't shine on the same ol' dog's ass every day.

—DARRELL ROYAL

Life is a series of inspired follies. The difficulty is to find them to do. Never lose a chance: it doesn't come every day.

—GEORGE BERNARD SHAW

I am open to receive With every breath I breathe.

—MICHAEL SUN

The sun! The sun! And all we can become!

—THEODORE ROETHKE

We are wide-eyed in contemplating the possibility that life may exist elsewhere in the universe, but we wear blinders when contemplating the possibilities of life on earth.

—NORMAN COUSINS

Many are called but few get up.

—OLIVER HERFORD

There is no security in this life. There is only opportunity.

—DOUGLAS MACARTHUR

A wise man will make more opportunities than he finds.

—FRANCIS BACON

A pessimist is one who makes difficulties of his opportunities; an optimist is one who makes opportunities of his difficulties.

—REGINALD B. MANSELL

The opportunity that God sends does not wake up him who is asleep.

—SENEGALESE PROVERB

Many do with opportunities as children do at the seashore, they fill their little hands with sand, and then let the grains fall through, one by one, till all are gone.

—THOMAS JONES

Observe the opportunity.

—ECCLESIASTICUS (4:20)

There are joys which long to be ours. God sends ten thousand truths, which come about us like birds seeking inlet; but we are shut up to them, and so they bring us nothing, but sit and sing awhile upon the roof, and then fly away.

—HENRY WARD BEECHER

When life gives you oranges, enjoy. When life gives you lemons, make lemonade.

—ANONYMOUS

There's so much speculating going on that a lot of us never get around to living. Life is always walking up to us and saying, "Come on in, the living's fine," and what do we do? Back off and take its picture.

—RUSSELL BAKER

Learn to listen. Opportunity could be knocking at your door very softly.

—FRANK TYGER

Problems are a chance for you to do your best.

—DUKE ELLINGTON

Never regard study as a duty, but as the enviable opportunity to learn to know the liberating influence of beauty in the realm of the spirit for your own personal joy and to the profit of the community to which your later work belongs.

—ALBERT EINSTEIN

Watch out for emergencies. They are your big chance!

—FRITZ REINER

OPTIMISM

I am not a pessimist; to perceive evil where it exists is, in my opinion, a form of optimism.

—ROBERTO ROSSELLINI

"Optimism," said Candide, "is a mania for maintaining that all is well when things are going badly."

—VOLTAIRE

An optimist may see a light where there is none, but why must the pessimist always run to blow it out?

—MICHEL DE SAINT-PIERRE

PAIN
See also GRIEF, ILLNESS, SUFFERING

It would be a great thing to understand pain in all its meanings.

—PETER MERE LATHAM

One word Frees us of all the weight and pain of life: That word is love.

—SOPHOCLES

PARENTS
See also FAMILY, FAMILY VALUES

I grew up to have my father's looks, my father's speech patterns, my father's posture, my father's opinions, and my mother's contempt for my father.

—JULES FEIFFER

If your parents didn't have any children, there is a good chance that you won't have any.

—CLARENCE DAY

I knew I was an unwanted baby when I saw that my bath toys were a toaster and a radio.

—JOAN RIVERS

My parents put a live Teddy bear in my crib.

—WOODY ALLEN

The only reason I always try to meet and know the parents better is because it helps me to forgive their children.

—LOUIS JOHANNOT

ARTHUR DENT: You know, it's at times like this, when I'm stuck in a Volgon air lock with a man from Betelgeuse, about to die of asphyxiation in deep space, that I really wish I'd listened to what my mother told me when I was young. *FORD PREFECT:* Why? What did she tell you? *ARTHUR:* I don't know; I didn't listen.

—*THE HITCHHIKER'S GUIDE TO THE GALAXY*

My mother had a great deal of trouble with me, but I think she enjoyed it.

—MARK TWAIN

If you really want to hear about it, the first thing you'll probably want to know is where I was born, and what my lousy childhood was like, and how my parents were occupied and all before they had me, and all that David Copperfield kind of crap, but I don't feel like going into it.

—J. D. SALINGER
THE CATCHER IN THE RYE

PASSION

If you want to win anything—a race, your self, your life—you have to go a little berserk.

—GEORGE SHEEHAN

There is no end. There is no beginning. There is only the infinite passion of life.

—FEDERICO FELLINI

PATIENCE

If you want to doctor life, maybe you need to be patient.

—KUNGFUCIOUS

Learn the art of patience. Apply discipline to your thoughts when they become anxious over the outcome of a goal. Impatience breeds anxiety, fear, discouragement and failure. Patience creates confidence, decisiveness and a rational outlook, which eventually leads to success.

—BRIAN ADAMS

I'm extraordinarily patient provided I get my own way in the end.

—MARGARET THATCHER

Thinking to get at once all the gold the goose could give, he killed it and opened it only to find—nothing.

—AESOP

No thing great is created suddenly, any more than a bunch of grapes or a fig. If you tell me that you desire a fig, I answer you that there must be time. Let it first blossom, then bear fruit, then ripen.

—EPICTETUS

Dear God, I pray for patience. And I want it *right now!*

—OREN ARNOLD

PEACE

They shall beat their swords into plowshares, and their spears into pruninghooks: nation shall not lift up sword against nation, neither shall they learn war any more.

—ISAIAH 2:4

Of one thing I am certain, the body is not the measure of healing—peace is the measure.

—GEORGE MELTON

First keep the peace within yourself, then you can also bring peace to others.

—THOMAS À KEMPIS

Nothing can bring you peace but yourself.

—RALPH WALDO EMERSON

We shall find peace. We shall hear the angels, we shall see the sky sparkling with diamonds.

—ANTON CHEKHOV

Lord, make me an instrument of Your peace. Where there is hatred let me sow love; where there is injury, pardon; where there is doubt, faith; where there is despair, hope; where there is darkness, light; and where there is sadness, joy.

—FRANCIS OF ASSISI

Peace I leave with you; my peace I give you. I do not give to you as the world gives. Do not let your hearts be troubled and do not be afraid.

—JESUS OF NAZARETH
John 14:27

PERCEPTION

It is the commonest of mistakes to consider that the limit of our power of perception is also the limit of all there is to perceive.

—C. W. LEADBEATER

PERFECTION

Have no fear of perfection— you'll never reach it.

—SALVADOR DALI

Nothing would be done at all if a man waited until he could do it so well that no one could find fault with it.

—CARDINAL NEWMAN

PERSEVERANCE
Also See DETERMINATION

Results! Why, man, I have gotten a lot of results. I know several thousand things that won't work.

—THOMAS EDISON

I think and think for months and years. Ninety-nine times, the conclusion is false. The hundredth time I am right.

—ALBERT EINSTEIN

Never give in. Never. Never. Never. Never.

—WINSTON CHURCHILL

Keep walking and keep smiling.

—TINY TIM

Fall seven times, stand up eight.

—JAPANESE PROVERB

Nothing I do can't be done by a ten-year-old—with fifteen years of practice.

—HARRY BLACKSTONE, JR.

Pick yourself up, dust yourself off, start all over again.

—DOROTHY FIELDS

I will neither yield to the song of the siren nor the voice of the hyena, the tears of the crocodile nor the howling of the wolf.

—GEORGE CHAPMAN

Victory belongs to the most persevering.

—NAPOLEON BONAPARTE

To dry one's eyes and laugh at a fall, And baffled, get up and begin again.

—ROBERT BROWNING

By perseverance the snail reached the ark.

—CHARLES HADDON SPURGEON

Perseverance is more prevailing than violence; and many things which cannot be overcome when they are together, yield themselves up when taken little by little.

—PLUTARCH

PHILANTHROPY
See also CHARITY, GIVING, SERVICE

Philanthropy is the refuge of people who wish to annoy their fellow creatures.

—OSCAR WILDE

We often excuse our own want of philanthropy by giving the name of fanaticism to the more ardent zeal of others.

—HENRY WADSWORTH LONGFELLOW

Philanthropy is commendable, but it must not cause the philanthropist to overlook the circumstances of economic injustice which make philanthropy necessary.

—DR. MARTIN LUTHER KING, JR.

Surplus wealth is a sacred trust which its possessor is bound to administer in his lifetime for the good of the community.

—ANDREW CARNEGIE

PHYSICIANS
See also HEALING, ILLNESS, MEDICINE

Some patients, though conscious that their condition is perilous, recover their health simply through their contentment with the goodness of the physician.

—HIPPOCRATES

Honor a physician with the honor due unto him for the uses which ye may have of him: for the Lord hath created him.

—ECCLESIASTICUS 38:1

My doctor is wonderful. Once, in 1955, when I couldn't afford an operation, he touched up the X-rays.

—JOEY BISHOP

It is a good idea to "shop around" before you settle on a doctor. Ask about the condition of his Mercedes. Ask about the competence of his mechanic. Don't be shy! After all, you're paying for it.

—DAVE BARRY

We have not lost faith, but we have transferred it from God to the medical profession.

—GEORGE BERNARD SHAW

PITY

Let no one underestimate the need of pity. We live in a stony universe whose hard, brilliant forces rage fiercely.

—THEODORE DREISER

PLANNING

If I had known my son was going to be president of Bolivia, I would have taught him to read and write.

—ENRIQUE PENARANDA'S MOTHER

You've got to be very careful if you don't know where you are going, because you might not get there.

—YOGI BERRA

I always wanted to be somebody, but I should have been more specific.

—LILY TOMLIN

I prefer Hostess fruit pies to pop-up toaster tarts because they don't require as much cooking.

—CARRIE SNOW

PLEASURE
See also HAPPINESS

I can think of nothing less pleasurable than a life devoted to pleasure.

—JOHN D. ROCKEFELLER, JR.

Life affords no higher pleasure than that of surmounting difficulties, passing from one step of success to another, forming new wishes and seeing them gratified.

—SAMUEL JOHNSON

The greatest pleasure in life is doing what people say you cannot do.

—WALTER BAGEHOT

Abstainer, *n.* A weak person who yields to the temptation of denying himself a pleasure.

—AMBROSE BIERCE

The greatest pleasure I know is to do a good action by stealth, and to have it found out by accident.

—CHARLES LAMB

Every human mind feels pleasure in doing good to another.

—THOMAS JEFFERSON

His renown has been purchased, not by deeds of violence and blood, but by the diligent dispensation of pleasure.

—WASHINGTON IRVING

There is no pleasure in having nothing to do; the fun is in having lots to do and not doing it.

—MARY WILSON LITTLE

Go to your business, pleasure, whilst I go to my pleasure, business.

—WILLIAM WYCHERLEY

POETRY

Genuine poetry can communicate before it is understood.

—T. S. ELIOT

Poetry is not an assertion of truth, but the making of that truth more real to us.

—T. S. ELIOT

POLITICS

Ninety percent of the politicians give the other ten percent a bad reputation.

—HENRY KISSINGER

I used to say that politics was the second oldest profession, and I have come to know that it bears a gross similarity to the first.

—RONALD REAGAN
one year before he won the presidency

Nobody could sleep with Dick. He wakes up during the night, switches on the lights, speaks into his tape recorder, or takes notes—it's impossible.

—PAT NIXON

Public life is regarded as the crown of a career, and to young men it is the worthiest ambition. Politics is still the greatest and the most honorable adventure.

—JOHN BUCHAN

Politics is the grim jockeying for position, the ceaseless trading, the deliberate use of words not for communication but to screen intention. In short, a splendidly exciting game for those who play it.

—GORE VIDAL

If you're going to play the game properly, you'd better know every rule.

—BARBARA JORDAN

My choice early in life was either to be a piano player in a whorehouse or a politician. And to tell the truth, there's hardly any difference.

—HARRY S. TRUMAN

POSITIVE FOCUSING

I am looking for a lot of men who have an infinite capacity to not know what can't be done.

—HENRY FORD

Dust is a protective coating for fine furniture.

—MARIO BUATTA

I discovered the "something" in "nothing."

—BARBRA STREISAND

One should sympathize with the joy, the beauty, the color of life—the less said about life's sores the better.

—OSCAR WILDE

Try thinking of love or something.

—CHRISTOPHER FRY

If we open a quarrel between the past and the present, we shall find that we have lost the future.

—WINSTON CHURCHILL

You've got to accentuate the positive, eliminate the negative, latch on to the affirmative.

—JOHNNY MERCER

I think it's very important to be positive about everything in your life that's negative. You can turn a twist on it.

—BARBRA STREISAND

An adventure is only an inconvenience, rightly considered.

—G. K. CHESTERTON

Aunt Maggie was every bit as worried as Mother but they'd take turns cheering each other up. Both of them were confirmed pessimists but never at the same time. Whichever one picked up the pessimism first evidently had a claim on it. The other would automatically assume the role of optimist, although always with a certain lack of conviction.

—STEVE ALLEN

The sorrow of knowing that there is evil in the best, is far out-balanced by the joy of discovering that there is good in the worst.

—DR. AUSTEN FOX RIGGS

Some people are always grumbling because roses have thorns; I am thankful that thorns have roses.

—ALPHONSE KARR

A humorist is a man who feels bad but who feels good about it.

—DON HEROLD

Alas, she married another; they frequently do; I hope she is happy—because I am.

—ARTEMUS WARD

You put up with a few inconvenience when you live in a condemned building.

—REVEREND JIM IGNATOWSKI
TAXI

I can either complain about my mother not believing in me, or I can tell you it served me in some way to become who I am.

—BARBRA STREISAND

Of course I wouldn't say anything about her unless I could say something good. And, oh boy, is this good . . .

—BILL KING

I keep the telephone of my mind open to peace, harmony, health, love and abundance. Then, whenever doubt, anxiety or fear try to call me, they keep getting a busy signal—and soon they'll forget my number.

—EDITH ARMSTRONG

POSITIVE THINKING

The apprehension of the good Gives but the greater feeling to the worse.

—WILLIAM SHAKESPEARE

POVERTY

LOVEY HOWELL: You know, I really wouldn't mind being poor, if it weren't for one thing. *THURSTON HOWELL III:* What is that, my dear? *LOVEY:* Poverty.

It's no shame being poor, but it's no great honor, either.

—SHELDON HARNICK

Poverty is no disgrace to a man, but it is confoundedly inconvenient.

—SYDNEY SMITH

Poverty of course is no disgrace, but it is damned annoying.

—WILLIAM PITT

It's no disgrace to be poor, but it might as well be.

—ELBERT HUBBARD

Honest poverty is a gem that even a king might be proud to call his own, but I wish to sell out.

—MARK TWAIN

Poverty is very good in poems but very bad in the house; very good in maxims and sermons but very bad in practical life.

—HENRY WARD BEECHER

I used to think I was poor. Then they told me I wasn't poor, I was needy. Then they told me it was self-defeating to think of myself as needy. I was deprived. Then they told me that underprivileged was overused. I was disadvantaged. I still don't have a dime. But I have a great vocabulary.

—JULES FEIFFER

I've always been after the trappings of great luxury, you see, I really, really have. But all I've got hold of are the trappings of great poverty. I've got hold of the wrong load of trappings, and a rotten load of trappings they are too, ones I could have very well done without.

—PETER COOK

PRAYER
See also RELIGION, WORSHIP

Give us grace and strength to forbear and to persevere. Give us courage and gaiety and the quiet mind.

—Robert Louis Stevenson

When the gods choose to punish us, they merely answer our prayers.

—OSCAR WILDE

I have never made but one prayer to God, a very short one: "O Lord, make my enemies ridiculous." And God granted it.

—VOLTAIRE

Serving God is doing good to man, but praying is thought an easier service and therefore more generally chosen.

—BENJAMIN FRANKLIN

O ye Gods, grant us what is good whether we pray for it or not, but keep evil from us even though we pray for it.

—PLATO

I am just going to pray for you at St. Paul's, but with no very lively hope of success.

—SYDNEY SMITH

Prayer gives a man the opportunity of getting to know a gentleman he hardly ever meets. I do not mean his maker, but himself.

—WILLIAM INGE

Practical prayer is harder on the soles of your shoes than on the knees of your trousers.

—AUSTIN O'MALLEY

PRIDE

Alas, I know if I ever became truly humble, I would be proud of it.

—BENJAMIN FRANKLIN

RALPH KRAMDEN: I promise you this, Norton. I'm gonna learn. I'm gonna learn from here on in how to swallow my pride. *ED NORTON:* That ought not to be too hard. You've learned how to swallow everything else.

—*THE HONEYMOONERS*

PROBLEMS

It often happens that I wake at night and begin to think about a serious problem and decide I must tell the Pope about it. Then I wake up completely and remember that I *am* the Pope.

—POPE JOHN XXIII

My problem lies in reconciling my gross habits with my net income.

—ERROL FLYNN

PROCRASTINATION
See also INACTION

If you trap the moment before it's ripe, The tears of repentance you'll certainly wipe; But if once you let the ripe moment go You can never wipe off the tears of woe.

—WILLIAM BLAKE

Delay is the deadliest form of denial.

—C. NORTHCOTE PARKINSON

Things may come to those who wait, but only the things left by those who hustle.

—ABRAHAM LINCOLN

Everything comes to him who hustles while he waits.

—THOMAS EDISON

Give me chastity and continence, but not just now.

—ST. AUGUSTINE

He who waits to do a great deal of good at once, will never do anything.

—SAMUEL JOHNSON

My holy of holies is the human body, health, intelligence, talent, inspiration, love, and the most absolute freedom imaginable, freedom from violence and lies, no matter what form the latter two take. Such is the program I would adhere to if I were a major artist.

—ANTON CHEKHOV

Do not put off till tomorrow what can be enjoyed today.

—JOSH BILLINGS

Most people put off till tomorrow that which they should have done yesterday.

—EDGAR WATSON HOWE

Never put off till tomorrow what you can do the day after tomorrow.

—MARK TWAIN

He who hesitates is poor.

—ZERO MOSTEL

He who hesitates is a damned fool.

—MAE WEST

PROGRESS

The art of progress is to preserve order amid change and to preserve change amid order.

—ALFRED NORTH WHITEHEAD

PROMISES

He promised me earrings, but he only pierced my ears.

—ARABIAN SAYING

PROSPERITY
See also WEALTH

I wish you all sorts of prosperity with a little more taste.

—ALAIN RENÉ LESAGE

Beloved, I wish above all things that thou mayest prosper and be in health, even as thy soul prospereth.

—3 JOHN 2

Prosperity is only an instrument to be used, not a deity to be worshiped.

—CALVIN COOLIDGE

First he bought a '57 Biscayne and put it in a ditch. He drank up all the rest, that sonofabitch.

—JONI MITCHELL

Peace be within thy walls, and prosperity within thy palaces.

—PSALM 122:7

Few of us can stand prosperity. Another man's, I mean.

—MARK TWAIN

PUBLIC OPINION

Its name is Public Opinion. It is held in reverence. It settles everything. Some think it is the voice of God. Loyalty to petrified opinion never yet broke a chain or freed a human soul.

—MARK TWAIN

You may talk of the tyranny of Nero and Tiberius; but the real tyranny is the tyranny of your next-door neighbor. Public opinion is a permeating influence, and it exacts obedience to itself; it requires us to think other men's thoughts, to speak other men's words, to follow other men's habits.

—WALTER BAGEHOT

Public opinion is compounded of folly, weakness, prejudice, wrong feeling, right feeling, obstinacy, and newspaper paragraphs.

—ROBERT PEEL

PURPOSE
See also DREAMS, GOALS

Strong lives are motivated by dynamic purposes.

—KENNETH HILDEBRAND

Nothing contributes so much to tranquilizing the mind as a steady purpose—a point on which the soul may fix its intellectual eye.

—MARY WOLLSTONECRAFT SHELLEY

Here is the test to find whether your mission on earth is finished: If you're alive, it isn't.

—RICHARD BACH

Perfections of means and confusion of goals seem—in my opinion—to characterize our age.

—ALBERT EINSTEIN

Since I was twenty-four there never was any vagueness in my plans or ideas as to what God's work was for me.

—FLORENCE NIGHTINGALE

The great use of life is to spend it for something that will outlast it.

—WILLIAM JAMES

You have to know what you want to get.

—GERTRUDE STEIN

Ours is a world where people don't know what they want and are willing to go through hell to get it.

—DON MARQUIS

Many persons have a wrong idea of what constitutes true happiness. It is not attained through self-gratification but through fidelity to a worthy purpose.

—HELEN KELLER

All men should try to learn before they die what they are running from, and to, and why.

—JAMES THURBER

As Miss America, my goal is to bring peace to the entire world and then to get my own apartment.

—JAY LENO

Not the fruit of experience, but experience itself, is the end.

—WALTER PATER

Try not to become a man of success, but rather try to become a man of value.

—ALBERT EINSTEIN

The very purpose of existence is to reconcile the glowing opinion we hold of ourselves with the appalling things that other people think about us.

—QUENTIN CRISP

Man's main task in life is to give birth to himself, to become what he potentially is.

—ERICH FROMM

The real distinction is between those who adapt their purposes to reality and those who seek to mould reality in the light of their purposes.

—HENRY KISSINGER

Anyone can revolt. It is more difficult silently to obey our own inner promptings, and to spend our lives finding sincere and fitting means of expression for our temperament and our gifts.

—GEORGES ROUAULT

My function in life was to render clear what was already blindingly conspicuous.

—QUENTIN CRISP

The purpose of life is a life of purpose.

—ROBERT BYRNE

Often people attempt to live their lives backwards; they try to have more things, or more money, in order to do more of what they want, so they will be happier. The way it actually works is the reverse. You must first be who you really are, then do what you need to do, in order to have what you want.

—MARGARET YOUNG

I just want to do God's will. And He's allowed me to go to the mountain. And I've looked over, and I've seen the promised land. So I'm happy tonight. I'm not worried about anything. I'm not fearing any man.

—MARTIN LUTHER KING, JR
the night before his death

To live content with small means; to seek elegance rather than luxury, and refinement rather than fashion; to be worthy, not respectable, and wealthy, not rich; to study hard, think quietly, talk gently, act frankly; to listen to stars and birds, to babes and sages, with open heart; to bear all cheerfully, do all bravely, await occasions, hurry never. In a word, to let the spiritual, unbidden and unconscious, grow up through the common. This is to be my symphony.

—WILLIAM HENRY CHANNING

What would you attempt to do if you knew you could not fail?

—DR. ROBERT SCHULLER

Human beings seem to have an almost unlimited capacity to deceive themselves and to deceive themselves into taking their own lies for the truth. One's only task is to realize oneself.

—R. D. LAING

Man's main task in life is to give birth to himself, to become what he potentially is. The most important product of his effort is his own personality.

—ERICH FROMM

You will become as small as your controlling desire; as great as your dominant aspiration.

—JAMES ALLEN

Man's task is to become conscious of the contents that press upwards from the unconscious . . . As far as we can discern, the sole purpose of human existence is to kindle a light in the darkness of mere being.

—C. G. JUNG

This is the true joy in life, the being used for a purpose recognized by yourself as a mighty one; the being thoroughly worn out before you are thrown on the scrap heap; the being a force of nature instead of a feverish selfish little clod of ailments and grievances complaining that the world will not devote itself to making you happy.

—GEORGE BERNARD SHAW

There is then a simple answer to the question "What is the purpose of our individual lives?" They have whatever purpose we succeed in putting into them.

—A. J. AYER

From his cradle to his grave a man never does a single thing which has any first and foremost object but one— to secure peace of mind, spiritual comfort, for himself.

—MARK TWAIN

What do people want? They want to be themselves, they want to reach their own potential. Some of them want men, some of them want women, some of them want neither, some of them want a pet turtle. The bottom line is self-expression.

—PAUL KRASSNER

Live all you can; it's a mistake not to. It doesn't so much matter what you do in particular, so long as you have your life. If you haven't had that, what have you had?

—HENRY JAMES

Someday I want to be rich. Some people get so rich they lose all respect for humanity. That's how rich I want to be.

—RITA RUDNER

The real difference between men is energy. A strong will, a settled purpose, an invincible determination, can accomplish almost anything; and in this lies the distinction between great men and little men.

—THOMAS FULLER

When you feel in your gut what you are and then dynamically pursue it—don't back down and don't give up—then you're going to mystify a lot of folks.

—BOB DYLAN

The only difference between a caprice and a lifelong passion is that a caprice lasts a little longer.

—OSCAR WILDE

I don't continually question my reason to live. It's just a state of being. The real question is what you're doing with the living you're doing, and what you want to do with that living.

—MICK JAGGER

He who has a why to live can bear almost any how.

—FRIEDRICH NIETZSCHE

The secret of success is constancy to purpose.

—BENJAMIN DISRAELI

A man needs a purpose for real health.

—SHERWOOD ANDERSON

I want death to find me planting my cabbages.

—MICHEL DE MONTAIGNE

The destiny of mankind is not decided by material computation. We learn that we are spirits, not animals, and that something is going on in space and time, and beyond space and time, which, whether we like it or not, spells duty.

—WINSTON CHURCHILL

Lord, make me an instrument of Your peace. Where there is hatred let me sow love; where there is injury, pardon; where there is doubt, faith; where there is despair, hope; where there is darkness, light; and where there is sadness, joy.

—FRANCIS OF ASSISI

The man who is tenacious of purpose in a rightful cause is not shaken from his firm resolve by the frenzy of his fellow citizens clamoring for what is wrong, or by the tyrant's threatening countenance.

—HORACE

How many cares one loses when one decides not to be something but to be someone.

—COCO CHANEL

Follow your bliss.

—JOSEPH CAMPBELL

How could there be any question of acquiring or possessing, when the one thing needful for a man is to *become*—to be at last, and to die in the fullness of his being.

—ANTOINE DE SAINT-ÉXUPÉRY

Great men are instruments by which the Highest One works out his designs; light-radiators to give guidance and blessing to the travelers of time.

—MOSES HARVEY

The boy gathers materials for a temple, and then when he is thirty concludes to build a woodshed.

—HENRY DAVID THOREAU

Be not simply good; be good for something.

—HENRY DAVID THOREAU

Great minds have purposes, others have wishes.

—WASHINGTON IRVING

If you look good and dress well, you don't need a purpose in life.

—ROBERT PANTE

No wind favors him who has no destined port.

—MICHEL DE MONTAIGNE

In life, as in football, you won't go far unless you know where the goalposts are.

—ARNOLD GLASOW

There are few moments during her recital when one can relax and feel confident that she will make her goal, which is the end of the song.

—PAUL HUME

The high prize of life, the crowning fortune of a man, is to be born with a bias to some pursuit which finds him in employment and happiness.

—RALPH WALDO EMERSON

When a fantasy turns you on, you're obligated to God and nature to start doing it—right away.

—STEWART BRAND

After a time, you may find that having is not so pleasing a thing, after all, as wanting. It is not logical, but it is often true.

—SPOCK
STAR TREK

Lots of times you have to pretend to join a parade in which you're not really interested in order to get where you're going.

—GEORGE MORLEY

Take care to get what you like, or you will end by liking what you get.

—GEORGE BERNARD SHAW

I cannot believe that the purpose of life is to be "happy." I think the purpose of life is to be useful, to be responsible, to be honorable, to be compassionate. It is, above all, to matter: to count, to stand for something, to have made some difference that you lived at all.

—LEO ROSTEN

But I have raised you up for this very purpose, that I might show you my power and that my name might be proclaimed in all the earth.

—EXODUS 9:16

The man who plants and the man who waters have one purpose.

— I CORINTHIANS 3:8

It is the paradox of life that the way to miss pleasure is to seek it first. The very first condition of lasting happiness is that a life should be full of purpose, aiming at something outside self.

—HUGH BLACK

Yes there is a meaning; at least for me, there is one thing that matters—to set a chime of words tinkling in the minds of a few fastidious people.

— LOGAN PEARSALL SMITH

We live very close together. So, our prime purpose in this life is to help others. And if you can't help them at least don't hurt them.

—DALAI LAMA

Grasp all, lose all.

—FOURTEENTH-CENTURY PROVERB

The true profession of a man is to find his way to himself.

—HERMANN HESSE

First, have a definite, clear, practical ideal—a goal, an objective. Second, have the necessary means to achieve your ends—wisdom, money, materials and methods. Third, adjust all your means to that end.

—ARISTOTLE

What is my loftiest ambition? He answered: I've always wanted to throw an egg into an electric fan.

—OLIVER HERFORD

QUOTATIONS

He ranged his tropes, and preached up patience; Backed his opinion with quotations.

—MATTHEW PRIOR

I hate quotations.

—RALPH WALDO EMERSON

REALITY

I stopped believing in Santa Claus when my mother took me to see him in a department store, and he asked for my autograph.

—SHIRLEY TEMPLE

I am certain of nothing but the holiness of the heart's affections, and the truth of imagination.

—JOHN KEATS

The one unchangeable certainty is that nothing is un-changeable or certain.

—JOHN F. KENNEDY

I do not know whether I was then a man dreaming I was a butterfly, or whether I am now a butterfly dreaming I am a man.

—CHUANG-TZU

REAPING WHAT WE SOW

The person who sows seeds of kindness enjoys a perpet-ual harvest.

—ANONYMOUS

It's what each of us sows, and how, that gives to us character and prestige. Seeds of kindness, goodwill, and human understanding, planted in fertile soil, spring up into deathless friendships, big deeds of worth, and a memory that will not soon fade out. We are all sowers of seeds—and let us never forget it!

—GEORGE MATTHEW ADAMS

For it is in giving that we receive.

—FRANCIS OF ASSISI

The first small sacrifice of this sort leads the way to others, and a single hand's turn given heartily to the world's great work helps one amazingly with one's own small tasks.

—LOUISA M. ALCOTT

Service to a just cause rewards the worker with more real happiness and satisfaction than any other venture of life.

—CARRIE CHAPMAN CATT

Do not judge, and you will not be judged. Do not condemn, and you will not be condemned. Forgive, and you will be forgiven. Give, and it will be given to you. For with the measure you use, it will be measured to you.

—JESUS OF NAZARETH
Luke 6:37–38

Charity is twice blessed—it blesses the one who gives and the one who receives.

—ANONYMOUS

There never was a person who did anything worth doing who did not receive more than he gave.

—HENRY WARD BEECHER

The quality of mercy is not strained, It droppeth as the gentle rain from heaven Upon the place beneath: it is twice blessed; It blesseth him that gives and him that takes.

—WILLIAM SHAKESPEARE

The greatest reward for serving others is the satisfaction found in your own heart.

—ANONYMOUS

RECEIVING

The art of acceptance is the art of making someone who has just done you a small favor wish that he might have done you a greater one.

—RUSSELL LYNES

Blessed are those who can give without remembering and take without forgetting.

—ELIZABETH BIBESCO

I know what I have given you. I do not know what you have received.

—ANTONIO PORCHIA

RECEPTIVITY
See also OPPORTUNITY

Life moves on, whether we act as cowards or heros. Life has no other discipline to impose, if we would but realize it, than to accept life unquestioningly. Everything we shut our eyes to, everything we run away from, everything we deny, denigrate or despise, serves to defeat us in the end. What seems nasty, painful, evil, can become a source of beauty, joy and strength, if faced with an open mind. Every moment is a golden one for him who has the vision to recognize it as such.

—HENRY MILLER

I can believe anything, provided it is incredible.

—OSCAR WILDE

Try everything once except incest and folk dancing.

—THOMAS BEECHAM

Let your hook always be cast. In the pool where you least expect it, will be a fish.

—OVID

Always keep a window in the attic open; not just cracked: open.

—HENRY JAMES

I only have "yes" men around me. Who needs "no" men?

—MAE WEST

Let us open up our natures, throw wide the doors of our hearts and let in the sunshine of good will and kindness.

—O. S. MARDEN

REGRET

Regret for the things we did can be tempered by time; it is regret for the things we did not do that is inconsolable.

—SYDNEY J. HARRIS

When such as I cast out remorse So great a sweetness flows into the breast We must laugh and we must sing, We are blest by everything, Everything we look upon is blest.

—W. B. YEATS

I coulda had class. I coulda been a contender. I coulda been somebody. Instead of a bum, which is what I am.

—MARLON BRANDO

Regret for time wasted can become a power for good in the time that remains, if we will only stop the waste and the idle, useless regretting.

—ARTHUR BRISBANE

Regret is an appalling waste of energy; you can't build on it; it's only good for wallowing in.

—KATHERINE MANSFIELD

RELATIONSHIPS

The easiest kind of relationship for me is with ten thousand people. The hardest is with one.

—JOAN BAEZ

Almost all of our relationships begin and most of them continue as forms of mutual exploitation, a mental or physical barter, to be terminated when one or both parties run out of goods.

—W. H. AUDEN

Once the realization is accepted that even between the *closest* human beings infinite distances continue to exist, a wonderful living side by side can grow up, if they succeed in loving the distance between them which makes it possible for each to see the other whole against the sky.

—RAINER MARIA RILKE

RICK: I mean, what AM I supposed to call you? My "Girl Friend"? My "Companion"? My "Roommate"? Nothing sounds quite right! *JOANIE:* How about your "Reason for Living"? *RICK:* No, no, I need something I can use around the office.

—GARRY TRUDEAU
DOONESBURY

It's relaxing to go out with my ex-wife because she already knows I'm an idiot.

—WARREN THOMAS

The perfect lover is one who turns into a pizza at 4:00 a.m.

—CHARLES PIERCE

It is explained that all relationships require a little give and take. This is untrue. Any partnership demands that we give and give and give and at the last, as we flop into our graves exhausted, we are told that we didn't give enough.

—QUENTIN CRISP

I recommend having no relationships except those easily borne and disposed of; I recommend limiting one's involvement in other people's lives to a pleasantly scant minimum.

—QUENTIN CRISP

It is better to be hated for what you are than loved for what you are not.

—ANDRÉ GIDE

RELIGION
See also GOD, PRAYER, WORSHIP

My religion consists of a humble admiration of the illimitable superior spirit who reveals himself in the slight details we are able to perceive with our frail and feeble mind.

—ALBERT EINSTEIN

I was told that the Chinese said they would bury me by the Western Lake and build a shrine to my memory. I have some slight regret that this did not happen, as I might have become a god, which would have been very *chic* for an atheist.

—BERTRAND RUSSELL

Men talk of "finding God," but no wonder it is difficult;
He is hidden in that darkest hiding-place, your heart.
You yourself are a part of him.

—CHRISTOPHER MORLEY

You must believe in God, in spite of what the clergy say.

—BENJAMIN JOWETT

It is the test of a good religion whether you can joke
about it.

—G. K. CHESTERTON

The world embarrasses me, and I cannot dream That
this watch exists and has no watchmaker.

—VOLTAIRE

You *dare* to dicker with your pontiff?

—REX HARRISON TO CHARLTON HESTON,
THE AGONY AND THE ECSTASY

Belief is a wise wager. If you gain, you gain all; if you
lose, you lose nothing. Wager then, without hesitation,
that He exists.

—BLAISE PASCAL

To believe in God is impossible—not to believe in him is
absurd.

—VOLTAIRE

I could not say I believe. I know! I have had the experience of being gripped by something that is stronger than
myself, something that people call God.

—CARL JUNG

There is no higher religion than human service. To work
for the common good is the greatest creed.

—ALBERT SCHWEITZER

Giving away a fortune is taking Christianity too far.

—CHARLOTTE BINGHAM

I'm going to take the moment to contemplate most of the Western religions. I'm looking for something soft on morality, generous with holidays, and with a very short initiation period.

—DAVID ADDISON
MOONLIGHTING

I do benefits for all religions—I'd hate to blow the hereafter on a technicality.

—BOB HOPE

Looking for loopholes.

—W. C. FIELDS
an atheist his entire life, asked on his
deathbed why he was reading the Bible

RESPONSIBILITY

After ecstasy, the laundry.

—ZEN STATEMENT

My philosophy is that not only are you responsible for your life, but doing the best at this moment puts you in the best place for the next moment.

—OPRAH WINFREY

Well, if you've got work to do, Wallace, I don't want to interfere. I was reading an article in the paper the other day where a certain amount of responsibility around the home was good character training. Good-bye, Mr. and Mrs. Cleaver.

—EDDIE HASKELL
LEAVE IT TO BEAVER

The price of greatness is responsibility.

—WINSTON CHURCHILL

Character—the willingness to accept responsibility for one's own life—is the source from which self-respect springs.

—JOAN DIDION

When the freedom they wished for most was freedom from responsibility, then Athens ceased to be free and was never free again.

—EDITH HAMILTON

Do you realize the responsibility I carry? I'm the only person standing between Richard Nixon and the White House.

—JOHN F. KENNEDY

We don't care. We don't have to. We're the phone company.

—LILY TOMLIN'S ERNESTINE

REST

Sometimes I sits and thinks and sometimes I just sits.

—SATCHEL PAIGE

How beautiful it is to do nothing, and then rest afterward.

—SPANISH PROVERB

Most of the evils in life arise from man's being unable to sit still in a room.

—BLAISE PASCAL

True silence is the rest of the mind; it is to the spirit what sleep is to the body, nourishment and refreshment.

—WILLIAM PENN

Laziness is nothing more than the habit of resting before you get tired.

—JULES RENARD

It is impossible to enjoy idling thoroughly unless one has plenty of work to do.

—JEROME KLAPKA JEROME

REVENGE

When lovely woman stoops to folly, And finds too late that men betray, What charm can soothe her melancholy? What art can wash her guilt away? The only art her guilt to cover, To hide her shame from every eye, To give repentance to her lover, And wring his bosom, is—to die.

—OLIVER GOLDSMITH

Revenge is often like biting a dog because the dog bit you

—AUSTIN O'MALLEY

RISK
See also ACTION, CHOICE

If you want a place in the sun, you must leave the shade of the family tree.

—OSAGE SAYING

One doesn't discover new lands without consenting to lose sight of the shore for a very long time.

—ANDRÉ GIDE

One can never consent to creep when one feels an impulse to soar.

—HELEN KELLER

Every man has the right to risk his own life in order to save it.

—JEAN-JACQUES ROUSSEAU

Don't play for safety—it's the most dangerous thing in the world.

—HUGH WALPOLE

Be daring, be different, be impractical; be anything that will assert integrity of purpose and imaginative vision against the play-it-safers, the creatures of the commonplace, the slaves of the ordinary.

—CECIL BEATON

There are risks and costs to a program of action, but they are far less than the long-range risks and costs of comfortable inaction.

—JOHN F. KENNEDY

The president has so much good publicity potential that hasn't been exploited. He should just sit down one day and make a list of all the things that people are embarrassed to do that they shouldn't be embarrassed to do, and then do them all on television.

—ANDY WARHOL
suggestion for President Kennedy

Take calculated risks. That is quite different from being rash.

—GEORGE PATTON

Often the difference between a successful man and a failure is not one's better abilities or ideas, but the courage that one has to bet on his ideas, to take a calculated risk—and to act.

—MAXWELL MALTZ

Try a thing you haven't done three times. Once, to get over the fear of doing it. Twice, to learn how to do it. And a third time to figure out whether you like it or not.

—VIRGIL THOMSON

Fortune sides with him who dares.

—VIRGIL

Don't be afraid to go on an occasional wild goose chase. That's what wild geese are for.

—ANONYMOUS

You can't expect to hit the jackpot if you don't put a few nickels in the machine.

—FLIP WILSON

Even God lends a hand to honest boldness.

—MENANDER

"Come to the edge," he said. They said, "We are afraid." "Come to the edge," he said. They came. He pushed them . . . And they flew.

—GUILLAUME APOLLINAIRE

There are seasons, in human affairs, when new depths seem to be broken up in the soul, when new wants are unfolded in multitudes, and a new and undefined good is thirsted for. There are periods when to dare, is the highest wisdom.

—WILLIAM ELLERY CHANNING

Don't be afraid to take a big step if one is indicated. You can't cross a chasm in two small jumps.

—DAVID LLOYD GEORGE

Make no little plans; they have no magic to stir men's blood.

—DANIEL HUDSON BURNHAM

Once more unto the breach, dear friends, once more.

—WILLIAM SHAKESPEARE

I can say, "I am terribly frightened and fear is terrible and awful and it makes me uncomfortable, so I won't do that because it's uncomfortable." Or I could say "Get used to being uncomfortable. It is uncomfortable doing something that's risky." But so what? Do you want to stagnate and just be comfortable?

—BARBRA STREISAND

A man of courage never needs weapons, but he may need bail.

—ETHEL WATTS MUMFORD

ROMANTIC LOVE
See also SEX

Romantic love is mental illness. But it's a pleasurable one. It's a drug. It distorts reality, and that's the point of it. It would be impossible to fall in love with someone that you really *saw*.

—FRAN LEBOWITZ

In real love you want the other person's good. In romantic love you want the other person.

—MARGARET ANDERSON

The message that "love" will solve all of our problems is repeated incessantly in contemporary culture—like a philosophical tom tom. It would be closer to the truth to say that love is a contagious and virulent disease which leaves a victim in a state of near imbecility, paralysis, profound melancholia, and sometimes culminates in death.

—QUENTIN CRISP

My silks and fine array, My smiles and languished air, By love are driv'n away; And mournful lean Despair Brings me yew to deck my grave: Such end true lovers have.

—WILLIAM BLAKE

Doris, I think I'm in love with you. I mean, it's crazy. Really crazy! I mean I don't even know if you've read *The Catcher in the Rye*.

—BERNARD SLADE

In 1862, as token of love and remorse, Dante Gabriel Rossetti buried a sheaf of original manuscript poems with his dear departed wife, Elizabeth Siddal. In 1869, having reconsidered his romantic gesture, Dante Gabriel Rossetti exhumed his wife, retrieved and subsequently published the buried poems.

—JON WINOKUR

If the man and woman walk off into the sunset hand-in-hand in the last reel, it adds $10 million to the box office.

—GEORGE LUCAS
advice to Steven Spielberg

Even though the labels stripper and congressman are completely incongruous, there was never anything but harmony in our hearts.

—FANNE FOX
about her relationship with Congressman Wilbur Mills

Love: that's self-love *à deux.*

—MADAME DE STAËL

What a recreation it is to be in love! It sets the heart aching so delicately, there's no taking a wink of sleep for the pleasure of the pain.

—GEORGE COLMAN THE YOUNGER

It's curious how, when you're in love, you yearn to go about doing acts of kindness to everybody. I am bursting with a sort of yeasty benevolence these days, like one of those chaps in Dickens.

—P. G. WODEHOUSE

It's an extra dividend when you like the girl you're in love with.

—CLARK GABLE

One exists with one's husband—one lives with one's lover.

—HONORÉ DE BALZAC

To say that you can love one person all your life is just like saying that one candle will continue burning as long as you live.

—LEO TOLSTOY

Older woman, younger man! Popular wisdom claims that this particular class of love affair is the most poignant, tender, poetic, exquisite one there is, altogether the choicest on the menu.

—DORIS LESSING

I can understand companionship. I can understand bought sex in the afternoon. I cannot understand the love affair.

—GORE VIDAL

Love is the same as *like* except you feel sexier. And more romantic. And also more annoyed when he talks with his mouth full. And you also resent it more when he interrupts you. And you also respect him less when he shows any weakness. And furthermore, when you ask him to pick you up at the airport and he tells you he can't do it because he's busy, it's only when you love him that you hate him.

—JUDITH VIORST

Out upon it, I have loved Three whole days together; And am like to love three more, If it prove fair weather.

—JOHN SUCKLING

When you're in love it's the most glorious two-and-a-half days of your life.

—RICHARD LEWIS

Ecstasy cannot last, but it can carve a channel for something lasting.

—E. M. FORSTER

RULES
See also WORDS TO LIVE BY

HOW TO BEHAVE IN AN ELEVATOR
1. Face forward.
2. Fold hands in front.
3. Do not make eye contact.
4. Watch the numbers.
5. Don't talk to anyone you don't know.
6. Stop talking with anyone you do know when anyone you don't know enters the elevator.
7. Avoid brushing bodies.

—LAYNE LONGFELLOW

A cardinal rule of politics—never get caught in bed with a live man or a dead woman.

—J. R. EWING

RULE A: Don't. RULE A1: Rule A does not exist. RULE A2: Do not discuss the existence or non-existence of Rules A, A1 or A2.

—R. D. LAING

Rule #1: Don't sweat the small stuff. Rule #2: It's all small stuff.

—DR. MICHAEL MANTELL

Is forbidden to steal towels, please. If you are not person to do such is please not to read notice.

—SIGN IN TOKYO HOTEL

Exit according to rule, first leg and then head. Remove high heels and synthetic stockings before evacuation: Open the door, take out the recovery line and throw it away.

—RUMANIAN NATIONAL AIRLINES
EMERGENCY INSTRUCTIONS

The ideas I stand for are not mine. I borrowed them from Socrates. I swiped them from Chesterfield. I stole them from Jesus. And I put them in a book. If you don't like their rules, whose would you use?

—DALE CARNEGIE

You are a member of the British royal family. We are *never* tired, and we all *love* hospitals.

—QUEEN MARY

Mirrors should reflect a little before throwing back images.

—JEAN COCTEAU

To change one's life: Start immediately. Do it flamboyantly. No exceptions.

—WILLIAM JAMES

Never be possessive. If a female friend lets on that she is going out with another man, be kind and understanding. If she says she would like to go out with the Dallas Cowboys, including the coaching staff, the same rule applies. Tell her: "Kath, you just go right ahead and do what you feel is right." Unless you actually care for her, in which case you must see to it that she has no male contact whatsoever.

—BRUCE JAY FRIEDMAN

Never get a mime talking. He won't stop.

—MARCEL MARCEAU

A few strong instincts and a few plain rules suffice us.

—RALPH WALDO EMERSON

Do to others as you would have them do to you.

—LUKE 6:31

A new command I give you: Love one another. As I have loved you, so you must love one another. By this all men will know that you are my disciples, if you love one another.

—JESUS OF NAZARETH
John 13:34–35

Woe to you, teachers of the law and Pharisees, you hypocrites! You give a tenth of your spices—mint, dill and cummin. But you have neglected the more important matters of the law—justice, mercy and faithfulness. You should have practiced the latter, without neglecting the former.

— JESUS OF NAZARETH
Matthew 23:23

In reading and writing, you cannot lay down rules until you have learnt to obey them. Much more so in life.

—MARCUS ANTONINUS

The best rules to form a young man are: to talk a little, to hear much, to reflect alone upon what has passed in company, to distrust one's own opinions, and value others' that deserve it.

—WILLIAM TEMPLE

There are two golden rules for an orchestra: start together and finish together. The public doesn't give a damn what goes on in between.

—THOMAS BEECHAM

We started off trying to set up a small anarchist community, but people wouldn't obey the rules.

—ALAN BENNETT

Never burn an uninteresting letter is the first rule of British aristocracy.

—FRANK MOORE COLBY

That old law about "an eye for an eye" leaves everybody blind.

—MARTIN LUTHER KING, JR.

People who live in glass houses have to answer the bell.

—BRUCE PATTERSON

Most of us, by the time we're up on the rules, are generally too old to play.

—PAPPY MAVERICK

The rules which experience suggests are better than those which theorists elaborate in their libraries.

—R. S. STORRS

Laws are not invented; they grow out of circumstances.

—AZARIAS

His face was filled with broken commandments.

—JOHN MASEFIELD

Life is like music; it must be composed by ear, feeling and instinct, not by rule. Nevertheless one had better know the rules, for they sometimes guide in doubtful cases, though not often.

—SAMUEL BUTLER

You got to know the rules before you can break 'em. Otherwise, it's no fun.

—SONNY CROCKETT
MIAMI VICE

It's a good idea to obey all the rules when you're young, just so you'll have the strength to break them when you're old.

—MARK TWAIN

There is no useful rule without an exception.

—THOMAS FULLER

There are those whose sole claim to profundity is the discovery of exceptions to rules.

—PAUL ELDRIDGE

Any fool can make a rule, and every fool will mind it.

—HENRY DAVID THOREAU

His life was formal; his actions seemed ruled with a ruler.

—CHARLES LAMB

The golden rule is that there are no golden rules. Do not do unto others as you would they should do unto you; their tastes may not be the same.

—GEORGE BERNARD SHAW

The great rule is not to talk about money with people who have much more or much less than you.

—KATHARINE WHITEHORN

SANCTUARY

My special place. It's a place no amount of hurt and anger Can deface. I put things back together there It all falls right in place—In my special space My special place.

—JONI MITCHELL

A harbor, even if it is a little harbor, is a good thing, since adventures come into it as well as go out, and the life in it grows strong, because it takes something from the world and has something to give in return.

—SARAH ORNE JEWETT

We must reserve a back shop all our own, entirely free, in which to establish our real liberty and our principal retreat and solitude.

—MICHEL DE MONTAIGNE

SATISFACTION

Pat and I have the satisfaction that every dime that we've got is honestly ours. I should say this, that Pat doesn't have a mink coat. But she does have a respectable Republican cloth coat, and I always tell her that she would look good in anything.

—RICHARD M. NIXON

SECURITY

If money is your hope for independence you will never have it. The only real security that a man can have in this world is a reserve of knowledge, experience and ability.

—HENRY FORD

Life is either a daring adventure or nothing. Security does not exist in nature, nor do the children of men as a whole experience it. Avoiding danger is no safer in the long run than exposure.

—HELEN KELLER

SELF
See Alo INDIVIDUALITY

Don't try to take on a new personality; it doesn't work.

—RICHARD M. NIXON

You have to leave the city of your comfort and go into the wilderness of your intuition. What you'll discover will be wonderful. What you'll discover will be yourself.

—ALAN ALDA

When you stop drinking, you have to deal with this marvelous personality that started you drinking in the first place.

—JIMMY BRESLIN

This above all: to thine own self be true, And it must follow, as the night the day, Thou canst not then be false to any man.

—WILLIAM SHAKESPEARE

A musician must make music, an artist must paint, a poet must write, if he is to be ultimately at peace with himself.

—ABRAHAM MASLOW

To know oneself, one should assert oneself.

—ALBERT CAMUS

Nobody can be exactly like me. Sometimes even I have trouble doing it.

—TALLULAH BANKHEAD

When we see men of a contrary character, we should turn inwards and examine ourselves.

—CONFUCIUS

Trying to define yourself is like trying to bite your own teeth.

—ALAN WATTS

To be one's self, and unafraid whether right or wrong, is more admirable than the easy cowardice of surrender to conformity.

—IRVING WALLACE

The most important thing is to be *whatever* you are without shame.

—ROD STEIGER

I don't have a warm personal enemy left. They've all died off. I miss them terribly because they helped define me.

—CLARE BOOTH LUCE

If egotism means a terrific interest in one's self, egotism is absolutely essential to efficient living.

—ARNOLD BENNETT

Selfness is an essential fact of life. The thought of non-selfness, precise sameness, is terrifying.

—LEWIS THOMAS

You can't change the music of your soul.

—KATHARINE HEPBURN

The last quarter of a century of my life has been pretty constantly and faithfully devoted to the study of the human race—that is to say, the study of myself, for in my individual person I am the entire human race compacted together. I have found that there is no ingredient of the race which I do not possess in either a small way or a large way.

—MARK TWAIN

It's not only the most difficult thing to know one's self, but the most inconvenient.

—JOSH BILLINGS

If people can be educated to see the lowly side of their own natures, it may be hoped that they will also learn to understand and to love their fellow men better. A little less hypocrisy and a little more tolerance toward oneself can only have good results in respect for our neighbor; for we are all too prone to transfer to our fellows the injustice and violence we inflict upon our own natures.

—CARL JUNG

Resolve to be thyself: and know, that he Who finds himself, loses his misery.

—MATTHEW ARNOLD

I have little patience with anyone who is not self-satisfied. I am always pleased to see my friends, happy to be with my wife and family, but the high spot of every day is when I first catch a glimpse of myself in the shaving mirror.

—ROBERT MORLEY

Self-reverence, self-knowledge, self-control, These three alone lead life to sovereign power.

—ALFRED, LORD TENNYSON

Be thine own palace, or the world's thy jail.

—JOHN DONNE

I have tried to state the need we have to recognise this aspect of health: the non-communicating central self, forever immune from the reality principle, and forever silent. Here communication is not non-verbal; it is like the music of the spheres, absolutely personal. It belongs to being alive. And in health, it is out of this that communication naturally arises.

—D. W. WINNICOTT

Romance and work are great diversions to keep you from dealing with yourself.

—CHER

He is rich or poor according to what he *is*, not according to what he *has*.

—HENRY WARD BEECHER

Everyone is necessarily the hero of his own life story.

—JOHN BARTH

Believe nothing, no matter where you read it, or who said it—even if I have said it—unless it agrees with your own reason and your own common sense.

—BUDDHA

The greatest thing in the world is to know how to belong to oneself.

—MICHEL DE MONTAIGNE

Make the most of yourself, for that is all there is of you.

—RALPH WALDO EMERSON

Characters do not change. Opinions alter, but characters are only developed.

—BENJAMIN DISRAELI

Evolution is the law of life, and there is no evolution save toward Individualism.

—OSCAR WILDE

What good is it for a man to gain the whole world, and yet lose or forfeit his very self?

—JESUS OF NAZARETH
Luke 9:25

Delight is to him—a far, far upward, and inward de-light—who against the proud gods and commodores of this earth, ever stands forth his own inexorable self.

—HERMAN MELVILLE
MOBY DICK

Our deeds determine us, as much as we determine our deeds.

—GEORGE ELIOT

SELF-CONFIDENCE
See also SELF-ESTEEM

The longer I live the more I see that I am never wrong about anything, and that all the pains I have so humbly taken to verify my notions have only wasted my time.

—GEORGE BERNARD SHAW

We confide in our strength, without boasting of it; we respect that of others, without fearing it.

—THOMAS JEFFERSON

Calm self-confidence is as far from conceit as the desire to earn a decent living is remote from greed.

—CHANNING POLLOCK

Early in life I had to choose between honest arrogance and hypocritical humility. I chose honest arrogance and have seen no occasion to change.

—FRANK LLOYD WRIGHT

All my shows are great. Some of them are bad. But they're all great.

—LORD GRADE

Dignity consists not in possessing honors, but in the consciousness that we deserve them.

—ARISTOTLE

Self-confidence is the first requisite to great undertakings.

—SAMUEL JOHNSON

I have great faith in fools—self-confidence my friends call it.

—EDGAR ALLAN POE

He only is a great man who can neglect the applause of the multitude and enjoy himself independent of its favor.

—JOSEPH ADDISON

SELF-CONTROL

Man who man would be, Must rule the empire of himself.

—PERCY BYSSHE SHELLEY

SELF-DECEPTION

You're obviously suffering from delusions of adequacy.

—ALEXIS CARRINGTON
DYNASTY

Most of our platitudes notwithstanding, self-deception remains the most difficult deception. The tricks that work on others count for nothing in that very well-lit back alley where one keeps assignations with oneself: no winning smiles will do here, no prettily drawn lists of good intentions.

—JOAN DIDION

The first and worst of all frauds is to cheat oneself.

—GAMALIEL BAILEY

SELF-DESTRUCTION

Practically all human misery and serious emotional turmoil are quite unnecessary—not to mention unethical. You, unethical? When you make yourself severely anxious or depressed, you are clearly acting against *you* and are being unfair and unjust to *yourself*.

—ALBERT ELLIS

SELF-ESTEEM
See also SELF-CONFIDENCE, SELF-LOVE

Last night at twelve I felt immense, But now I feel like thirty cents.

—GEORGE ADE

My vigor, vitality and cheek repel me. I am the kind of woman I would run from.

—NANCY, LADY ASTOR

I've been promoted to middle management. I never thought I'd sink so low.

—TIM GOULD

It's surprising how many persons go through life without ever recognizing that their feelings toward other people are largely determined by their feelings toward themselves, and if you're not comfortable within yourself, you can't be comfortable with others.

—SYDNEY J. HARRIS

Self-respect is a question of recognizing that anything worth having has a price.

—JOAN DIDION

So much is a man worth as he esteems himself.

—FRANÇOIS RABELAIS

Ofttimes nothing profits more Than self-esteem, grounded on just and right Well managed.

—JOHN MILTON

I cannot love anyone if I hate myself. That is the reason why we feel so extremely uncomfortable in the presence of people who are noted for their special virtuousness, for they radiate an atmosphere of the torture they inflict on themselves. That is not a virtue but a vice.

—CARL JUNG

I just look in the mirror and I say "God, it's really fantastic, the Lord really gave me something." So why on earth should I cover any of it up.

—EDY WILLIAMS

Humility is not my forte, and whenever I dwell for any length of time on my own shortcomings, they gradually begin to seem mild, harmless, rather engaging little things.

—MARGARET HALSEY

The superior man will not manifest either narrow-mindedness or the want of self-respect.

—MENCIUS

We can secure other people's approval, if we do right and try hard; but our own is worth a hundred of it.

—MARK TWAIN

It is suddenly all right to be a hairdresser. No one really knows how this happened.

—TONY LANG

I have a memory like an elephant. In fact, elephants often consult me.

—NOËL COWARD

To feel themselves in the presence of true greatness many men find it necessary only to be alone.

—TOM MASSON

So Harry says, "You don't like me any more. Why not?" And he says, "Because you've got so terribly pretentious." And Harry says, "Pretentious? *Moi?*"

—JOHN CLEESE & CONNIE BOOTH

SELF-HELP

See also CARING FOR YOURSELF

Satisfaction will come to those who please themselves.

—ARNOLD LOBEL

God changes not what is in a people, until they change what is in themselves.

—KORAN

Prayer indeed is good, but while calling on the gods a man should himself lend a hand.

—HIPPOCRATES

The spirit of self-help is the root of all genuine growth in the individual; and, exhibited in the lives of many, it constitutes the true source of national vigor and strength. Help from without is often enfeebling in its effects, but help from within invariably invigorates.

—SAMUEL SMILES

We can endure neither our evils nor their cures.

—LIVY

A noble person attracts noble people, and knows how to hold on to them.

—JOHANN WOLFGANG VON GOETHE

I know of no more encouraging fact than the unquestionable ability of man to elevate his life by conscious endeavor.

—HENRY DAVID THOREAU

Thanks be to God, since my leaving drinking of wine, I do find myself much better, and do mind my business better, and do spend less money, and less time lost in idle company.

—SAMUEL PEPYS

If you want to lift yourself up, lift up someone else.

—BOOKER T. WASHINGTON

It is one of the beautiful compensations of this life that no one can sincerely try to help another without helping himself.

—CHARLES DUDLEY WARNER

When you find yourself overpowered, as it were, by melancholy, the best way is to go out and do something kind to somebody or other.

— JOHN KEBLE

Lock up your house, go across the railroad tracks, and find someone in need and do something for him.

—KARL MENNINGER
advice for someone who feels a nervous breakdown coming on

SELF-KNOWLEDGE

Your vision will become clear only when you can look into your own heart. Who looks outside, dreams; who looks inside, awakes.

—CARL JUNG

Any life, no matter how long and complex it may be, is made up of a single moment—the moment in which a man finds out, once and for all, who he is.

—JORGE LUIS BORGES

But if a man happens to find himself he has a mansion which he can inhabit with dignity all the days of his life.

—JAMES MICHENER

SELF-LOVE
See also SELF-CONFIDENCE, SELF-ESTEEM

To love oneself is the beginning of a lifelong romance.

—OSCAR WILDE

The last time I saw him he was walking down Lover's Lane holding his own hand.

—FRED ALLEN

No one is born prejudiced against others, but everyone is born prejudiced in favor of himself.

—DAVID STAFFORD-CLARK, M.D.

Would you hurt a man keenest, strike at his self-love.

—LEW WALLACE
BEN HUR

He fell in love with himself at first sight and it is a passion to which he has always been faithful.

—ANTHONY POWELL

SELF-SUFFICIENCY

Poor is the man whose pleasures depend on the permission of another.

—MADONNA

The consuming desire of most human beings is deliberately to plant their whole life in the hands of some other person. I would describe this method of searching for happiness as immature. Development of character consists solely in moving toward self-sufficiency.

—QUENTIN CRISP

All hatred driven hence, The soul recovers radical innocence And learns at last that it is self-delighting, Self-appeasing, self-affrighting, And that its own sweet will is Heaven's will.

—W. B. YEATS

No one can build his security upon the nobleness of another person.

—WILLA CATHER

In battle or business, whatever the game, In law or in love, it is ever the same; In the struggle for power, or the scramble for pelf, Let this be your motto— Rely on yourself! For, whether the prize be a ribbon or throne, The victor is he who can go it alone!

—JOHN GODFREY SAXE
THE GAME OF LIFE

He was the only really independent person—boy or man—in the community, and by consequence he was tranquilly and continuously happy and was envied by all the rest of us.

—MARK TWAIN
of Tom Blankenship, real-life model for Huckleberry Finn

Why be influenced by a person when you already are one?

—MARTIN MULL

I shun father and mother and wife and brother when my genius calls me.

—RALPH WALDO EMERSON

Even in the common affairs of life, in love, friendship, and marriage, how little security have we when we trust our happiness in the hands of others!

—WILLIAM HAZLITT

There is no dependence that can be sure but a dependence upon one's self.

—JOHN GAY

My sense of my own importance to myself is tremendous. I am all I have, to work with, to play with, to suffer
and to enjoy. It is not the eyes of others that I am wary
of, but my own.

—NOËL COWARD

In the choice of a horse and a wife, a man must please
himself, ignoring the opinion and advice of friends.

—GEORGE JOHN WHYTE-MELVILLE

Lean too much upon the approval of people, and it becomes a bed of thorns.

—TEHYI HSIEH

If a man is in health, he doesn't need to take anybody
else's temperature to know where he is going.

—E. B. WHITE

CLIFF CLAVEN: You ever heard of the lone wolf, Carla?
The lone wolf, *c'est moi.* A man by himself, needing no
one. I touch no one, no one touches me. I am a rock. I
am an island. *CARLA TORTELLI:* You am a boob.

—CHEERS

He is his own best friend, and takes delight in privacy;
whereas the man of no virtue or ability is his own worst
enemy and is afraid of solitude.

—ARISTOTLE

SELFISHNESS

Selfishness is not living as one wishes to live, it is asking
others to live as one wishes to live.

—OSCAR WILDE

Egotist, *n.* A person of low taste, more interested in himself than in me.

—AMBROSE BIERCE

Don't be selfish. If you have something you do not want, and know someone who has no use for it, give. In this way you can be generous without expenditure of self-denial and also help another to be the same.

— ELBERT HUBBARD

SERVICE
See also CHARITY, GIVING, GOOD DEEDS

If it is not mere rhetoric and you really mean what you say when you say, "I will do anything you want me to do!", then let us have a real though minor trial: will you learn shorthand as soon as possible? It is a skill worth having anyway.

—DELMORE SCHWARTZ
to Elizabeth Pollet

When you make a world tolerable for yourself you make a world tolerable for others.

—ANAIS NIN

There is nothing to make you like other human beings so much as doing things for them.

—ZORA NEALE HURSTON

Men become attached to us not by reason of the services we render them, but by reason of the services they render us.

—EUGÈNE LABICHE

Knowing sorrow well, I learn the way to succor the distressed.

—VERGIL

The sage does not accumulate for himself. The more he uses for others, the more he has himself. The more he gives to others, the more he possesses of his own. The Way of Heaven is to benefit others and not to injure.

—LAO-TZU

If things are not going well with you, begin your effort at correcting the situation by carefully examining the service you are rendering, and especially the spirit in which you are rendering it.

—ROGER BABSON

It is hideous and coarse to assume that we can do something for others—and it is vile not to endeavor to do it.

—EDWARD DAHLBERG

Often we can help each other most by leaving each other alone; at other times we need the hand-grasp and the word of cheer.

—ELBERT HUBBARD

These are the times that try men's souls. The summer soldier and the sunshine patriot will, in this crisis, shrink from the service of their country; but he that stands it now, deserves the love and thanks of man and woman.

—THOMAS PAINE

All service ranks the same with God.

—ROBERT BROWNING

They serve God well, who serve his creatures.

—CAROLINE NORTON

In the New Testament it is taught that willing and voluntary service to others is the highest duty and glory in human life. The men of talent are constantly forced to serve the rest. They make the discoveries and inventions, order the battles, write the books, and produce the works of art. The benefit and enjoyment go to the whole. There are those who joyfully order their own lives so that they may serve the welfare of mankind.

—W. G. SUMNE

To give and not to count the cost; To fight and not to heed the wounds; To toil and not to seek for rest; To labour and not ask for any reward Save that of knowing that we do Thy will.

—IGNATIUS LOYOLA

Make a joyful noise unto the Lord, all ye lands. Serve the Lord with gladness: come before his presence with singing.

—PSALM 100:1–2

If anyone wants to be first, he must be the very last, and the servant of all.

—JESUS OF NAZARETH
Mark 9:35

One of the most amazing things ever said on this earth is Jesus' statement: "He that is greatest among you shall be your servant." Nobody has one chance in a billion of being thought really great after a century has passed except those who have been the servants of all. That strange realist from Bethlehem knew that.

—HARRY EMERSON FOSDICK

For I was hungry and you gave me something to eat, I was thirsty and you gave me something to drink, I was a stranger and you invited me in, I needed clothes and you clothed me, I was sick and you looked after me, I was in prison and you came to visit me . . . I tell you the truth, whatever you did for one of the least of these brothers of mine, you did for me.

—JESUS OF NAZARETH
Matthew 25:35–36, 40

The measure of a man is not the number of his servants but in the number of people whom he serves.

—DR. PAUL D. MOODY

I am not influenced by the expectation of promotion or pecuniary reward. I wish to be useful, and every kind of service necessary for the public good, becomes honorable by being necessary.

—NATHAN HALE

There is a place for everyone, man and woman, old and young, hale and halt; service in a thousand forms is open. There is no room now for the dilettante, the weakling, for the shirker, or the sluggard. From the highest to the humblest tasks, all are of equal honor; all have their part to play.

—WINSTON CHURCHILL

The noblest service comes from nameless hands, And the best servant does his work unseen.

—OLIVER WENDELL HOLMES

If we do not lay out ourselves in the service of mankind whom should we serve?

—ABIGAIL ADAMS

Service is nothing but love in work clothes.

—ANONYMOUS

Then choose for yourselves this day whom you will serve . . . But as for me and my household, we will serve the Lord.

—JOSHUA 24:15

SERVICE (MISGUIDED)

The little entourage of friends and relatives whom she completely dominated was fond of saying, "Becky would give you the shirt off her back." And it was true. The only trouble was that she neglected to take it off first, and what you found on your back was not only Becky's shirt but Becky too.

—MARGARET HALSEY

Herbert was so benevolent, so merciful a man that, in his mistaken passion, he would have held an umbrella over a duck in a shower of rain.

—DOUGLAS JERROLD

The bird thinks it is an act of kindness to give the fish a lift in the air.

—RABINDRANATH TAGORE

Which of you if his son asks for bread, will give him a stone? Or if he asks for a fish, will give him a snake?

—JESUS OF NAZARETH
Matthew 7:9–10

SEX
See also MARRIAGE, ROMANTIC LOVE

The important thing in acting is to be able to laugh and cry. If I have to cry, I think of my sex life. If I have to laugh, I think of my sex life.

—GLENDA JACKSON

Love is the drug which makes sexuality palatable in popular mythology.

—GERMAINE GREER

The only reason I would take up jogging is so that I could hear heavy breathing again.

—ERMA BOMBECK

Personally, I like sex and I don't care what a man thinks of me as long as I get what I want from him—which is usually sex.

—VALERIE PERRINE

Love is the answer, but while you are waiting for the answer, sex raises some pretty good questions.

—WOODY ALLEN

Wink, wink, nudge, nudge, say no more, know what I mean?

—ERIC IDLE
MONTY PYTHON'S FLYING CIRCUS

Were kisses all the joys in bed, one woman would another wed.

—WILLIAM SHAKESPEARE

Many mothers are wholly ignorant of the almost universal prevalence of secret vice, or self-abuse, among the young. Why hesitate to say firmly and without quibble that personal abuse lies at the root of much of the feebleness, paleness, nervousness, and good-for-nothingness of the entire community?

—DR. J. H. KELLOGG
the inventor of Kellogg's Corn Flakes
in a warning against Grape Nuts

The next time you feel the desire [to masturbate] coming on, don't give way to it. If you have the chance, just wash your parts in cold water and cool them down.

—ROBERT BADEN-POWELL
to Boy Scouts

The only reason I feel guilty about masturbation is that I do it so badly.

—DAVID STEINBERG

I would rather score a touchdown than make love to the prettiest girl in the United States.

—PAUL HORNUNG

When a woman unhappily yoked talks about the soul with a man not her husband, it isn't the soul they are talking about.

—DON MARQUIS

On stage I make love to 25,000 people; then I go home alone.

—JANIS JOPLIN

I'm saving the bass player for Omaha.

—JANIS JOPLIN

Your idea of fidelity is not having more than one man in bed at the same time.

—FREDERIC RAPHAEL

Love is the self-delusion we manufacture to justify the trouble we take to have sex.

—DAN GREENBURG

What is a promiscuous person? It's usually someone who is getting more sex than you are.

—VICTOR LOWNES

Voyeurism is a healthy, non-participatory sexual activity—the world *should* look at the world.

—DESMOND MORRIS

Sex is like having dinner: sometimes you joke about the dishes, sometimes you take the meal seriously.

—WOODY ALLEN

She gave me a smile I could feel in my hip pocket.

—RAYMOND CHANDLER

I wrote the story myself. It's all about a girl who lost her reputation but never missed it.

—MAE WEST

Once you know what women are like, men get kind of boring. I'm not trying to put them down, I mean I like them sometimes as people, but sexually they're dull.

—RITA MAE BROWN

Self-abuse is the most certain road to the grave.

—GEORGE M. CALHOUN, M.D., 1855

Hey, don't knock masturbation. It's sex with someone I love.

—WOODY ALLEN

Masturbation! The amazing availability of it!

—JAMES JOYCE

A woman occasionally is quite a serviceable substitute for masturbation. It takes an abundance of imagination, to be sure.

—KARL KRAUS

I like making love myself and I can make love for about three minutes. Three minutes and I need eight hours sleep, and a bowl of Wheaties.

—RICHARD PRYOR

DORIS DAY [to Rock Hudson]: Mr. Allen, this may come as a shock to you, but there are some men who don't end every sentence with a proposition.

—*PILLOW TALK*

For flavor, instant sex will never supersede the stuff you have to peel and cook.

—QUENTIN CRISP

Let's take coitus out of the closet and off the altar and put it in the continuum of human behaviour.

—JOHN UPDIKE

SHARING
See also GIVING

If wisdom were offered me with the proviso that I should keep it shut up and refrain from declaring it, I should refuse. There's no delight in owning anything unshared.

—SENECA

Not what we give, but what we share, for the gift without the giver is bare.

—JAMES RUSSELL LOWELL

Even children followed with endearing wile, and plucked his gown, to share the good man's smile.

—OLIVER GOLDSMITH

Friends share all things.

—PYTHAGORAS
between theorems

I think that, as life is action and passion, it is required of a man that he should share the passion and action of his time.

—OLIVER WENDELL HOLMES, JR.

SILENCE

A man is known by the silence he keeps.

—OLIVER HERFORD

Silence is wonderful to listen to.

—THOMAS HARDY

Carlyle finally compressed his Gospel of Silence into thirty handsome octavos.

—JOHN MORLEY

SIN
See also EVIL

The wages of sin are death, but by the time taxes are taken out, it's just sort of a tired feeling.

—PAULA POUNDSTONE

To err is human—but it feels divine.

—MAE WEST

If any of you is without sin, let him be the first to throw a stone at her.

—JESUS OF NAZARETH
John 8:7

Fifty-four-year-old Ellsworth Donald Griffith told a Des Moines, Iowa judge that he was too old to go to prison, and asked instead for a public stoning for his conviction for terrorizing his former employer. His one condition was that only those without sin be allowed to cast stones. The judge sentenced him to 5 years in prison.

—WORLD ALMANAC & BOOK OF FACTS

SOLITUDE

We're all in this alone.

—LILY TOMLIN

When you close your doors, and make darkness within, remember never to say that you are alone, for you are not alone; nay, God is within, and your genius is within. And what need have they of light to see what you are doing?

—EPICTETUS

Pray that your loneliness may spur you into finding something to live for, great enough to die for.

—DAG HAMMARSKJÖLD

That I am totally devoid of sympathy for, or interest in, the world of groups is directly attributable to the fact that *my* two greatest needs and desires—smoking ciga-rettes and plotting revenge—are basically solitary pur-suits.

—FRAN LEBOWITZ

To me, the sea is like a person—like a child that I've known a long time. It sounds crazy, I know, but when I swim in the sea I talk to it. I never feel alone when I'm out there.

—GERTRUDE EDERLE
thirty years after becoming the first
woman to swim the English Channel

I love tranquil solitude And such society as is quiet, wise, and good.

—PERCY BYSSHE SHELLEY

The nurse of full-grown souls is solitude.

—JAMES RUSSELL LOWELL

It is easy in the world to live after the world's opinion; it is easy in solitude to live after our own; but the great man is he who in the midst of the crowd keeps with perfect sweetness the independence of solitude.

—RALPH WALDO EMERSON

The best way to study human nature is when nobody else is present.

—TOM MASSON

SPENDING

Annual income twenty pounds, annual expenditure nineteen nineteen six, result happiness. Annual income twenty pounds, annual expenditure twenty pounds ought and six, result misery.

—CHARLES DICKENS
DAVID COPPERFIELD

When I had my operation, the doctor gave me a local anesthetic. I couldn't afford the imported kind.

—*LAUGH-IN*

First he bought a '57 Biscayne and put it in a ditch; He drank up all the rest, that sonofabitch.

—JONI MITCHELL

SPIRIT

I am the maker of my own fortune. I think of the Great Spirit that rules this universe.

—CHIEF TECUMSEH

STATISTICS

Do not put your faith in what statistics say until you have carefully considered what they do not say.

—WILLIAM W. WATT

I could prove God statistically.

—GEORGE GALLUP

STINGINESS

If my hands are fully occupied in holding on to something, I can neither give nor receive.

—DOROTHEE SÖLLE

There is an ordinary proverb for this: "Stinginess does not enrich; charity does not impoverish."

—GLÜCKEL OF HAMELN

It is with narrow-souled people as with narrow-necked bottles: the less they have in them the more noise they make in pouring it out.

—ALEXANDER POPE

STUPIDITY

Only two things are infinite, the universe and human stupidity, and I'm not sure about the former.

—ALBERT EINSTEIN

This . . . reminds me of the way they used to weigh hogs in Texas. They would get a long plank, put it over a cross-bar, and somehow tie the hog on one end of the plank. They'd search all around till they found a stone that would balance the weight of the hog and they'd put that on the other end of the plank. Then they'd guess the weight of the stone.

—JOHN DEWEY

STYLE

God is really only another artist. He invented the giraffe, the elephant, the ant. He has no real style. He just goes on trying other things.

—PABLO PICASSO

Style is knowing who you are, what you want to say, and not giving a damn.

—GORE VIDAL

You can convert your style into riches.

—QUENTIN CRISP

It's no good running a pig farm badly for thirty years while saying, "Really I was meant to be a ballet dancer." By that time, pigs will be your style.

—QUENTIN CRISP

The Argentinians believed in Mrs. Perón. So much so, that when she died, they petitioned the pope to make her a saint. His Holiness declined. But if he'd consented, what a triumph for style that would have been. A double fox stole, ankle-strapped shoes, and eternal life. Nobody's ever had that.

—QUENTIN CRISP

If Quentin Crisp had never existed it is unlikely that anyone would have had the nerve to invent him.

—ANONYMOUS REVIEWER

SUCCESS
See also ACCOMPLISHMENT, ACTION, GOALS, RISK

Men are born to succeed, not to fail.

—HENRY DAVID THOREAU

Success is simply a matter of luck. Ask any failure.

—EARL WILSON

Eighty percent of success is showing up.

—WOODY ALLEN

It matters not whether you win or lose; what matters is whether *I* win or lose.

—DARIN WEINBERG

To laugh often and much; to win the respect of intelligent people and the affection of children; to earn the appreciation of honest critics and endure the betrayal of false friends; to appreciate beauty; to find the best in others; to leave the world a bit better, whether by a healthy child, a garden patch or a redeemed social condition; to know even one life has breathed easier because you have lived. This is to have succeeded.

—HARRY EMERSON FOSDICK

When you get there, there is no there there. But there will be a pool.

—DAVID ZUCKER

Procrastination is the fear of success. People procrastinate because they are afraid of the success that they know will result if they move ahead now. Because success is heavy, carries a responsibility with it, it is much easier to procrastinate and live on the "someday I'll" philosophy.

—DENIS WAITLEY

What's money? A man is a success if he gets up in the morning and goes to bed at night and in between does what he wants to do.

—BOB DYLAN

JANE HATHAWAY: Chief, haven't you heard of the saying "It's not whether you win or lose, it's how you play the game"? *MR. DRYSDALE:* Yes, I've heard it. And I consider it one of the most ridiculous statements ever made.

—*THE BEVERLY HILLBILLIES*

The method of the enterprising is to plan with audacity, and execute with vigor; to sketch out a map of possibilities; and then to treat them as probabilities.

—BOVEE

Always bear in mind that your own resolution to success is more important than any other one thing.

—ABRAHAM LINCOLN

Losers visualize the penalties of failure. Winners visualize the rewards of success.

—DR. ROB GILBERT

There's nothing to winning, really. That is, if you happen to be blessed with a keen eye, an agile mind, and no scruples whatsoever.

—ALFRED HITCHCOCK

Success is not the result of spontaneous combustion. You must set yourself on fire.

—REGGIE LEACH

The real secret of success is enthusiasm.

—WALTER CHRYSLER

There is only one success— to be able to spend your life in your own way.

—CHRISTOPHER MORLEY

It is a rough road that leads to the heights of greatness.

—SENECA

Act as if it were impossible to fail.

—DOROTHEA BRANDE

The Wright brothers flew right through the smoke screen of impossibility.

—CHARLES F. KETTERING

Let us be thankful for the fools. But for them the rest of us could not succeed.

—MARK TWAIN

The common idea that success spoils people by making them vain, egotistic, and self complacent is erroneous— on the contrary it makes them, for the most part, humble, tolerant and kind. Failure makes people bitter and cruel.

—W. SOMERSET MAUGHAM

The secret of success is constancy to purpose.

—BENJAMIN DISRAELI

When you get right down to the root of the meaning of the word "succeed," you find it simply means to follow through.

—F. W. NICHOL

No man is a failure who is enjoying life.

—WILLIAM FEATHER

Can success change the human mechanism so completely between one dawn and another? Can it make one feel taller, more alive, handsomer, uncommonly gifted and indomitably secure with the certainty that this is the way life will always be? It can and it does!

—MOSS HART

The man who lives for himself is a failure. Even if he gains much wealth, position or power he still is a failure. The man who lives for others has achieved true success. A rich man who consecrates his wealth and his position to the good of humanity is a success. A poor man who gives of his service and his sympathy to others has achieved true success even though material prosperity or outward honors never come to him.

—NORMAN VINCENT PEALE

The moral flabbiness born of the bitch-goddess SUCCESS. That—with the squalid cash interpretation put on the word success—is our national disease.

—WILLIAM JAMES

You can't win any game unless you are ready to win.

—CONNIE MACK

There's no secret about success. Did you ever know a successful man that didn't tell you all about it?

—KIN HUBBARD

It is easy to get everything you want, provided you first learn to do without the things you can not get.

—ELBERT HUBBARD

Success didn't spoil me; I've always been insufferable.

—FRAN LEBOWITZ

There's always room at the top— after the investigation.

—OLIVER HERFORD

The successful people are the ones who can think up things for the rest of the world to keep busy at.

—DON MARQUIS

I started out with nothing. I still have most of it.

—MICHAEL DAVIS

We are not interested in the possibilities of defeat.

—QUEEN VICTORIA

WILBUR POST: I'm counting on you to win tomorrow, but if you don't, be a good sport—lose with a smile. *MR. ED:* I'd rather win with a sneer!

—*MR. ED*

If at first you don't succeed, you're running about average.

—M. H. ALDERSON

SUFFERING

Suffering is not a prerequisite for happiness.

—JUDY TATELBAUM

The man who fears suffering is already suffering from what he fears.

—MICHEL DE MONTAIGNE

We are healed of a suffering only by experiencing it to the full.

—MARCEL PROUST

I was much further out than you thought And not waving but drowning.

—STEVIE SMITH

Pain is inevitable. Suffering is optional.

—M. KATHLEEN CASEY

Nothing can be attained without suffering but at the same time one must begin by sacrificing suffering.

—GURUDJIEFF

Many, amid great affluence, are utterly miserable.

—TACITUS

SUICIDE

I know a man who gave up smoking, drinking, sex, and rich food. He was healthy right up to the time he killed himself.

—JOHNNY CARSON

I don't think suicide is so terrible. Some rainy winter Sunday when there's a little boredom, you should always carry a gun. Not to shoot yourself, but to know exactly that you're always making a choice.

—LINA WERTMULLER

Human life consists in mutual service. No grief, pain, misfortune or "broken heart" is excuse for cutting off one's life while any power of service remains. But when all usefulness is over, when one is assured of an unavoidable and imminent death, it is the simplest of human rights to choose a quick and easy death in place of a slow and horrible one.

—CHARLOTTE PERKINS GILMAN

TECHNOLOGY

Concerns for man and his fate must always form the chief interest of all technical endeavors. Never forget this in the midst of your diagrams and equations.

—ALBERT EINSTEIN

Any sufficiently advanced technology is indistinguishable from magic.

—ARTHUR C. CLARKE

Computers are useless. They can only give you answers.

—PABLO PICASSO

TEMPTATION

My temptation is quiet.

—W. B. YEATS

I can resist everything except temptation.

—OSCAR WILDE

Why comes temptation, but for man to meet And master and make crouch beneath his foot, And so be pedestaled in triumph?

—ROBERT BROWNING

Blessed is the man that endureth temptation: for when he is tried, he shall receive the crown of life.

—JAMES 1:12

A good many young writers make the mistake of enclosing a stamped, self-addressed envelope, big enough for the manuscript to come back in. This is too much of a temptation to the editor.

—RING LARDNER

Do you really think it is weakness that yields to temptation? I tell you that there are terrible temptations which it requires strength, strength and courage, to yield to.

—OSCAR WILDE

TEN COMMANDMENTS

I know a fellow who's as broke as the Ten Commandments.

—JOHN MARQUAND

Say what you will about the Ten Commandments, you must always come back to the pleasant fact that there are only ten of them.

—H. L. MENCKEN

THERAPY

The future may teach us how to exercise a direct influence by means of particular chemical substances, upon the amount of energy and their distribution in the apparatus of the mind. It may be that there are other undreamed of possibilities of therapy.

—SIGMUND FREUD

I told my wife the truth. I told her I was seeing a psychiatrist. Then she told *me* the truth: that she was seeing a psychiatrist, two plumbers and a bartender.

—RODNEY DANGERFIELD

MRS. BAKERMAN: Dr. Hartley, if you're looking for a new member of our group, I know a nice schizophrenic. *MR. PETERSON:* Or how about a manic-depressive? At least you know they'll be fun half the time.

—*THE BOB NEWHART SHOW*

THINKING

See also IMAGINATION, MEMORY,
THE MIND, NEGATIVE THINKING

Aristotle was famous for knowing everything. He taught that the brain exists merely to cool the blood and is not involved in the process of thinking. This is true only of certain persons.

—WILL CUPPY

Whenever he thought about it, he felt terrible. And so, at last, he came to a fateful decision. He decided not to think about it.

—ANONYMOUS

A man is not idle because he is absorbed in thought. There is a visible labor and there is an invisible labor.

—VICTOR HUGO

I have found power in the mysteries of thought.

—EURIPIDES

Thus only can you gain the secret isolated joy of the thinker, who knows that, a hundred years after he is dead and forgotten, men who never heard of him will be moving to the measure of his thought—the subtle rapture of a postponed power, which the world knows not because it has no external trappings, but which to his prophetic vision is more real than that which commands an army.

—OLIVER WENDELL HOLMES, JR.

Thought takes man out of servitude, into freedom.

—HENRY WADSWORTH LONGFELLOW

Thinking is an experimental dealing with small quantities of energy, just as a general moves miniature figures over a map before setting his troops in action.

—SIGMUND FREUD

Every good thought you think is contributing its share to the ultimate result of your life.

—GRENVILLE KLEISER

Great men are they who see that spiritual is stronger than any material force, that thoughts rule the world.

—RALPH WALDO EMERSON

The highest possible stage in moral culture is when we recognize that we ought to control our thoughts.

—CHARLES DARWIN

The ancestor of every action is a thought.

—RALPH WALDO EMERSON

I have had a good many more uplifting thoughts, creative and expansive visions, while soaking in comfortable baths in well-equipped American bathrooms than I have ever had in any cathedral.

—EDMUND WILSON

Heavy thoughts bring on physical maladies.

—MARTIN LUTHER

You've got to watch your mind all the time or you'll awaken and find a strange picture on your press.

—LORD BUCKLEY

TIME

The great French Marshall Lyautey once asked his gardener to plant a tree. The gardener objected that the tree was slow growing and would not reach maturity for 100 years. The Marshall replied, "In that case, there is no time to lose; plant it this afternoon!"

—JOHN F. KENNEDY

If you don't have enough time to accomplish something, consider the work finished once it's begun.

—JOHN CAGE

I've been on a calendar, but I've never been on time.

—MARILYN MONROE

Next week there can't be any crisis. My schedule is already full.

—HENRY A. KISSINGER

Most modern calendars mar the sweet simplicity of our lives by reminding us that each day that passes is the anniversary of some perfectly uninteresting event.

—OSCAR WILDE

They always say that time changes things, but you actually have to change them yourself.

—ANDY WARHOL

I went on a diet, swore off drinking and heavy eating, and in fourteen days I lost two weeks.

—JOE E. LEWIS

Tomorrow is the most important thing in life. Comes into us at midnight very clean. It's perfect when it arrives and it puts itself in our hands. It hopes we've learned something from yesterday.

—JOHN WAYNE

You will never "find" time for anything. If you want time you must make it.

—CHARLES BUXTON

Follow your desire as long as you live; do not lessen the time of following desire, for the wasting of time is an abomination to the spirit.

—PTAHHOTEP

To every thing there is a season, and a time to every purpose under the heaven. A time to be born, and a time to die; a time to plant, and a time to pluck up that which is planted; A time to kill, and a time to heal; a time to break down, and a time to build up; A time to weep, and a time to laugh; a time to mourn, and a time to dance; A time to cast away stones, and a time to gather stones together; A time to embrace, and a time to refrain from embracing; A time to get, and a time to lose; a time to keep, and a time to cast away; A time to rend, and a time to sew; a time to keep silence, and a time to speak; A time to love, and a time to hate; a time of war, and a time of peace.

—ECCLESIASTES 3:1–8

Only time can heal your broken heart, just as only time can heal his broken arms and legs.

—MISS PIGGY

Everything happens to everybody sooner or later, if there is time enough.

—GEORGE BERNARD SHAW

TOLERANCE

Tolerance is the oil which takes the friction out of life.

—WILBERT E. SCHEER

TRUST

Just trust yourself, then you will know how to live.

—JOHANN WOLFGANG VON GOETHE

So, if you have not been trustworthy in handling worldly wealth, who will trust you with true riches?

—LUKE 16:11

TRUTH

I don't want any yes-men around me. I want everybody to tell me the truth even if it costs them their jobs.

—SAMUEL GOLDWYN

My mind is made up, don't try and confuse me with the facts.

—OLD SAYING

Facts do not cease to exist because they are ignored.

— ALDOUS HUXLEY

A paranoid is a man who knows *a little* of what's going on.

—WILLIAM S. BURROUGHS

Men stumble over the truth from time to time, but most pick themselves up and hurry off as if nothing happened.

—WINSTON CHURCHILL

From error to error, one discovers the entire truth.

—SIGMUND FREUD

In the province of the mind, what one believes to be true either is true or becomes true.

—JOHN LILLY

Whoever undertakes to set himself up as a judge in the field of truth and knowledge is shipwrecked by the laughter of the Gods.

—ALBERT EINSTEIN

In seeking truth you have to get both sides of a story.

—WALTER CRONKITE

Believe those who are seeking the truth; doubt those who find it.

—ANDRÉ GIDE

Truth has no special time of its own. Its hour is now—always.

—ALBERT SCHWEITZER

The opposite of a correct statement is a false statement. But the opposite of a profound truth may well be another profound truth.

—NIELS BOHR

There is nothing so powerful as truth—and often nothing so strange.

—DANIEL WEBSTER

If error is corrected whenever it is recognized as such, the path of error is the path of truth.

—HANS REICHENBACH

Keep the other person's well-being in mind when you feel an attack of soul-purging truth coming on.

—BETTY WHITE

Rather than love, than money, than fame, give me truth.

—HENRY DAVID THOREAU

And I will ask the Father, and he will give you another Counselor to be with you forever— the Spirit of truth. The world cannot accept him, because it neither sees him nor knows him. But you know him, for he lives with you and will be in you.

—JESUS OF NAZARETH
John 14:16–17

The visionary denies the truth to himself, the liar only to others.

—FRIEDRICH NIETZSCHE

The truth is what is, what should be is a dirty lie.

—LENNY BRUCE

The illusions of hope are apt to close one's eyes to the painful truth.

—HARRY F. BANKS

UNANSWERED QUESTIONS

Undoubtedly we have no questions to ask which are unanswerable. We must trust the perfection of the creation so far as to believe that whatever curiosity the order of things has awakened in our minds, the order of things can satisfy.

—RALPH WALDO EMERSON

Why is a carrot more orange than an orange?

—AMBOY DUKES

It's an unanswered question, but let us still believe in the dignity and importance of the question.

—TENNESSEE WILLIAMS

Sexual harassment at work—is it a problem for the self-employed?

—VICTORIA WOOD

If lawyers are disbarred and clergymen defrocked, doesn't it follow that electricians can be delighted; musicians denoted; cowboys deranged; models deposed; tree surgeons debarked and dry cleaners depressed?

—VIRGINIA OSTMAN

Why is this thus? What is the reason of this thusness?

—ARTEMUS WARD

Why do they call them tellers? They never tell you anything. They just ask questions. And why do they call it interest? It's boring. And another thing—how come the Trust Department has all their pens chained to the table?

—COACH ERNIE PANTUSSO
CHEERS

I'm only the Pope, what can I do?

—POPE JOHN XXIII

I know the answer! The answer lies within the heart of all mankind! The answer is twelve? I think I'm in the wrong building.

—LUCY VAN PELT
PEANUTS

I was gratified to be able to answer promptly. I said I don't know.

—MARK TWAIN

UNDERSTANDING

The most incomprehensible thing about the world is that it is comprehensible.

—ALBERT EINSTEIN

Everything that irritates us about others can lead us to an understanding of ourselves.

—CARL JUNG

Understanding a person does not mean condoning; it only means that one does not accuse him as if one were God or a judge placed above him.

—ERICH FROMM

UNHAPPINESS

See also DISSATISFACTION, SUFFERING

Unhappiness is in not knowing what we want and killing ourselves to get it.

—DON HEROLD

Cast away care; he that loves sorrow Lengthens not a day, nor can buy tomorrow.

—THOMAS DEKKER

Sob, heavy world, Sob as you spin, Mantled in mist, remote from the happy.

—W. H. AUDEN
THE AGE OF ANXIETY

Well, isn't life a picnic? I get to be miserable forever. I'm just going to have to mope and be unhappy and then one day I'll die.

—STEPHANIE VANDERKELLAN
NEWHART

UNWORTHINESS

"If you can't do it." "You're not good enough!" "Don't even try!" "Who do you think you are?" "You'll never make it!" "Settle down!" "You don't deserve it!" "Somebody better than you should have it!"

—JACK CANFIELD
quoting the vulture of unworthiness sitting on your shoulder

You have no idea what a poor opinion I have of myself— and how little I deserve it.

—W. S. GILBERT

Unworthiness (Continued)

FERDINAND: Wherefore weep you? *MIRANDA:* At mine unworthiness, that dare not offer What I desire to give; and much less take What I shall die to want.

—WILLIAM SHAKESPEARE
THE TEMPEST

Thank you for the present, but what's wrong with the stuff?

—STEPHEN SONDHEIM

I refuse to join any club that would have me as a member.

—GROUCHO MARX

WEALTH
See also ABUNDANCE, MONEY, PROSPERITY, SPENDING

I don't know much about being a millionaire, but I'll bet I'd be *darling* at it.

—DOROTHY PARKER

A man is rich in proportion to the number of things which he can afford to let alone.

—HENRY DAVID THOREAU

If I were rich I'd have the Time that I lack To sit in the Synagogue and pray, And maybe have a seat by the Eastern Wall. And I'd discuss the Holy Books With the learned men Seven hours every day. That would be the sweetest thing of all.

—SHELDON HARNICK
FIDDLER ON THE ROOF

Riches are not from an abundance of worldly goods, but from a contented mind.

—MOHAMMED

A man's true wealth is the good he does in this world.

—ANONYMOUS

Seek wealth, it's good.

—IVAN BOESKY

I care for riches, to make gifts To friends, or lead a sick man back to health With ease and plenty. Else small aid is wealth For daily gladness; once a man be done With hunger, rich and poor are all as one.

—EURIPIDES

I only want enough to keep body and soul apart.

—DOROTHY PARKER

I have no riches but my thoughts, yet these are wealth enough for me.

—SARA TEASDALE

The use of riches is better than their possession. Riches do not make one rich but busy.

—FERNANDO DE ROJAS

Riches are a good handmaid, but the worst mistress.

—FRANCIS BACON

A man is rich in proportion to the number of things which he can afford to let alone.

—HENRY DAVID THOREAU

That's the state to live and die in! R-r-rich!

—CHARLES DICKENS

Wealth is not in making money, but in making the man while he is making money.

—JOHN WICKER

Wealth to us is not mere material for vain glory but an opportunity for achievement; and poverty we think it no disgrace to acknowledge but a real degradation to make no effort to overcome.

—THUCYDIDES

Pearls around the neck—stones upon the heart.

—YIDDISH PROVERB

Watching for riches consumeth the flesh, and the care thereof driveth away sleep.

—ECCLESIASTICUS 31:1

Banks are failing all over the country, but not the sand banks, solid and warm and streaked with bloody blackberry vines. You may run on them as much as you please, even as the crickets do . . .

—HENRY DAVID THOREAU

If a man own land, the land owns him.

—RALPH WALDO EMERSON

Wealth is not without its advantages and the case to the contrary, although it has often been made, has never proved widely persuasive.

—JOHN KENNETH GALBRAITH

Natural wealth is limited and easily obtained; the wealth defined by vain fancies is always beyond reach.

—EPICURUS

It ain't so much trouble to get rich as it is to tell when we have got rich.

—JOSH BILLINGS

I am indeed rich, since my income is superior to my expense, and my expense is equal to my wishes.

—EDWARD GIBBON

That man is the richest whose pleasures are the cheapest.

— HENRY DAVID THOREAU

We live in a vastly complex society which has been able to provide us with a multitude of material things, and this is good, but people are beginning to suspect that we have paid a high spiritual price for our plenty.

—EUELL GIBBONS

Seek not proud riches, but such as thou mayest get justly, use soberly, distribute cheerfully, and leave contentedly.

—FRANCIS BACON

Be not penny-wise: riches have wings, and sometimes they fly away of themselves; sometimes they must be set flying to bring in more.

—FRANCIS BACON

You may say to yourself, "My power and the strength of my hands have produced this wealth for me." But remember the Lord your God, for it is he who gives you the ability to produce wealth, and so confirms his covenant which he swore to your forefathers, as it is today.

—DEUTERONOMY 8:17-18

The Pluto-American Anti-Defamation League said it will bring pressure to bear on media to up-grade the image of incredibly rich people. The newly-formed group, which hopes to combat negative portrayals of incredibly rich people on television and in print, cited the crucial role that incredibly rich people have played in American history, and hopes to restore incredible richness as a "positive aspect of American life."

—OFF THE WALL STREET JOURNAL

WHAT YOU READ IN THE PAPER

MARTIANS BUILD TWO IMMENSE CANALS IN TWO YEARS! Vast Engineering Works Accomplished in an Incredibly Short Time by Our Planetary Neighbors

—*NEW YORK TIMES*
front-page headline August 27, 1911

The French army is still the best all-around fighting machine in Europe.

—*TIME*
June 12, 1939

Comet Kohoutek promises to be the celestial extravaganza of the century.

—*NEWSWEEK*
November 5, 1973

For the majority of people, smoking has a beneficial effect.

—DR. IAN G. MACDONALD
Newsweek, Nov. 18, 1963

Everything you read in the newspaper is absolutely true except for the rare story of which you happen to have first-hand knowledge.

—ERWIN KNOLL

WISDOM

We don't receive wisdom; we must discover it for ourselves after a journey that no one can take for us or spare us.

—MARCEL PROUST

Be wiser than other people, if you can, but do not tell them so.

—LORD CHESTERFIELD

For the very true beginning of wisdom is the desire of discipline; and the care of discipline is love.

—WISDOM OF SOLOMON 6:17

Wisdom entereth not into a malicious mind.

—FRANÇOIS RABELAIS

We should be careful to get out of an experience only the wisdom that is in it and stop there; lest we be like the cat that sits down on a hot stove lid. She will never sit down on a hot stove lid again and that is well; but also she will never sit down on a cold one any more.

—MARK TWAIN

The only medicine for suffering, crime, and all the other woes of mankind, is wisdom.

—T. H. HUXLEY

The philosophies of one age have become the absurdities of the next, and the foolishness of yesterday will become the wisdom of tomorrow.

—WILLIAM OSLER
MONTREAL MEDICAL JOURNAL

Wisdom is the power that enables us to use knowledge for the benefit of ourselves and others.

—THOMAS J. WATSON

A wise man's heart guides his mouth.

—PROVERBS 16:23

The latter part of a wise man's life is taken up in curing the follies, prejudices, and false opinions he had contracted in the former.

—JONATHAN SWIFT

A short saying oft contains much wisdom.

—SOPHOCLES

To profit from good advice requires more wisdom than to give it.

—JOHN CHURTON COLLINS

The wise and moral man Shines like a fire on a hilltop, Making money like the bee, Who does not hurt the flower.

—PALI CANON

WOMEN

I buy women shoes, and they use them to walk away from me.

—MICKEY ROONEY

Are women books? says Hodge, then would mine were an Almanack, to change her every year.

—BENJAMIN FRANKLIN

American women expect to find in their husbands a perfection that English women only hope to find in their butlers.

—W. SOMERSET MAUGHAM

We can call each other girls, chicks, broads, birds and dames with equanimity. Many of us prefer to do so since the word "woman," being two syllables, is long, unwieldy, and earnest. But a man must watch his ass. Never may a man be permitted to call any female a "chick." He may call you a broad or a dame only if he is a close friend and fond of John Garfield movies. The term "bird," generally used by fatuous Englishmen, is always frowned upon.

—CYNTHIA HEIMEL

You can't be happy with a woman who pronounces both d's in Wednesday.

—PETER DE VRIES

WONDER
See also APPRECIATION, GRATITUDE

The world will never starve for want of wonders, but for want of wonder.

—G. K. CHESTERTON

There are only two ways to live your life. One is as though nothing is a miracle. The other is as though everything is a miracle.

—ALBERT EINSTEIN

WORDS TO LIVE BY
See also RULES

Condoms aren't completely safe. A friend of mine was wearing one and got hit by a bus.

—BOB RUBIN

Don't ask the barber whether you need a haircut.

—DANIEL S. GREENBERG

If you cannot catch a bird of paradise, better take a wet hen.

—NIKITA KHRUSCHEV

Never eat anything whose listed ingredients cover more than one-third the package.

—JOSEPH LEONARD

Write injuries in dust, benefits in marble.

—BENJAMIN FRANKLIN

People will accept your ideas much more readily if you tell them Benjamin Franklin said it first.

—DAVID H. COMINS

Let your intentions create your methods and not the other way around.

—THE AUTHOR
although Benjamin Franklin said it first

Never keep up with the Joneses. Drag them down to your level. It's cheaper.

—QUENTIN CRISP

You can't tell your friend if you've been cuckolded. Even if he doesn't laugh at you, he may put the information to personal use.

—MICHEL DE MONTAIGNE

Put all your eggs in one basket and WATCH THAT BASKET!

—MARK TWAIN

It is easier to get forgiveness than permission.

—STUART'S LAW OF RETROACTION

Never go to a doctor whose office plants have died.

—ERMA BOMBECK

Don't go to piano bars where young, unemployed actors get up and sing. Definitely don't be a young, unemployed actor who gets up and sings.

—TONY LANG

Live simply that others may simply live.

—ELIZABETH SEATON

Murder is always a mistake. One should never do anything that one cannot talk about after dinner.

—OSCAR WILDE

Always obey your superiors—if you have any.

—MARK TWAIN

Dare to be naive.

—R. BUCKMINSTER FULLER

Never underestimate a man who overestimates himself.

—FRANKLIN D. ROOSEVELT

Hope for the best, prepare for the worst, and shoot down the middle.

—PRAGMATIC CREED

The race is not always to the swift, nor the battle to the strong, but that's the way to bet.

—DAMON RUNYON

One does not moisten a stamp with the Niagara Falls.

—P. W. R. FOOT

This warning from the New York City Department of Health Fraud: Be suspicious of any doctor who tries to take your temperature with his finger.

—DAVID LETTERMAN

No leg's too short to reach the ground.

—LYNDON IRVING

She that knows why knows wherefore.

—JIM SNELL

He digs deepest who deepest digs.

—ROGER WODDIS

My dear, I don't care what they do, so long as they don't do it in the street and frighten the horses.

—MRS. PATRICK CAMPBELL

Never call a man a fool; borrow from him.

—ADDISON MIZNER

If it might break, don't go near it.

—HERBERT STEIN

Go through the motions anyway; you might get lucky.

—THOMAS MAGNUM

When you handle yourself, use your head; when you handle others, use your heart.

—DONNA REED

When the telephone rings, it is against the law not to answer it.

—RING LARDNER

Comments from the public are always welcome in courts of law. When you start speaking, an usher will call "Silence in court" to ensure that you are heard without interruption.

—PETER ALEXANDER

WORDS TO LIVE BY WHEN IN ENGLAND

London barbers are delighted to shave patrons' armpits.

—GENERAL KNOWLEDGE

Most foreign tourists know that in London they are encouraged to take a piece of fruit, free of charge, from any open-air stall or display.

—MICHAEL LIPTON

Women are not allowed upstairs on buses; if you see a woman there ask her politely to descend.

—DAVID GORDON

Try the famous echo in the British Museum Reading Room.

—GERARD HOFFNUNG

On first entering an Underground train, it is customary to shake hands with every passenger.

—R. J. PHILLIPS

WORK

When love and skill work together, expect a masterpiece.

—JOHN RUSKIN

By working faithfully eight hours a day, you may eventually get to be a boss and work twelve hours a day.

—ROBERT FROST

The heights by great men reached and kept Were not attained by sudden flight, But they, while their companions slept, Were toiling upward in the night.

—HENRY WADSWORTH LONGFELLOW

I don't have anything against work. I just figure, why deprive somebody who really enjoys it?

—DOBIE GILLIS

NAPOLEON SOLO: Are you free? *ILLYA KURAKIN:* No man is free who has to work for a living. But I am available.

—*THE MAN FROM UNCLE*

It is your work in life that is the ultimate seduction.

—PABLO PICASSO

We can lick gravity, but sometimes the paperwork is overwhelming.

—WERNHER VON BRAUN
discussing the business side of putting a man on the moon

Work is much more fun than fun.

—NOËL COWARD

The more I want to get something done, the less I call it work.

—RICHARD BACH

Work seven days a week and nothing can stop you.

—JOHN MOORES

If you have a job without aggravations, you don't have a job.

—MALCOLM FORBES

The trouble with the rat race is that even if you win, you're still a rat.

—LILY TOMLIN

The price one pays for pursuing any profession or calling is an intimate knowledge of its ugly side.

—JAMES BALDWIN

One of the symptoms of an approaching nervous break-down is the belief that one's work is terribly important.

—BERTRAND RUSSELL

Men for the sake of getting a living forget to live.

—MARGARET FULLER

Only a fool would make the bed every day.

—NANCY SPAIN

What the hell do you want to work for somebody else for? Work for yourself!

—IRVING BERLIN
refusing to hire the young George Gershwin

INTERVIEWER: Your Holiness, how many people work in the Vatican? *POPE JOHN XXIII:* About half.

The best way to do field work is not to come up for air until you're done.

—MARGARET MEAD

He who labors diligently need never despair, for all things are accomplished by diligence and labor.

—MENANDER

Tradition cannot be inherited, and if you want it you must obtain it by great labor.

—T. S. ELIOT

If the grass is greener in the other fellow's yard, let him worry about cutting it.

—FRED ALLEN

The expectations of life depend upon diligence; the mechanic that would perfect his work must first sharpen his tools.

—CONFUCIUS

Dear, never forget one little point: It's my business. You just work here.

—ELIZABETH ARDEN
to her husband

I've made so many movies playing a hooker that they don't pay me in the regular way any more. They leave it on the dresser.

—SHIRLEY MACLAINE

Work consists of whatever a body is obliged to do. Play consists of whatever a body is not obliged to do.

—MARK TWAIN

If you cannot work with love but only with distaste, it is better that you should leave your work.

—KHALIL GIBRANIT

Every really able man, in whatever direction he work, if you talk sincerely with him, considers his work, however much admired, as far short of what it should be.

— RALPH WALDO EMERSON

In order that people may be happy in their work, these three things are needed: They must be fit for it. They must not do too much of it. And they must have a sense of success in it.

—JOHN RUSKIN

Work keeps us from three great evils: boredom, vice, and need.

—VOLTAIRE

There is no substitute for hard work.

—THOMAS EDISON

All work is as seed sown; it grows and spreads, and sows itself anew.

—THOMAS CARLYLE

In the morning, when you are sluggish about getting up, let this thought be present: "I am rising to a man's work."

—MARCUS AURELIUS

The return from work must be the satisfaction which that works brings you and the world's need of that work. With this, life is heaven, or as near heaven as you can get. Without this, with work which you despise, which bores you, and which the world does not need, this life is hell.

—WILLIAM EDWARD BURGHARDT DuBOIS

I don't like work—no man does—but I like what is in work: the chance to find yourself. Your own reality for yourself, not for others; what no other man can ever know.

—JOSEPH CONRAD

I will work in my own way, according to the light that is in me.

—LYDIA MARIA CHILD

Work is love made visible.

—KHALIL GIBRAN

A great many people have asked how I manage to get so much work done and still keep looking so dissipated.

—ROBERT BENCHLEY

The natural dignity of our work, its unembarrassed kindness, its insight into life, its hold on science—for these privileges, and for all that they bring with them, up and up, high over the top of the tree, the very heavens open, preaching thankfulness.

—STEPHEN PAGET

Good for the body is the work of the body, good for the soul the work of the soul, and good for either is the work of the other.

—HENRY DAVID THOREAU

Thunder is good, thunder is impressive; but it is lightning that does the work.

—MARK TWAIN

The eye of the master will do more work than both his hands.

—BENJAMIN FRANKLIN

Andy, you gits up at noon, then you rushes to get dressed, then you rushes to the restaurant for breakfast. After you eat, you rushes to the park to take a nap, after you take your nap then you rushes back to eat again; then you rushes home, rushes to get undressed and then you rushes to bed. I tell ya Andy, there's just so much a body can stand.

—KINGFISH
AMOS 'N' ANDY

I do most of my work sitting down; that's where I shine.

—ROBERT BENCHLEY

The superstition that all our hours of work are a minus quantity in the happiness of life, and all the hours of idleness are plus ones, is a most ludicrous and pernicious doctrine, and its greatest support comes from our not taking sufficient trouble, not making a real effort, to make work as near pleasure as it can be.

—LORD BALFOUR

I go on working for the same reason that a hen goes on laying eggs.

—H. L. MENCKEN

All in all I'd rather have been a judge than a miner. And what is more, being a miner, as soon as you are too old and tired and sick and stupid to do the job properly, you have to go. Well, the very opposite applies with judges.

—PETER COOK

Blessed is that man who has found his work.

—ELBERT HUBBARD

Work is the true elixir of life. The busiest man is the happiest man. Excellence in any art or profession is attained only by hard and persistent work. Never believe that you are perfect. When a man imagines, even after years of striving, that he has attained perfection, his decline begins.

—THEODORE MARTIN
at age ninety-two

Thinking is hard work.

—THOMAS EDISON

The law of work does seem utterly unfair—but there it is, and nothing can change it; the higher the pay in enjoyment the worker gets out of it, the higher shall be his pay in money also.

—MARK TWAIN

So far I've found that most high-level executives prefer the boardroom to the Bahamas. They don't really enjoy leisure time; they feel their work is their leisure.

—WILLIAM THEOBALD

Work is our sanity, our self respect, our salvation. So far from being a curse, work is the greatest blessing.

—HENRY FORD

It is only the farmer who faithfully plants seeds in the Spring, who reaps a harvest in the Autumn.

—B. C. FORBES

Gardens are not made by singing "Oh, how beautiful," and sitting in the shade.

—RUDYARD KIPLING

I am a great believer in luck, and I find the harder I work the more I have of it.

—STEPHEN LEACOCK

Don't stay in bed . . . unless you make money in bed.

—GEORGE BURNS

I like work; it fascinates me; I can sit and look at it for hours.

—JEROME KLAPKA JEROME

Lazy hands make a man poor, but diligent hands bring wealth.

—PROVERBS 10:4

WORRY
See also ANXIETY, FEAR

What? Me Worry?

—ALFRED E. NEWMAN

We are, perhaps, uniquely among the earth's creatures, the worrying animal. We worry away our lives, fearing the future, discontent with the present, unable to take in the idea of dying, unable to sit still.

—LEWIS THOMAS

One way to get high blood pressure is to go mountain climbing over molehills.

—EARL WILSON

Worries go down better with soup than without.

—YIDDISH PROVERB

WORSHIP
See also GOD, PRAYER, RELIGION

Serve God, that He may do the like for you.

—THE TEACHING FOR MERIKARE

Has God forgotten all I have done for him?

—LOUIS XIV
(Louis also said, when a coach arrived
precisely on time, "I *almost* had to wait.")

Some men worship rank, some worship heroes, some worship power, some worship God, and over these ideals they dispute—but they all worship money.

—MARK TWAIN

I meditated for hours on end. Chanted. I was finding God all over the place. He kept ditching me. You gotta understand, I thought I was on my way to Nirvana. All I ended up with was recurrent flashbacks of the original Mouseketeers.

—REVEREND JIM IGNATOWSKI
TAXI

One of the hardest things for any man to do is to fall down on the ice when it is wet and then get up and praise the Lord.

—JOSH BILLINGS

WORTHINESS

It is difficult to make a man miserable while he feels he is worthy of himself and claims kindred to the great God who made him.

—ABRAHAM LINCOLN

Be free, all worthy spirits, and stretch yourselves, for greatness and for height.

—GEORGE CHAPMAN

As my Great Aunt Maude always said, to own a priceless treasure one must first be worthy of it.

—ARTEMUS GORDON
THE WILD, WILD WEST

Worth begets in base minds, envy; in great souls, emulation.

—HENRY FIELDING

MAN: Do you belong here? *FONZIE:* I belong everywhere.

—HAPPY DAYS

We are stardust, we are golden, and we've got to get ourselves back to the garden.

—JONI MITCHELL

Worth seeing? Yes, but not worth going to see.

—SAMUEL JOHNSON

WRITING

A powerful agent is the right word. Whenever we come upon one of those intensely right words the resulting effect is physical as well as spiritual, and electrically prompt.

—MARK TWAIN

Type faster.

—ISAAC ASIMOV
when asked what he would do if he had only six months to live

In the afternoons, Gertrude Stein and I used to go antique hunting in the local shops, and I remember once asking her if she thought I should become a writer. In the typically cryptic way we were all enchanted with, she said, "No." I took that to mean yes and sailed for Italy the next day.

—WOODY ALLEN

Go on writing plays, my boy. One of these days one of these London producers will go into his office and say to his secretary, 'Is there a play from Shaw this morning?" and when she says, "No," he will say, "Well, then we'll have a start on the rubbish." And that's your chance, my boy.

— GEORGE BERNARD SHAW
when a young playwright asked
whether he should continue writing plays

The writer's only responsibility is to his art. He will be completely ruthless if he is a good one. He has a dream. Everything goes by the board: honor, pride, decency, security, happiness, all, to get the book written. If a writer has to rob his mother, he will not hesitate; the "Ode on a Grecian Urn" is worth any number of old ladies.

—WILLIAM FAULKNER

Writing is easy. All you do is stare at a blank sheet of paper until drops of blood form on your forehead.

—GENE FOWLER

If you want to be a writer—stop talking about it and sit down and write!

—JACKIE COLLINS

It took me fifteen years to discover that I had no talent for writing, but I couldn't give it up because by then I was too famous.

—ROBERT BENCHLEY

I keep six honest serving men (They taught me all I knew); Their names are What and Why and When And How and Where and Who.

—RUDYARD KIPLING

Every man has one thing he can do better than anyone else and usually it is reading his own handwriting.

—G. NORMAN COLLIE

One may not have written it well enough for others to know, but you're in love with truth when you discover it at the point of a pencil. That, in and by itself, is one of the few rare pleasures in life.

—NORMAN MAILER

Beware of the man who denounces women writers; his penis is tiny & cannot spell.

—ERICA JONG

I hope that one or two immortal lyrics will come out of all this tumbling around.

—POET LOUISE BOGAN
on her love affair with poet Theodore Roethke

It's the good girls who keep the diaries; the bad girls never have the time.

—TALLULAH BANKHEAD

Why don't you write books people can read?

—NORA JOYCE
to her husband, James

When I want to read a book, I write one.

—BENJAMIN DISRAELI

I always say, keep a diary and someday it'll keep you.

—MAE WEST

Unprovided with original learning, unformed in the habits of thinking, unskilled in the arts of composition, I resolved—to write a book.

—EDWARD GIBBON

Writing is turning one's worst moments into money.

—J. P. DONLEAVY

I'm not happy when I'm writing, but I'm more unhappy when I'm not.

—FANNIE HURST

ZEAL

Zeal is very blind, or badly regulated, when it encroaches upon the rights of others.

—QUESNEL

Zeal is fire without light.

—ENGLISH PROVERB

Experience shows that success is due less to ability than to zeal. The winner is he who gives himself to his work, body and soul.

—CHARLES BUXTON

An Overview

THIS BOOK IS BASED ON A SINGLE IDEA: *You should be allowed to do whatever you want with your own person and property, as long as you don't physically harm the person or property of another.*

Simple. Seemingly guaranteed to us by that remarkable document known as the United States Constitution and its even more remarkable Bill of Rights. And yet, it's not the way things are.

Roughly half of the arrests and court cases in the United States each year involve consensual crimes—actions that are against the law, but directly harm no one's person or property except, possibly, the "criminal's."

More than 750,000 people are in jail *right now* because of something they did, something that did not physically harm the person or property of another. In addition, more than 3,000,000 people are on parole or probation for consensual crimes. Further, more than 4,000,000 people are arrested *each year* for doing something that hurts no one but, potentially, themselves.

The injustice doesn't end there, of course. Throwing people in jail is the extreme. If you can throw people in jail for something, you can fire them for the same reason. You can evict them from their apartments. You can deny them credit. You can expel them from schools. You can strip away their civil rights, confiscate their property, and destroy their lives—just because they're different.

> *No loss by flood and lightning,*
> *no destruction of cities and temples*
> *by hostile forces of nature,*
> *has deprived man*
> *of so many noble lives and impulses*
> *as those which his intolerance*
> *has destroyed.*
>
> HELEN KELLER

At what point does behavior become so unacceptable that we should tell our government to lock people up? The answer, as explored in this book: We lock people up only when they physically harm the person or property of a nonconsenting other.

Contained in this answer is an important assumption. After a certain age, our persons and property belong to us.

Yes, if we harm ourselves, it may *emotionally* harm others. That's unfortunate, but not grounds for putting us in jail. If it were, every time we stopped dating person A in order to date person B, we would run the risk of going to jail for hurting person A. If person B were hurt by our being put in jail, person A could be put in jail for hurting person B. This would, of course, hurt person A's mother, who would see to it that person B would go to jail. Eventually, we'd all be in jail. As silly as that situation sounds, it is precisely the logic used by some to protect the idea of consensual crimes.

Arguments in favor of laws against any consensual activity are usually variations of "It's not *moral!*" And where does the objector's sense of morality come from? For the most part, his or her religion. Some claim "cultural values" as the basis of morality, but where does this set of cultural values come from? The sharing of a similar religion.*

To a large degree, we have created a legal system that is, to quote Alan Watts, "clergymen with billy clubs." Says Watts:

The police have enough work to keep them busy regulat-

---

*Laws that are primarily based on the rules of society and not the rules of religion are discussed in the chapter, "Separation of Society and State."

Excerpts from *Ain't Nobody's Business If You Do*

> *That which we call sin in others is experiment for us.*
>
> RALPH WALDO EMERSON

ing automobile traffic, preventing robberies and crimes of violence and helping lost children and little old ladies find their way home. As long as the police confine themselves to such activities they are respected friends of the public. But as soon as they begin inquiring into people's private morals, they become nothing more than armed clergymen.

Please don't think I'm against religion. I'm not. *Individual* morality based on religious or spiritual beliefs can be invaluable. It can be an excellent guide for *one's own life.* Religious belief, however, is a terrible foundation for deciding who does and does not go to jail.

If people physically harm your person or your property, they go to jail. If not, they don't. Every other behavior we would like them to follow (for their own good or our own comfort) must be achieved through education or persuasion—not force of law.

In exchange for extending this tolerance to others, we know that unless we physically harm another's person or property, we will not be put in jail. This assurance gives us the boundaries within which we can live our lives. It allows us to explore, to take risks, and—as long as we risk only our own person and property—we know that at least one risk we won't be taking is the risk of being thrown in jail.

With such freedom, of course, comes responsibility. As we take risks, bad things will occasionally happen—that's why they're called risks. At that point, we must learn to shrug and say, "That's life," not, "Why isn't there a law against this? Why isn't the government protecting me from every possible negative occurrence I might get myself into?" When we, as adults, consent to do something—unless we are being deceived—we become responsible for the outcome.

We must become involved, educated, aware consumers—and teach our children to be the same. Just because some activity is available, and just because we won't be thrown in jail for doing it, doesn't mean it is necessarily harmless.

If it's not the government's job to protect us from our own actions (and whoever said the government is equipped to do that anyway when the government can't seem to buy a toilet seat for less than $600?), then the job returns to where it always has been: with us.

⚖ ⚖ ⚖

Consensual crimes are sometimes known as *victimless crimes* because it's hard to find a clear-cut victim. The term *victimless crimes,* however, has been so thoroughly misused in recent years that, as a description, it has become almost meaningless. One criminal after another has claimed that his or hers was a victimless crime, while one self-appointed moralist after another has claimed that truly victimless crimes do, indeed, have victims. It seems easier to use the lesser-known phrase *consensual crimes* than to rehabilitate the better-known phrase *victimless crimes*.

What are the consensual crimes? Before listing the most popular ones, I want to point out that the regulators of our morality have spent a lot of money making them all sound *just terrible*. The propaganda against consensual crimes has tainted the very words, so that even reading them can make one uneasy.

On the other hand, the consensual crimes themselves have had nothing but word-of-mouth to get their message across. Considering the vast PR campaign against them, they've done pretty well—each of them seems to be flourishing.

Please keep in mind that I am not advocating any of the consensual crimes. Some of them are harmful to the person doing them. Others are only potentially harmful to the doer. Still others are simply lifestyle choices.

No matter how harmful doing them may be to the doer,

> It has been my experience that folks who have no vices have very few virtues.
>
> ABRAHAM LINCOLN

however, it makes no sense to *put people in jail* for doing things that do not physically harm the person or property of another. Further, the government has no right to put people in jail unless they do harm the person or property of another. The United States Constitution and its Bill of Rights—the "supreme law of the land"—prohibit it.*

People often use the word *legal* too loosely. They fail to give sufficient thought as to what *legal* and *illegal* really mean. When we say a given activity should be illegal, what we're saying is that if someone takes part in that activity, we should *put that person in jail.* When it comes to consensual crimes, when people say, "It should be illegal," what they usually mean is, "That's not right," "That's not a good idea," or "That's immoral." When using the word *illegal,* it's important to remember how forceful the force of law truly is. We are all entitled, of course, to our opinions about certain activities, but do we really want to lock up people who don't go along with our opinions?

We all have the right to be different. The laws against consensual activities take away that right. If we let anyone lose his or her freedom without just cause, we have all lost our freedom.

With this thought in mind, here are the most popular consensual crimes: gambling, recreational drug use, religious drug use, prostitution, pornography and obscenity, violations of marriage (adultery, fornication, cohabitation, bigamy, polyg-

*If you are a citizen of a country other than the United States, this book still applies. Your country is almost certainly a signatory of the United Nations Declaration of Human Rights, which also guarantees the freedom of individual expression.

amy), homosexuality, regenerative drug use, unorthodox medical practices ("Quacks!"), unconventional religious practices ("Cults!"), unpopular political views ("Commies!"), suicide and assisted suicide, transvestism, not using safety devices (such as motorcycle helmets and seat belts), public drunkenness, jaywalking, and loitering and vagrancy (as long as they don't become trespassing or disturbing the peace).

Even if you don't want to take part in any of the consensual crimes, working to remove the consensual crimes from the books has a trickle-down effect of tolerance, acceptance, and freedom for the things you do want to do. (This may be one trickle-down theory that actually works.)

While exploring the extremes of social prejudice, we can explore our personal prejudices as well. I suggest that, when we want to put people in jail for what they do to their own person or property, our individual tolerance and compassion probably needs a little aerobic exercise.

But this isn't just *my* idea. Here's how another person—a carpenter by training—put it:

> Why do you look at the speck of sawdust in your brother's eye and pay no attention to the plank in your own eye? How can you say to your brother, "Brother, let me take the speck out of your eye," when you yourself fail to see the plank in your own eye? You hypocrite, first take the plank out of your eye, and then you will see clearly to remove the speck from your brother's eye.

That, of course, was said by Jesus of Nazareth, that dear misunderstood man most people use as the authority to "lock the bastards up."*

The fact that his idea would be so controversial 2,000 years later, and more than 200 years after we formed a government based on "life, liberty and the pursuit of happiness," shows how much work we have to do.

---

*Those who have their Bibles handy can read all about it in Matthew 7:3–5 and Luke 6:41–42. Much more on people's misrepresentation of Jesus in the chapter, "Consensual Crimes and the Bible."

> *My definition of a free society is a society where it is safe to be unpopular.*
>
> ADLAI E. STEVENSON

⚖️ ⚖️ ⚖️

Here's the condensed list of reasons why having laws against consensual activities is not a good idea (each point has a chapter of its own later in the book):

It's un-American! America is based on personal freedom and on the strength of diversity, not on unnecessary limitation and slavish conformity. The American dream is that we are all free to live our lives as we see fit, providing we do not physically harm the person or property of another.

It's unconstitutional. The United States Constitution and its Bill of Rights clearly give us the right to pursue our lives without the forced intervention of moralists, do-gooders, and busybodies.

Laws against consensual activities violate the separation of church and state. The Constitution guarantees that not only can we freely practice the religion of our choice, but also that the government will not impose religion upon us. Almost all the arguments in favor of maintaining laws against consensual activities have a religious foundation. The government is then asked to enforce these religious beliefs by arresting the nonbelievers and putting them in jail.

Laws against consensual activities are opposed to the principles of private property, free enterprise, capitalism, and the open market. If everything thus far has sounded hopelessly liberal, here's a nice conservative argument: Our economic system is based on the sanctity of private property. What you own is your own business; you can give it away, trade it, or sell it for a profit or a loss—none of which is the government's business. This is the system known as capitalism. We recently fought (and won) a forty-five-year cold-and-hot war against communism to maintain it. For the government to say that certain things cannot be owned, bought, given away, traded, or sold is a direct violation of both the sanctity of private property and the fundamental principles of capitalism.

It's expensive. We're spending more than fifty *billion* dollars per year catching and jailing consensual "criminals." In addition, we're losing at least an additional $150 billion in potential tax revenues. In other words, each man, woman, and child in this country is paying $800 per year to destroy the lives of 5,000,000 fellow citizens. If we did nothing else but declare consensual crimes legal, the $200,000,000,000 we'd save each year could wipe out the national debt in twenty years, or we could reduce personal income tax by one-third. Another economic high point: moving the underground economy of consensual crimes aboveground would create 6,000,000 tax-paying jobs. And then there's the matter of interest. The $50 billion we spend jailing consensual "criminals" is not just spent; it's *borrowed.* The national debit grows larger. Six percent interest compounded over thirty years adds $250 billion to that $50 billion figure—a dandy legacy for our progeny.

Lives are destroyed. Yes, by taking part in consensual crimes, people may destroy their own lives. This is unfortunate, but it is their choice. The problem with making consensual activities crimes, however, is that the government moves in and by force destroys the life of the consensual "criminal." And this destruction is almost guaranteed. A single arrest and conviction, even without a jail sentence, can permanently affect one's ability to get employment, housing, credit, education, and insurance. In addition, there is the emotional, financial, and physical trauma of arrest, trial, and conviction. If any significant amount of jail time is added to this governmental torture, an individual's life is almost certainly ruined.

Consensual crimes encourage *real* crimes. Because consensual crimes are against the law, taking part in them costs significantly more than is necessary. In order to pay these artificially inflated prices, some of those who take part in consensual

> *The government of the*
> *United States*
> *is not, in any sense,*
> *founded on the Christian religion.*
>
> GEORGE WASHINGTON
> TREATY OF TRIPOLI
> 1796

crimes go out and commit *real* crimes: mugging, robbery, burglary, forgery, embezzlement, and fraud. If the consensual activities were cheap, real crimes would decrease significantly. In addition, to someone who is regularly breaking a law against a consensual activity, all laws start to seem unimportant.

Consensual crimes corrupt law enforcement. Asking the police to enforce a crime that does not have a clear-cut victim makes a travesty of law enforcement. The law enforcement system is based on a *perpetrator* and a *victim*. With consensual crimes, perpetrator and victim are the same person. Whom are the police supposed to protect? Theoretically, they arrest the perpetrator to protect the victim. With a consensual crime, when the perpetrator goes to jail, the victim goes too. It's a sham that demoralizes police, promotes disrespect for the law, and makes arresting real criminals more difficult. It's sad that the enforcement of laws against consensual crimes has turned one of the true heroes of our society, the honest cop, into an endangered species.

The cops can't catch 'em; the courts can't handle 'em; the prisons can't hold 'em. As it is, the police are catching less than 20% of the real criminals—those who do harm the person or property of others. There is simply no way that the police can even make a dent in the practice of consensual crimes. (Because consensual crimes have no victims, they are seldom reported to the police.) Even if the police could catch all the consensual criminals, the courts couldn't possibly process them. The courts, already swamped with consensual crime cases, can't handle any more. Real criminals walk free every day to rape, rob, and murder again because the courts are so busy finding consensual criminals guilty of hurting no one but themselves. And even if the courts could process them, the prisons are already full; most are operating at more than 100% capacity. To free cells for consensual criminals, real criminals are put on the street every day.

Consensual crimes promote organized crime. Organized crime grew directly out of an earlier unsuccessful attempt to legislate morality: Prohibition. Whenever something is desired by tens of millions of people each day, there will be an organization to meet that desire. If fulfilling that desire is a crime, that organization will be organized crime. Operating outside the law as organized criminals do, they don't differentiate much between crimes with victims and crimes without victims. Further, the enormous amount of money at their disposal allows them to obtain volume discounts when buying police, prosecutors, witnesses, judges, juries, journalists, and politicians. And guess who finances some of those let's-get-tough-on-consensual-crime campaigns? You guessed it. Once consensual crimes are no longer crimes, organized crime is out of business.

Consensual crimes corrupt the freedom of the press. Reporting on consensual crimes has turned a good portion of the media into gossips, busybodies, and tattletales (the Hugh Grant Syndrome). With so much important investigation and reporting to be done concerning issues directly affecting the lives of individuals, the nation, and the world, should we be asking one of our most powerful assets—the free press—to report who's doing what, when, where, how, and how often with other consenting whom's?

Laws against consensual activities teach irresponsibility. If we maintain that it is the government's job to keep illegal anything that might do us harm, it implies that anything not illegal is harmless. This is certainly not the case.

Laws against consensual activities are too randomly enforced to be either a deterrent or fair. The laws against consensual crimes provide almost no deterrent whatsoever. In fact, their very illegality sometimes makes consensual crimes

Excerpts from *Ain't Nobody's Business If You Do*

> *If we've learned anything
> in the past quarter century,
> it is that we cannot
> federalize virtue.*
>
> PRESIDENT GEORGE BUSH
> 1991

fascinating, glamorous, and irresistible. If the chances of being caught at something are only, say, one in ten million, that's hardly a deterrent.

Laws against consensual activities discriminate against minorities and the poor. In selecting which consensual activities should and should not be crimes, the views of the poor and minorities are seldom considered. Therefore, many consensual activities that the mostly white, male, heterosexual, affluent, Christian lawmakers have deemed illegal do not necessarily reflect the preferences or experiences of minority groups. Further, the laws against consensual activities are not uniformly enforced—the poor and minorities, for a variety of reasons, tend to receive the brief end of the stick.

Problems sometimes associated with consensual activities cannot be solved while they're crimes. Some people take part in consensual crimes as a symptom of, or escape from, deeper problems. These problems are not easily addressed until we dispense with the irrational, illogical, and transparently inaccurate myth that participation in the currently illegal consensual activities is always wrong. It wasn't until after Prohibition, for example, that those who had real drinking problems could see, admit to, and do something about them. Maintaining the fallacy that participation in illegal consensual activities is always wrong keeps those for whom it is wrong from doing something constructive about it.

We have more important things to worry about. The short list of national and global problems more deserving of our precious resources includes: *real* crime (robbery, rape, murder—the chances are one in four that you or someone in your household will be "touched," as they say, by a violent crime this year), abducted children (more than 400,000 abducted children each year), insurance fraud (a $100 billion per-year problem that adds from 10% to 30% to all insurance premiums), illiteracy (one in seven American adults is functionally illiterate; one in twenty cannot fill out a job application), poverty (14.2% of the population—35.7 million people—live below the poverty level; a good number of these are children), pollution (all the pending environmental disasters cannot be summed up in a single parenthesis), our addiction to foreign oil (the Gulf War should have been called the Gulf-Standard-Mobil War), terrorism (the bombing of the World Trade Center was, in reality, a terrorist warning: the next time it might be an *atomic* bomb), AIDS (by the year 2000, the largest number of HIV-infected people will be heterosexual women), supposedly new government-regulated but not-really-regulated industries (the $500 billion savings and loan bailout is an obvious example) and last, but certainly not least, the national debt ($5 trillion, and growing faster than almost anything in this country other than intolerance).

It's hypocritical. To give but one obvious example: Cigarettes do more damage and cause roughly one hundred times the deaths of all of the consensual crimes combined. Each year, 500,000 people die as a direct result of smoking. And yet, cigarettes are perfectly legal, available everywhere, and heavily advertised; tobacco growers are government subsidized, and cigarette companies are free to use their influence on both politicians and the media (and, boy, do they ever). How can we tolerate such contradictions in this country? We are, as Thomas Wolfe pointed out, "making the world safe for hypocrisy."

Laws against consensual activities create a society of fear, hatred, bigotry, oppression, and conformity; a culture opposed to personal expression, diversity, freedom, choice, and growth. The prosecution of consensual crimes "trickles down" into ostracizing, humiliating, and scorning people who do things that are not quite against the law—but probably should be. "They're different; therefore, they're bad" seems to

Excerpts from *Ain't Nobody's Business If You Do*

be the motto for a large segment of our society. We are addicted to normalcy; even if it means we must lop off significant portions of ourselves, we must conform.

⚖ ⚖ ⚖

There's no need to accept the validity of all these arguments; the validity of any one is sufficient reason to wipe away all the laws against consensual activities.

In this book, we will explore each of the consensual crimes, asking not, "Is it good?" but, "Is it worth throwing someone in jail for?" We'll explore the prejudice about consensual crimes—the prejudices we have been conditioned to believe. You'll find that the number of lies within lies within lies is amazing.

Responsibility is the price of freedom. So is tolerance.

⚖ ⚖ ⚖

In the time it took you to read this overview, 342 persons were arrested for consensual crimes in the United States.

"If you can't remember the last time
you felt genuinely good,
please read this book."
Larry King

How to
Heal
Depression

By the co-authors of
How to Survive the Loss of a Love

Harold H. Bloomfield, M.D.
& Peter McWilliams

HARDCOVER
5½x8¼, 240 pages
$14.95
ISBN: 0-931580-34-0

PAPERBACK
4x7, 240 pages
$5.95
ISBN: 0-931580-61-7

AUDIO TAPES
Read by the authors
(with lots of classic blues songs)
Six cassettes, $19.95
ISBN: 0-931580-37-4

Authors' Notes

Welcome.

Our goal is to make this book brief, practical, and to-the-point.

The *last* thing a person with depression wants is an intricate tome, heavy with footnotes, citations, Latin words, and sentences such as "Depression is a biopsychosocial disorder, sometimes treated with monoamine oxidase inhibitors."

We have also included quotes from people, some well known and some not, across many cultures and centuries, to show that depression—and the desire to heal it—is a deeply human and universal experience.

Our approach to the treatment of depression is twofold. Each part is equally important.

• One is healing the brain, as current medical research points to biochemical imbalances in the brain as the seat of depression.

• The other is healing the mind—overcoming negative habits of thought and action which may cause, or be caused by, depression.

Treating the brain *and* the mind is the most effective way to heal depression. Recent medical and psychological breakthroughs make depression among the most successfully treatable of all serious illnesses.

Harold H. Bloomfield, M.D.
Peter McWilliams

As a confirmed melancholic,
I can testify that the best
and maybe the only antidote
for melancholia is action.
However, like most melancholics,
I also suffer from sloth.

EDWARD ABBEY

Excerpt from *How to Heal Depression*

About This Book

Our book is divided into four parts.

In Part I, **"Understanding Depression,"** we discuss what depression is (and is not); how you can be depressed without "feeling depressed"; and the possible causes of depression. There's even a short self-evaluation for depression, compliments of the National Institutes of Health (page 22).

In Part II, **"Healing the Brain,"** we look at the biological causes of depression and its medical treatment. This includes antidepressant medication, nutrition, exercise, and such strenuous activities as hot baths and massage. This is the domain of the psychiatrist, family doctor, and other healthcare specialists.

Part III we call **"Healing the Mind."** We explore unlearning mental habits either caused by or contributing to depression, while learning new mental patterns that tend to enhance effectiveness, well-being, and emotional freedom. We discuss exciting new short-term therapies (usually only ten to twenty sessions) that have proven to be highly successful in healing depression. This is the domain of the psychologist, psychiatrist, clinical social worker, and mental health professional.

The final section, Part IV, is **"As Healing Continues . . . ."** Although most people treated for depression find remarkable results within a short time, the complete healing of depression often continues for a while. There are ups and downs, lessons to be learned, new pathways to be explored.

Thank you for joining us on this healing journey.

One:
You Are Not Alone

- If you or someone you know is depressed, you are not alone.

- *That's* something of an understatement.

- One in twenty Americans currently suffers from a depression severe enough to require medical treatment.

- One person in five will have a depression at some time in his or her life.

- Depression in its various forms (insomnia, fatigue, anxiety, stress, vague aches and pains, etc.) is the most common complaint heard in doctors' offices.

- Two percent of all children and five percent of all adolescents suffer from depression.

- More than twice as many women are currently being treated for depression than men. (It is not known whether this is because women are more likely to be depressed, or whether men tend to deny their depression.)

- People over sixty-five are four times more likely to suffer depression than the rest of the population.

- Depression is the #1 public health problem in this country. Depression is an epidemic—an epidemic on the rise.

I am now experiencing myself
all the things that
as a third party
I have witnessed going on
in my patients—
days when I slink about
depressed.

SIGMUND FREUD

Three:
There Is No Need to Suffer

- More than eighty percent of the people with depression can be successfully treated.

- Long-term, expensive treatments are seldom necessary.

- Modern treatment for most depression is antidepressant medication and short-term "talk" therapy—usually just ten to twenty sessions.

- Treatment for depression is relatively inexpensive—but whatever the cost, it is more than made up for in increased productivity, efficiency, physical health, improved relationships, and enjoyment of life.

- Yes, life will always have its "slings and arrows of outrageous fortune," and, yes, they will hurt. But there's no need to suffer from depression as well.

Pain is inevitable.
Suffering is optional.

M. KATHLEEN CASEY

Ten:
The Symptoms of Depression

After careful evaluation, the National Institutes of Health developed the following checklist:

Symptoms of Depression Can Include

- ☐ Persistent sad or "empty" mood
- ☐ Loss of interest or pleasure in ordinary activities, including sex
- ☐ Decreased energy, fatigue, being "slowed down"
- ☐ Sleep disturbances (insomnia, early-morning waking, or oversleeping)
- ☐ Eating disturbances (loss of appetite and weight, or weight gain)
- ☐ Difficulty concentrating, remembering, making decisions
- ☐ Feelings of guilt, worthlessness, helplessness
- ☐ Thoughts of death or suicide, suicide attempts
- ☐ Irritability
- ☐ Excessive crying
- ☐ Chronic aches and pains that don't respond to treatment

In the Workplace, Symptoms of Depression Often May Be Recognized by

- ☐ Decreased productivity
- ☐ Morale problems
- ☐ Lack of cooperation
- ☐ Safety problems, accidents
- ☐ Absenteeism
- ☐ Frequent complaints of being tired all the time
- ☐ Complaints of unexplained aches and pains
- ☐ Alcohol and drug abuse

Symptoms of Mania Can Include

- ☐ Excessively "high" mood
- ☐ Irritability
- ☐ Decreased need for sleep
- ☐ Increased energy and activity
- ☐ Increased talking, moving, and sexual activity
- ☐ Racing thoughts
- ☐ Disturbed ability to make decisions
- ☐ Grandiose notions
- ☐ Being easily distracted

Excerpt from *How to Heal Depression*

Eleven:
Are You Depressed?

- *"A thorough diagnosis is needed if four or more of the symptoms of depression or mania persist for more than two weeks,"* say the National Institutes of Health, *"or are interfering with work or family life."*

- The symptoms on the facing page are *not* "just life." If four or more of the symptoms have been a regular part of your life for more than two weeks or regularly tend to interfere with your life, a consultation with a physician experienced in diagnosing and treating depression is in order.

- You need not suffer any longer. Treatment is readily available.

- *"With available treatment, eighty percent of the people with serious depression—even those with the most severe forms—can improve significantly,"* say the National Institutes of Health. *"Symptoms can be relieved, usually in a matter of weeks."*

- Please talk to your doctor. (And read on!)

A NEW EDITION COMPLETELY REVISED

#1 BEST SELLER

DO IT!
Let's Get Off Our Buts

A GUIDE TO LIVING YOUR DREAMS

IMPORTANT MESSAGE

Peter McWilliams

#1 BESTSELLER	FOLLOW	TERRIFIC
—New York Times	YOUR DREAMS	—Larry King
	—Detroit News	

INTRODUCTION:
How Do You Do?

We all have a dream, a heart's desire. Most have more than one. Some of us have an entire entourage. This is a book about discovering (or rediscovering) those dreams, how to choose which dreams to pursue, and practical suggestions for achieving them.

- By pursuing any *one* of our dreams, we can find fulfillment. We don't need to pursue them all.

- We don't have to *achieve* a dream in order to find fulfillment—we need only actively *pursue* the dream to attain satisfaction.

- By living our dream, we can contribute not only to ourselves, but to everyone and everything around us.

And yet, with all this good news, most people are not pursuing their dreams.

When we're not pursuing our dreams, we spend our time and abilities pursuing the things we *think* will make us happy, the things we *believe* will bring us fulfillment: the house, the car, the cashmere jump suit.

There's an old saying: "You can't get enough of what you don't really want." When the new car doesn't make us happy, we tend to blame the new car for not being "enough," and set our sights on a "better" new car. Surely *that* will make us happy.

Many people are so far away from living their dream *they have forgotten what their dream truly is.*

It is sad. It is unnecessary. It is wasteful. We have abandoned our heart's desire—and somewhere, deep down, we know it. Even if we don't remember quite what it is—we miss it.

Why aren't we living our dreams?

Because there is something we are trained to honor more than our dreams: the comfort zone. The comfort zone is all the things we have done often enough to feel comfortable doing again.

> *I stopped believing in Santa Claus*
> *when my mother took me to*
> *see him in a department store,*
> *and he asked for my autograph.*
>
> SHIRLEY TEMPLE

Whenever we do something new, it falls outside the barrier of the comfort zone. In even *contemplating* a new action, we feel fear, guilt, unworthiness, hurt feelings, and / or anger—all those things we generally think of as "uncomfortable."

When we feel uncomfortable enough long enough, we tend to feel discouraged (a form of exhaustion), and we return to thoughts, feelings and actions that are more familiar, more practiced, more predictable—more, well, *comfortable.*

The irony is that the feelings we have been taught to label "uncomfortable" are, in fact, among the very tools necessary to fulfill our dreams.

As it turns out, the bricks used to build the walls of comfort zone are made of gold.

Why don't we know this?

The training we received as children—which, for the most part, is fine for children—is not appropriate for adults. The guidelines of an independent, productive adult are not the same rules of a dependent, limited child. What is true for children can be

 Excerpt from *DO IT! Let's Get Off Our Buts*

counterproductive for adults. We live our lives as though it were a bicycle with the training wheels still on—limiting, entirely *too* safe, and somewhat boring.

We no longer believe in Santa Claus, but we still believe that "being uncomfortable" is reason enough not to do something new. The Easter Bunny hopped out of our lives years ago, yet we still let "what other people might think" affect our behavior. The tooth fairy was yanked from us long before adolescence, but we still feel we can justify any personal failure by finding someone or something outside ourselves to blame.

Most people are drifting along in a childish sleep. To live our dreams, we must wake up.

In reading that last sentence, do you feel your comfort zone being challenged? That will happen a lot in this book. That tingling we feel when we contemplate waking up and living our dreams we can label either "fear" or "excitement." If we call it fear, it's uncomfortable; we tend to find reasons not to read any further. If we call it excitement, we turn it into energy that makes the process of learning and doing active and enjoyable.

It's your choice. It's always your choice. Alas, many of us have delegated the choice to habits formed long ago, formed when we knew far less about life than we know now. We let habits formed when we were two or four or six or ten or fifteen control our lives today.

To change a habit requires work. Make no mistake about it: reading this book will not change your life, just as reading a guidebook to France will not show you France. It may give you a *sense* of France, perhaps, but France is France and can only be experienced through *action*.

And so it is with your dreams. This book will show you *how* to discover your dreams, *how* to select the dreams you choose to pursue, and *how* to fulfill those dreams—but if you don't *act* upon those *how's,* you will never see Paris from atop the Eiffel Tower.

> *Regret for the things we did*
> *can be tempered by time;*
> *it is regret for the things we*
> *did not do that is inconsolable.*
>
> SYDNEY J. HARRIS

Although fulfilling our dreams requires *work,* the process can also be *fun.* Which reminds me of a joke.

An Indian Chief greeted a friend by raising his hand in the traditional salute and saying, "Chance!"

"Chance?" his friend asked, "You must mean 'How!'"

"I know how," the Chief responded, "I'm looking for chance."

Please think of this book as your chance— a chance *you* are giving *yourself.* Imagine for a moment that you are powerful enough to have had this book written *just for you.* When you get a sense of that power, you'll know that you have all it takes to fulfill your dream. *Any* dream. *Your* dream.

F. Scott Fitzgerald met Joan Crawford at a Hollywood party. He told her he had been hired to write the screenplay for her next film. She looked him straight in the eye and said, "Write hard, Mr. Fitzgerald, write hard."

Imagine that I am looking you straight in the eye and saying, "Dream big, dear reader, dream big."

When we discover how easy it is to fulfill personal

dreams—even the ones that seem "really big" before the achievement of them—we are naturally inspired to fulfill even larger dreams.

Pursuing a Big Dream of your own choosing is the same amount of work as gathering more and more of the things you don't really want. You're going to spend the rest of your life doing *something*. It might as well be something *you* want to do.

"But what about money? But what about time? But what about this? But what about that?" There *are* a lot of buts to "get off," aren't there?

Let's return to the question I posed earlier: "How do you do?"

That's easy. You do by learning.

And how do you learn?

You learn by doing.

A chicken-and-egg conundrum, to be sure; yet one penetrated by this deceptively simple thought: "The willingness to do creates the ability to do."

For now, simply be *willing* to do. Be willing to do what it takes to read this book. That takes the willingness to finish this page and turn to the next. That takes the willingness to finish this paragraph. That takes the willingness to finish this sentence (which you have just done—congratulations!).

Where does the willingness come from?

From you.

As Joni Mitchell pointed out, "It all comes down to you."

I certainly agree, and would only add, "It all comes down to *do*."

A New Edition—
Completely Revised

LIFE 101

Everything We Wish We Had Learned About Life In School — But Didn't

Peter McWilliams

FABULOUS!
—Liz Smith

A GUIDE TO BUILDING SELF-ESTEEM
—Entertainment Weekly

PRACTICAL AND WITTY
—Detroit News

FINAL MARKS

INTRODUCTION TO LIFE

Welcome to life.

I call this book *LIFE 101* because it contains all the things I wish I had learned about life in school but, for the most part, did not.

After twelve (or more) years of schooling, we know how to figure the square root of an isosceles triangle (invaluable in daily life), but we might not know how to forgive ourselves and others.

We know what direction migrating birds fly in autumn, but we're not sure which way we want to go.

We have dissected a frog, but perhaps have never explored the dynamics of human relationships.

We know who wrote "To be or not to be, that is the question," but we don't know the answer.

We know what pi is, but we're not sure who we are.

We may know how to diagram a sentence, but we may not know how to love ourselves.

That our educational system is not designed to teach us the "secrets of life" is no secret. In school, we learn how to do everything—except how to live.

Maybe that's the way it should be. Unraveling life's "mysteries" and discovering life's "secrets" (which are, in fact, neither mysterious nor secretive) may take the courage and determination found only in a self-motivated pursuit.

You probably already know there's more to life than reading, 'riting, and 'rithmetic. I'm glad you learned reading, of course, or you wouldn't be able to read this book. I'm also glad I learned 'riting (such as it is).

And 'rithmetic? Well, as Mae West once said, "One and one is two, two and two are four, and five'll get you ten if you know how to work it." That's what this book is about: knowing how to work it, and having fun along the way.

Although a lot can be learned from adversity, most of the same

> *Only the curious will learn and*
> *only the resolute overcome*
> *the obstacles to learning.*
> *The quest quotient has*
> *always excited me more*
> *than the intelligence quotient.*
>
> EUGENE S. WILSON

lessons can be learned through enjoyment and laughter. If you're like me, you've probably had more than enough adversity. (After graduating from the School of Hard Knocks, I automatically enrolled in the University of Adversity.)

I agree with Alan Watts, who said, "I am *sincere* about life, but I'm not *serious* about it." If you're looking for serious, pedantic, didactic instruction, you will not find it here. I will—with a light heart—present hundreds of techniques and suggestions, and for each of them I make the same suggestion:

Give it a try.

If it works for you, fine—use it; it's yours. If it doesn't work for you, let it go and try other things that may. When you find things that *do* work for you, I advise you to follow Shakespeare's advice: "Grapple them to thy soul with hoops of steel."

Naturally, not everything in *LIFE 101* will be for you. If I say something you find not "true," please don't discount everything else in the book. It may be "true" for someone else. That same someone else might say, "What nonsense," about something which has you knowingly muttering, "How true." It's a big world;

> **Fred Sanford:** *Didn't you
> learn anything being my son?
> Who do you think I'm
> doing this all for?*
>
> **Lamont Sanford:** *Yourself.*
>
> **Fred:** *Yeah, you
> learned something.*

we are all at different points on our personal journeys. Life has many truths; take what you can use and leave the rest.

If you take from this book ten percent—any ten percent—and use it as your own, I'll consider my job well done.

Which brings me to the question: Who is the *real* teacher of LIFE 101? I'll get to that shortly. (Hint: It's certainly not me—or *I*, as the grammatically correct among us would say.) (Second hint: It is *definitely* not me.)

For now, welcome to *LIFE 101*. When you were born, you probably had quite a welcome, although you may have been too young to remember it. So, as you begin this "life," please feel welcome.

Although it may be "just a book," it's a book of ideas from my mind to yours; a book of best wishes from my heart to yours. As James Burke observed, "When you read a book, you hold another's mind in your hands." (So be careful!) Here's to our time together being intimate, enjoyable, and loving.

Welcome.

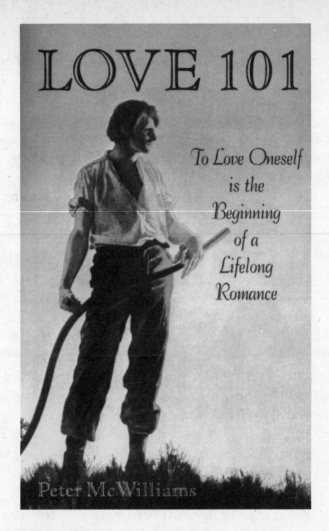

LOVE 101

To Love Oneself
is the
Beginning
of a
Lifelong
Romance

Peter McWilliams

Author's Notes

In the early 1970s, I went to the American Booksellers Association annual convention, where publishers rent booths at exorbitant rates and show their recent wares to the booksellers of America. At the Penguin booth, I saw a book entitled *Self Love*. It had an introduction by Alan Watts, who was then and is still my favorite philosopher. I was excited to discover a book about the love of oneself endorsed by him and published by such a distinguished house as Penguin—then known primarily for its reprints of the classics. As was the custom at ABA, complimentary copies were available. I took my copy and thanked the salesperson, a dignified British man who nodded his acceptance of my appreciation.

"I can really use this book," I said. "I'm very bad at self-love."

The sales representative smiled one of those smiles that doesn't go up at the edges, but merely makes one's mouth wider while perfectly horizontal.

"In fact, of all the things I need to work on," I continued, "I think self-love is the most essential." I was twenty-something at the time, and determined to be "open about my process." I could see, however, that saying I didn't know how to love myself made the Penguin sales representative a bit uncomfortable, so I said my good-bye.

"Thank you again," I said, extending my hand. As he shook it, I said, "In fact, I'm going up to my hotel room right now and read this." He dropped my hand.

The Penguin book on self-love was about the joys of masturbation.

➡

My seeking self-love in the early 1970s was sincere. Like many people, I had inhaled the book *How to Be Your Own Best Friend*. I read it clandestinely—it seemed to be as taboo a subject as that

> *The last time I saw him*
> *he was walking down Lover's Lane*
> *holding his own hand.*
>
> FRED ALLEN

other form of self-love. In 1971, the idea that one could be one's own friend, much less *best* friend, was radical.

Today, the notion that one can be the most significant love object in one's own life, is just as radical.

I certainly do not present myself as a pillar of self-loving, nor put myself on a pedestal labeled AN IDEAL SPECIMEN OF A SELF-LOVING PERSON. I'm just a person who has been struggling with the notion of loving himself since 1967. Twenty-eight years later, I finally feel as though I have *something* worth sharing; that I know enough about the subject to write a book on it; and, since there's something more to learn about everything, "The best way to learn about a subject," Benjamin Disraeli once said, "is to write a book about it."

Although your path and discoveries on the road to greater self-love will differ from mine, allow me to offer three personal observations:

1. God* is within you.**

---

*As you perceive him, her, or it to be, from God the Father, to Mother Nature, to Universal Mind, to the "illimitable superior spirit who reveals himself in the slight details we are able to perceive with our frail and feeble mind" (Einstein).

**For those who find this an anti-Christian statement, please consider this

2. You are lovable, *just as you are now.*

3. You *can* learn to love yourself, more and more each day.

In this book I will not be spending a great deal of time on point #1. The discovery of, defining of, relating to, and praise for God I will leave to you, God, and any number of excellent source materials on the subject. *LOVE 101* can be read by anyone, from devout fundamentalist to confirmed atheist, and he or she can learn enough about self-loving to proclaim, "Glory, hallelujah! I'm glad I read this book."

In the end, of course, we must all write our own book on how to love ourselves. Thanks for reading my book. My best and warmest wishes to you as you write your own.

Take good care,

> Peter McWilliams
> Los Angeles, California
> January 3, 1995

P.S. *LOVE 101: To Love Oneself Is the Beginning of a Lifelong Romance* was completed on January 3, 1995. Precisely one hundred years earlier—to the day—the curtain rose at London's Theatre Royal on Oscar Wilde's latest play, *An Ideal Husband.* As the third act opens, we find this stage direction:

> *Enter* LORD GORING *in evening dress with a button hole [flower in his lapel]. He is wearing a silk hat and Inverness cape. White-gloved, he carries a Louis Seize cane. His are all the delicate fopperies of fashion. One sees that he stands in immediate relation to modern life, makes it, indeed, and so masters it. He is the first well-dressed philosopher in the history of thought.*

Could Wilde possibly be describing himself? But of course. Goring addresses his butler:

> LORD GORING: You see, Phipps, fashion is what one wears oneself. Whereas unfashionable is what other people wear.
>
> PHIPPS: Yes, my lord.
>
> LORD GORING: Just as vulgarity is simply the conduct of other people.

from Jesus: "The kingdom of God is within you" (Luke 17:21).

> *Style is knowing who you are,*
> *what you want to say,*
> *and not giving a damn.*
>
> GORE VIDAL

PHIPPS: Yes, my lord.

LORD GORING [putting in new button hole]: And falsehoods the truths of other people.

PHIPPS: Yes, my lord.

LORD GORING: To love oneself is the beginning of a life-long romance.

PHIPPS: Yes, my lord.

And from that bit of typical Wilde dialogue comes the subtitle for this book.

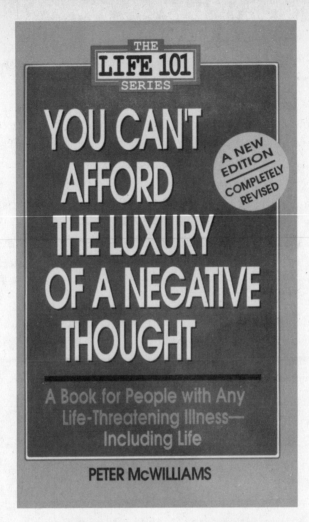

THE LIFE 101 SERIES

YOU CAN'T AFFORD THE LUXURY OF A NEGATIVE THOUGHT

A NEW EDITION
COMPLETELY REVISED

A Book for People with Any
Life-Threatening Illness—
Including Life

PETER McWILLIAMS

Introduction

This is not just a book for people with life-threatening illnesses. It's a book for anyone afflicted with one of the primary diseases of our time: negative thinking.

I come before you a certified expert on the subject: I'm a confirmed negaholic. I don't just see a glass that's half-full and call it half-empty; I see a glass that's completely full and worry that someone's going to tip it over.

Negative thinking is always expensive—dragging us down mentally, emotionally, and physically—hence, I refer to any indulgence in it as a *luxury*. When, however, we have the symptoms of a life-threatening illness—be it AIDS, heart trouble, cancer, high blood pressure, or any of the others—negative thinking is a *luxury* we can no longer afford.

I remember a bumper sticker from the 1960s—"Death Is Nature's Way of Telling You to Slow Down." Well, the signs of a life-threatening illness are nature's way of telling us to—as we say in California—lighten up.

Be easier on yourself. Think better of yourself. Learn to forgive yourself and others.

This is a book about getting behind on your worrying. Way, way behind. The further behind on your worrying you get, the further ahead you'll be.

My favorite quote on worry: "Worrying is a form of atheism." Second favorite: "Worrying is the interest paid on a debt you may not owe."

This is not so much a book to be read as it is a book to be *used*. It doesn't have to be read cover to cover. I like to think you can flip it open at any time to any page and get something of value from it. This is especially true of the second—and longest—section of the book.

This book has two sections: **The Disease** and **The Cure**.

> *We are, perhaps*
> *unique among the*
> *earth's creatures,*
> *the worrying animal.*
> *We worry away our lives,*
> *fearing the future,*
> *discontent with the present,*
> *unable to take in*
> *the idea of dying,*
> *unable to sit still.*
>
> LEWIS THOMAS

The disease is not any specific illness, but what I believe to be a precursor of all life-threatening illnesses—negative thinking.

The cure is not a wonder drug or a vaccination or The Magic Bullet. The cure is simple: (1) spend more time focusing on the positive things in your life *(Accentuate the Positive)*; (2) spend less time thinking negatively *(Eliminate the Negative)*; and (3) enjoy each moment *(Latch on to the Affirmative)*.

That's it. Simple, but far from easy.

It's the aim of this book to make the process simple and, if not easy, at least easier.

Please don't use anything in this book against yourself. Don't interpret anything I say in **The Disease** as blame. When I use the word *responsibility*, for example, I simply mean you have the *ability* to *respond*. (And you *are* responding or you wouldn't be reading this book.)

And please don't take any of the suggestions in **The Cure** as "musts," "shoulds," or "have-tos." Think of them as joyful activity, creative play, curious exploration—not as additional burdens in an already burdensome life.

This book is not designed to replace proper medical care. Please use this book *in conjunction with* whatever course of treatment your doctor or health-care provider prescribes.

You are far more powerful than you ever dreamed. As you discover and learn how to use your power, use it only for your upliftment and the upliftment of others.

You are a marvelous, wonderful, worthwhile person—just because you are. That's the point of view I'll be taking. Please join me for a while—an hour, a week, a lifetime—at that viewing point.

How to Survive the Loss of a Love

♥ ♥ ♥ ♥ ♥

Melba Colgrove, Ph.D.
Harold H. Bloomfield, M.D.
& Peter McWilliams

HARDCOVER
5½x8½, 212 pages, $10.00
ISBN: 0-931580-45-5

PAPERBACK
4x7, 212 pages, $5.95
ISBN: 0-931580-43-9

AUDIO TAPES
Read by the authors
Two cassettes, $11.95
ISBN: 0-931580-47-1

WORKBOOK
Surviving, Healing & Growing
7x10, 198 pages, $11.95
ISBN: 0-931580-46-3

When an emotional injury takes place,
the body begins a process
as natural as the healing
of a physical wound.

Let the process happen.
Trust the process.
Surrender to it.

Trust that nature will do the healing.
Know that the pain will pass,
and, when it passes,
you will be stronger,
happier, more sensitive and aware.

Excerpt from *How to Survive the Loss of a Love*

THE STAGES OF RECOVERY

- Recovering from a loss takes place in three distinct—yet over-lapping—stages.

- They are:

    —shock/denial/numbness
    —fear/anger/depression
    —understanding/acceptance/moving on

- Each stage of recovery is:

    —necessary
    —natural
    —a part of the healing process

the fear that I would
come home one day and
find you gone has turned
into the pain of the
reality.

"What will I do if it happens?"
I would ask myself.

What will I do
now that it
has?

Excerpt from *How to Survive the Loss of a Love*

One:
You Will Survive

- You *will* get better.

- No doubt about it.

- The healing process has a beginning, a middle, and an end.

- Keep in mind, at the beginning, that there *is* an end. It's not that far off. You *will* heal.

- Nature is on your side, and nature is a powerful ally.

- Tell yourself, often, "I am alive. I will survive."

- You are alive.

- You will survive.

in my sleep
I dreamed
you called. you said
you were moving back
with your old lover.
you said you thought a
phone call would be the
cleanest way to handle it,
"it" being that we could
never see each other
again, and that I should
understand why.
I moved to wake
myself and found I wasn't
sleeping after all.
my life became
a nightmare.

Excerpt from *How to Survive the Loss of a Love*

Five:
It's OK to Feel

- It's OK to feel numb. Expect to be in shock for awhile. This emotional numbness may be frightening.

- It's OK to fear. "Will I make it?" "Will I ever love again?" "Will I ever feel good about anything again?" These are familiar fears following a loss. It's OK to *feel* them, but, to the degree you can, don't *believe* them.

- It's OK to feel nothing. There are times when you'll have no feelings of any kind. That's fine.

- It's OK to feel anything. You may feel grief-stricken, angry, like a failure, exhausted, muddled, lost, beaten, indecisive, relieved, overwhelmed, inferior, melancholy, giddy, silly, loathful, full of self-hatred, envious, suicidal (feelings OK, actions not), disgusted, happy, outraged, in rage or *anything* else.

- *All* feelings are a part of the healing process.

- Let yourself heal. Let yourself feel.

Spring:
leaves grow.
love grows.

Summer:
love dies.
I drive away,
tears in my eyes.

Bugs commit suicide on my windshield.

Autumn:
leaves fall.
I fall.

Winter:
I die.
I drive away,
nothing in my eyes.

Snowflakes commit suicide on my windshield.

Excerpt from *How to Survive the Loss of a Love*

Seven:
You're Great!

- You are a good, whole, worthwhile human being.

- You are OK. You're more than OK, you're great.

- Your self-esteem may have suffered a jolt. Your thoughts may reflect some guilt, worry, condemnation or self-deprecation. These thoughts are just symptoms of the stress you are going through.

- There is no need to give negative thoughts about yourself the center of attention.

- Don't punish yourself with "if only's." ("*If only* I had [or hadn't] done this or that I wouldn't be in this emotional mess.") Disregard any thought that begins "If only . . ."

- You are much more than the emotional wound you are currently suffering. Don't lose sight of that.

- Beneath the surface turmoil:

    —you are good
    —you are whole
    —you are beautiful

    just because you are

I am Joy.
I am everything.
I can do all things but two:

1. forget that I love you.

2. forget that you no longer love me.

Excerpt from *How to Survive the Loss of a Love*

Twenty-five:
The Question of Suicide

- You may be having suicidal thoughts. They may or may not be as eloquent as *"to be or not to be,"* but they may arise.

- Know they are a natural symptom of the pain, and that there is no need to act on them.

- If you fear these impulses are getting out of hand, seek professional help *at once.* Call directory assistance and ask for the number of your local Suicide Prevention Hotline. Then call it. The people (almost entirely volunteers) are there to help. They *want* to help. Give them the gift of allowing them to do so.

- Don't turn the rage against yourself. (Although feeling rage is perfectly alright—after all, an utterly outrageous thing has happened to you.) Find a safe way to release it. Beat a pillow, cry, scream, stomp up and down, yell.

- Above all, suicide is silly. It's leaving the world series ten minutes into the first inning just because your favorite hitter struck out. It's walking out of the opera during the overture just because the conductor dropped his baton. It's . . . well, you get the picture. In this play called life, aren't you even a little curious about what might happen next?

- The feeling *will pass.* You can count on that. You *will* get better. *Much* better.

- We do promise you a rose garden. We just can't promise you it will be totally without thorns.

THE QUESTION OF SUICIDE:

Keep it a question.
it's not really an answer.

Excerpt from *How to Survive the Loss of a Love*

Ninety-three:
Your Happiness Is Up to You

- Happiness depends on your *attitude* toward what happens to you, not on what happens to you.

- It may sound revolutionary, but problems don't have to make you unhappy.

- This runs counter to our cultural programming—which tells us we *must* react in certain negative ways to certain "negative" events.

- Nonetheless, happiness is always our choice. That is a reality of life.

- Stop waiting for Prince Charming, Cinderella, more money, the right job, total health *or anything else* before you're happy.

- Stop waiting.

- Choose satisfaction.

- Be happy.

- Now.

I am worthy.

I am worthy of my life and
all the good that is in it.

I am worthy of
my friends and their friendship.

I am worthy of spacious skies, amber waves
of grain and purple mountain majesties
above the fruited plain. (I am worthy, too,
of the fruited plain.)

I am worthy of a degree of happiness
that could only be referred to as
"sinful" in less enlightened times.

I am worthy of creativity,
sensitivity and appreciation.

I am worthy of peace of mind, peace on Earth,
peace in the valley and a piece of the action.

I am worthy of God's presence in my life.

I am worthy
of my love.

Excerpt from *How to Survive the Loss of a Love*

INDEX

F

Fadden, Mary Toarmina
McWilliams 59
Fadiman, Clifton 177
Fantasy Island
Mr. Roarke 66
Faulkner, William 308
Feather, William 8, 274
Feiffer, Jules 198, 210
Fellini, Federico 199
Feltham, Owen 123
Fiddler on the Roof 288
Field, Eugene 86
Field, John Hancock 9
Fielding, Henry 307
Fields, Dorothy 202
Fields, W. C. 58, 112, 231
Fillmore, Charles 88
Fischer, Martin H. 72
Flaubert, Gustave 24
Fletcher, John 124
Flynn, Errol 212
Fontenelle, Bernard 117
Fonteyn, Margot 128
Foot, P. W. R. 297
Forbes, B. C. 106, 305
Forbes, Malcolm 191, 300
Ford, Henry 9, 78, 184, 20,
244, 304
Foreman, George 188
Forster, E. M. 238
Fosdick, Harry
Emerson 4, 93, 118,
260, 271

Fowler, Gene 124, 308
France, Anatole 70
Francis of Assisi . . . 201, 220, 225
Francis, Brendan 3
Frankfurter, Felix 109
Frankl, Viktor 35
Franklin, Benjamin . . 5, 7, 58-59,
74, 91-92, 109, 123,
147, 153, 178, 211,
294-296, 303
Freud, Anna 70
Freud, Sigmund 15, 19, 179,
279, 283
Friedman, Bruce Jay 10, 240
Fritz, Robert 36
Fromm, Erich . 98, 216, 218, 286
Frost, Robert 42, 69, 77,
122, 299
Fry, Christopher 26, 207
Fuller, Margaret 300
Fuller, R. Buckminster 1, 67,
103, 296
Fuller, Thomas 16, 32, 53,
105, 112, 162,
190, 219, 242
Furnas, J. J. 52

G

Gable, Clark 237
Gabor, Zsa Zsa 58, 65,
118, 171
Galbraith, John
Kenneth 65, 112
Galento, Tony Two-Ton 16
Gallup, George 269
Galton, Francis 12
Gandhi, Mahatma . . 88, 131, 147
Garbo, Greta 169

I